PLANTING DESIGN
ILLUSTRATED

Gang Chen

Outskirts Press, Inc.
Denver, Colorado

Outskirts Press
http://www.outskirtspress.com

ISBN-10: 1-4327-0379-X
ISBN-13: 978-1-4327-0379-0

Library of Congress Control Number: 2007921544

Outskirts Press and the "OP" logo are trademarks belonging to
Outskirts Press, Inc.

Printed in the United States of America

DEDICATION

To my parents, Zhuixian and Yugen, my wife Xiaojie, my daughters Alice, Angela and Amy.

TABLE OF CONTENTS

literature and painting; the use of bamboo in Chinese planting design embodies both the idea of "man and nature in one" and the dominant influence of literature and painting

PREFACE

Mr. Donald B., FASLA, CEO and Chairman of a well-known landscape design firm, accidentally read a copy of my original manuscript on planting design. He was amazed by what he read and encouraged me to seek the possibilities of getting the manuscript published. I never knew Donald before. He requested a friend of mine (an employee of his firm from whom he got a copy of my manuscript) to set up a lunch meeting with me. He told me in that meeting that he could not describe how impressed he was by my manuscript, and he felt like he had found a hidden treasure and loved to let others know about it and share it. He thought it was too good a piece to be left sitting on the shelf, and considered it to be a much needed piece in the field of planting design education and practice. In fact, he loved the manuscript so much that he requested my authorization for his firm to reproduce 6 copies of the manuscript for its in-house use. He also requested the every designer in his firm to read my manuscript and use the principles and concepts in their design.

Donald's firm is a well-known landscape design firm that designed many landscape projects in Las Vegas and other places, including Mirage Hotel, Bellagio Hotel, etc. Donald is a well-respected landscape architect and has over 50 years of experience in Landscape Design. He is a Fellow of American Society of Landscape Architects (FASLA, the most honorable and highest level of member of ASLA), his encouragement really gave me more confidence in trying to get my manuscript modified and published as a book.

I expanded my original manuscript to cover a broader range of gardens and added some basic but practical elements of planting design to meet the needs of a broader mainstream audience. Previous publications on various gardens treated them as isolated dot. I used planting design as a major linkage to connect the discussions of various styles of gardens in many different countries. I tried to connect the dots and find both differences and interactions. I compared different garden styles and noted the unique aspect of each garden style and its planting design but also tried to discover and generalize the common principles and concepts. I discussed design history, but not for history sake. The purpose is to find out how we can learn from history and use it in our practice today. I have analyzed historical development, framework, underlying principles and major trends of various gardens and their planting design, with special attention to their potential use in modern landscape practice and planting design. If you have little knowledge of planting design, you'll have a good understanding of the framework of planting design after you read this book. Even though you may not understand everything that you read at first, but you'll remember where the information is and can always come back to the section later after you gain more knowledge in landscape architecture. I also tried to look at the contemporary landscape education and practice from the angle of planting design, and tried to introduce landscape practice and planting design to ordinary readers.

Much effort has been put into this book to tailor it to fit the contemporary landscape education and practice in the U.S. and other countries. This book focuses on planting design, because that is the way landscape design professionals are trained in the U.S. and many other countries. That is also the way landscape design practice is done in landscape firms. It intends to cover pragmatic, useful principles and concepts and to assist landscape architects, design professionals and garden lovers in the U.S. and other countries to solve practical problems.

For both professional designers and ordinary garden lovers, this book can be a very useful resource. Various planting design principles and concepts are discussed in plain English. It can not only help ordinary garden lovers, novice landscape designers or landscape students to learn how to proceed in planting design, but also serve as a desktop reference book for seasoned landscape architects, architects and urban planners and other design professionals. It can assist ordinary people or armchair travelers to understand and appreciate a garden and its planting design at a higher and intellectual level.

For the students in hundreds of Landscape Architecture programs in colleges and universities, this book can be a textbook or reference book. There are few existing textbooks or reference books that systematically cover the academic and design aspect of planting design, while planting design is a main and mandatory course in all Landscape Architecture programs in colleges and universities. The level of planting design course varies and is affected greatly by the teachers of the course, who are often part-time lecturers from outside design firms and are at various academic levels. Some teachers did NOT teach planting design course well. They just showed some slides and finished planting design drawings, but they did NOT teach students HOW the planting concepts were developed and decided, what was the PROCESS, and what were the design principles, concepts and rules. There are no or very few existing "standard" books that are commonly used in planting design courses. Most of the time, each lecturer or teacher only copied pages from various books that they found interesting and used them.

There are many books on landscape architecture or gardening, they discuss plants or facts of gardens, but unfortunately, few of them really cover the DESIGN aspect of planting design or cover planting design principles and concepts, which is the most important aspect of planting design. The available books can be put into following categories:

a. **Coffee table books,** with pretty photos and some description, but no design principles or concepts. Much of the contents of these other books are description of the facts of the gardens, with little analysis of the design principles and concept. The ways that landscape architecture are taught and practiced are different from what these books described.

b. **"Dictionaries" or encyclopedia of plants** that tell people what the names and properties of the plants are, and their mature sizes and whether they are deciduous or evergreen, etc. One of the most famous of this kind of books is Sunset's "Western Garden Book" by Brenzel. It is sometimes called the "bible" of landscaping in the western United States. These kind of books can be useful AFTER the planting design concept is thought out and done, and can be used to choose the plants. For example, if I already decided, in a courtyard or a commercial plaza, to use a large tree, with about 40-feet-wide tree canopy, and this tree need to be deciduous, and then I can turn to these dictionaries or encyclopedias of plants to look for the appropriate plant. I can choose from many different kinds of trees to achieve the intended design effect, but the basic spatial concept will stay the same, **which has been decided even before I turn to a dictionary or encyclopedia style book.** More important than the dictionaries or encyclopedia of plants are the books that tell people about the design principles or concepts, basically the space design concepts and themes. This is where my book steps in to meet the needs. The effective use of planting design principles and concepts by the designers will determine the original concepts, layout, and spatial relations of various plants, which largely determine the final result of a garden design. We can use writing an article as an analogy to designing a garden: a good dictionary is important, but no one can learn how to write an article by merely reading a dictionary. More importantly, one needs to learn how to layout and organize an article and think out the theme, ideas and framework for the article before he starts to write.

c. **Horticulture books**, listing species, climate zones, soil amendments, etc. These books basically tell people how to plant trees and other plants and make sure they live and grow well and healthy.

Much of the content of existing books on landscape or gardens is description of the facts of the gardens, with little analysis of the planting design principles and concepts. Again, the ways that landscape architecture are taught and practiced are different from what these books described. In colleges and universities, landscape design's main courses are planting design and irrigation design (how to design and layout sprinkler systems for plants). In landscape design firms, their main design and constructions drawings are planting plans (planting design), and irrigation plans (these irrigation plans are often done by consultants outside of landscape firms). That may be the reason that the existing books on gardens have NOT been very appealing to the design professionals and students, because they did not focus on planting design. The books available that contained the word "planting design" often offer little design principles and concepts.

On the naturalistic planting design portion, this book uses Chinese gardens as case studies, yet it is different from other books on Chinese gardens, because other existing books did not focus on planting design. My book has been written to fit the basic needs of landscape architecture education and practice in many countries.

Planting design, like other kinds of art, is a cumulative process. We not only need to bring forward new ideas, but also need to inherit from the past. The challenge for us is not whether we should learn from history, but how to learn from history, how to differentiate what is constant and timeless and what is temporary and only has academic value.

In recent decades, with the development of the economy, the living standard of people has been raised rapidly. People are not satisfied with the existing housing anymore; they want to improve the quality of the whole living environment, including public space such as city parks, community parks, and streets; and semi-public areas like green belts inside residential districts, courtyards of apartments; and private space: their homes. Planting is one of the most important and effective landscape design measures to achieve this objective. But the current practice of planting design has lost its continuity with the splendid past. A major reason for this situation is the lack of contemporary landscape design theory, especially landscape theory focusing on planting design principles and concepts, with genuine understanding of traditional garden arts and analysis of previous successful planting design cases. In the meantime, existing planting literature does need to be generalized and straightened out so as to meet today's need.

Thus, the problem is to strive to establish a contemporary landscape planting design theory focusing on the principles and concepts, with its roots in traditional garden design theory and previous successful planting design cases, to fit the continuously growing needs of people.

It is the purpose of this book to (1) use existing materials to summarize the principles and concepts of planting design that were used consciously or unconsciously by previous garden designers; (2) use these principles to analyze some typical gardens and their uses of plants; (3) try to generalize some practical patterns of planting design; (4) evaluate the observations we have made and clarify the underlying theory behind the principles, rules and patterns; (5) make some judgment on the cohesive theoretical frame works explaining the observations and explore the possibilities of applying these principles and patterns in modern planting design under new conditions.

Even though planting is one of the basic elements of gardens, most researchers have neglected its design theory, and little comprehensive study of planting design theory focusing on the DESIGN principles and concepts has been done so far. Therefore, this book could be significant because no improvements and advances in planting design and its theory would be possible without comprehensive research into its tradition.

Few existing books have done a comprehensive discussion on planting design principles and concepts. Thus, this book could be beneficial to the formation of modern planting design theory. It could help to indicate the present and future trends of development in planting design. It could give both professional designers and ordinary garden lovers a better understanding of planting design principles and concepts, and it could also be valuable for the further development of planting design theory.

This book covers almost every aspect of planting design. I intend to focus on the principles and concepts that are universal and relevant to common problems in contemporary landscape and planting design education and practice. I have used some gardens in California as case studies and figures; that is simply because they are easily accessible to me. If other gardens were more accessible to me, I would have used them as case studies and figures as well. Even though many of the specialized case studies on naturalistic planting design are based on Chinese gardens, the principles, concepts and methodology discussed are universal and have great applications in other gardens: learning from nature; use literature, paintings and poems as sources of inspirations, etc. One can use the methodology learned from Chinese garden case studies to absorb from Shakespeare's works or any other great western literature, conceive creative concepts and create a naturalistic and yet very westernized garden. One can also get inspiration from American or English landscape painting and poems and use it as original concept in garden design, and create an American or English garden. This is confirmed by the comparative study of Chinese and Japanese gardens and their planting design, as well as a comparative study of Chinese and English naturalistic gardens and their planting design in later portion of the book.

I also intended to elevate the planting design to a higher level: we should not only consider functional, ecological and aesthetic aspect of planting design, but also include historical connotation, psychological effects, symbolic meanings and intellectual enjoyment in our concepts as well. I spent much effort in this book trying to achieve this goal.

Methodology for research of this book includes:

(1) Document Studies: a. ancient documents; b. contemporary plants and garden literature; c. documents in related disciplines: Aesthetics, Typology, Ecology, Philosophy, History, Literature, Arts, Botany, Geography, Climatology, Horticulture, Agriculture, etc.
(2) Interviews: Professionals of landscaping, of planting design, of aesthetics and of literature, etc., have been consulted for development of ideas and technical problems.
(3) Field trips: I have been to many of the gardens discussed in the book. The memory and impressions of these gardens and the materials gained in the field trips have been helpful for the development of the idea and the writing of the book. Some sketches and photographs gained in the field trips were used as figures in the book.
(4) Personal analysis, discoveries and opinions.

This book has been organized from the general to the specific, from theory to practice and from the past to present and future, with reference to context (historical, cultural, environmental, etc.) and with an emphasis on design principles and concepts.

The World Heritage Committee of United Nations Educational, Scientific and Cultural Organization has inscribed many of the gardens selected and discussed in this book as World Cultural Heritage Sites. These gardens include Versailles in France, Summer Palace, Summer Retreating Mountain Villa, and Suzhou Classical Gardens in China.

An annotated bibliography has been included at the end of the book; it lists almost all major landscape and garden books and gives a brief description and evaluation of each book.

I have compiled and drew from much information from many books and incorporated other design professionals' and my own experience, and discussed and analyzed the methodology on planting design and concepts. This is like how bees make honey: They collect materials and nutrition from many flowers (source books) and working hard to finally make honey, which is different from what it came from. This book is an attempt to develop a comprehensive framework and system in the field of planting design principles and concepts.

If this book can "cast a brick to attract jade" and promote research into planting design in different approaches and aspects, I'll feel satisfied.

Photos and line drawings are placed within the text immediate before or after the page that it is referred to.

All the names of the Chinese people, places and gardens are given in Pinyin, a system of romanization of Chinese according to the pronunciation of the words in Mandarin, the standard language used in China. When a quoted reference uses the older Wade-Giles system of romanization, the Pinyin equivalent will follow in parentheses at the first mention. A chart of the Pinyin alphabet, equivalent Wade-Giles letters and similar pronunciation in English is given in the end of the book.

For simplicity, when I use the word "he," it also implies "she."

If you have any comments, or if you have some good planting design drawings, photos and examples to be included in the next edition of this book, please send an e-mail to plantingdesign@yahoo.com

Sincerely,

Gang Chen

SECTION 1
BASIC PLANTING DESIGN PRINCIPLES AND CONCEPTS AND PLANTING DESIGN IN FORMAL GARDENS

CHAPTER 1
BASIC PLANTING DESIGN PRINCIPLES AND CONCEPTS

1. Comparing Planting Design in the Two Major Landscaping Systems

Planting design is the arrangement of plants to achieve the best aesthetic, functional, ecological and symbolic effect. Even though there are a variety of garden styles in the world, gardening and planting design can be put into two major landscaping systems: formal gardens and naturalistic gardens. The formal gardens are represented by Egyptian gardens, Persian gardens, Islamic gardens, Italian gardens, French gardens, some American gardens and some English gardens, etc. The naturalistic gardens are represented by Chinese traditional gardens, some English gardens, some Japanese gardens and some American gardens, etc.

When we discuss formal gardens, we always mention French gardens. We want to point out that French gardens are neither the first, nor the exclusive master of the formal gardens. There are many successful formal gardens in Italy, Britain, the United States, Canada and some Muslim countries, etc. The formal gardens can be sub-divided into the inward-looking Formal Courtyard Gardens and the outward-looking Villa and Formal Gardens categories. The distinction between the formal gardens and the naturalistic gardens is also not really clear-cut in some cases. For example, even though most of the Chinese gardens are naturalistic, we do see formal planting layout in some Chinese gardens. Japanese gardens have very nicely trimmed plants, a major feature in the formal gardens, yet they also share many naturalistic planting design principles with Chinese gardens. Not all English gardens are naturalistic either: early English gardens were in the European formal style. We are mainly using the term formal gardens and naturalistic gardens to describe the major schools and trends of planting design in this book.

The major characteristic of planting design in formal gardens is an emphasis on artificial beauty. The formal garden pattern is an extension of the architecture; its lines are controlled by architectural elements. The natural contour is often completely changed and the ground is leveled and built into terraces. Plants are organized in a symmetric, regular manner around axes. They are usually pruned into geometric shapes, and their locations, shape, and size often reflect geometric relationships and mathematical proportions. This is basically an objective approach, and its principles and concepts are similar to those of architectural design.

Naturalistic planting design shows completely different characteristics: it emphasizes naturalistic beauty. Even though gardens are designed and made by man, yet they must look like having been created by nature. Plants are organized in an irregular, asymmetric manner. Straight lines and geometric shapes are usually avoided in the layout and forms of plants. Naturalistic gardens and planting design showed a very strong tendency towards the creation of poetic atmosphere and picturesque scenes from the very beginning. They managed to achieve the artistic conception. This is probably because painters and poets did most of the gardening and planting in naturalistic gardens design in the past. This is basically an artistic, subjective approach, and the principles and concepts contrast with those of architectural design.

We are not saying one planting system is better than the other. In fact, each of the two planting design styles is very unique and has distinct characteristic. You need to make a decision about which planting design system to use based on what the actual project requirements and design objectives are. Sometimes, a combination of the two systems can be used also. The decision needs to be made according to the specific project condition.

2. How to approach a planting design problem

a. Fundamental concept, framework and outline of a planting design

This is the first step in planting design. Ask yourself the questions: What is the theme or purpose of this planting design project? What should be the fundamental concept? What can be the framework or outline of the planting design?

In recent years, "Genius Loci," (pronounced as "loh-kai") a Latin word has become very popular in Landscape Architecture education and practice. It means the particular spirit of a site. It is a belief that each site has a special importance, a particular meaning beyond function and beauty. This can be a very good way to start the fundamental concept for the planting design of a project. You can do various research works on the site's history and context and try to define the "Genius Loci" of the site and base the design on it. This is a general philosophical concept that came from ancient Western civilizations. This approach focuses on the studies of the objective site. In the naturalistic planting design portion of this book, we'll discuss in detail another important aesthetic concept, "Yi Jing." It is a concept that came from ancient Eastern civilizations. It emphasizes the combination of subjective ideas, thought and emotion with objective life, scenery and situation. You mingle your idea, thought and emotion with objective life, scenery and situation, so as to stimulate a similar emotional excitement. It can also be used to create the fundamental concept of a project. This approach focuses on the interaction between the designer's subjective ideas and the objective site condition.

The framework of planting design maybe revised several times. It should be well thought out before the next step of the design. It is one of the most important components and will determine the final result of the planting design. Some important decisions have to be made when setting the framework and outline of planting design. They include whether to use a formal planting design or to use a naturalistic planting design, and what the design intent is, etc.

b. Think of plants in generic terms

At the beginning stage of the planting design, you can think of plants in generic terms (lawn, ground cover, hedge, shrub and tree, etc.) and avoid confining your thoughts to specific plants. You may think of the spatial sequence and effect, and the general character of plants. Once this is decided, it will be very easy to choose plants. There are plenty of plant encyclopedia books, plant lists, and plant nursery catalogs to assist you to choose proper plants to achieve your design intent. Many of the local plant suppliers and nurseries are also willing to assist you in choosing plants.

In the front portion of this book, we'll try to discuss plants in generic terms, and the graphic will be abstractive and generic also. This section is to layout a general foundation of planting design principles and concepts. In later chapters of this book, we'll do detail and in-depth discussions of planting design. We'll also discuss some specific plants and their characteristic.

Every planting design can be thought out at four different scales: at the city scale, at the plaza/neighborhood scale, at the building scale and at the detail scale. Let's discuss each of the scale as following:

c. At city scale

You may consider your planting design project's relation to the entire city. This is the most important scale and is often missed by most designers. For example, the Mall at Washington DC is located at one of the most important axes of the city. This axis connects the Robert F. Kennedy Memorial Stadium, Lincoln Park, U.S. Capitol Hill, Washington Monument, National WWII Memorial and Lincoln Memorial. This means it would make a lot of sense to design the planting in the Mall as ceremonial, formal, and classical style, probably in a symmetric manner to reinforce this important axis. The size of the trees used probably need to be huge along the Mall to match the grand columns and other architectural components used in the U. S. Capitol Hill and Lincoln Memorial. The center area can be lawn or other low-rise plants so as not to block the view of U.S. Capital Hill, Washington Monument, and Lincoln Memorial along this axis. The overall theme of the planting design may be grand and dignified to demonstrate the great power of the federal government (Fig. 1.1). This planting design layout would also be consistent with Pierre l'Enfant's original overall city design concept in 1791 and the "Grand Avenue" (Boulevard) and wide and monumental public space that he intended to create and to symbolize that America is a nation with room to grow.

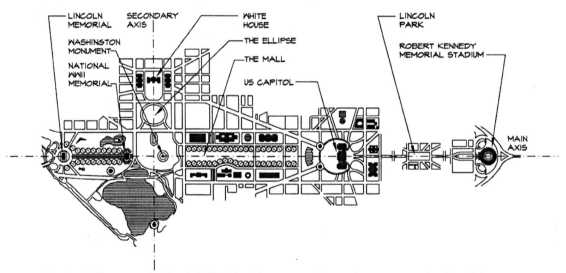

Fig. 1.1 The trees in the Mall, Washington DC can be symmetrical and huge to match overall city design concept

Central Park at New York is a global wonder of landscape design. It has experienced many changes in the past 150 years, yet the most fundamental concept and overall layout was decided in 1858 by the original designers, Frederick Law Olmsted and Calvert Vaux. At the City scale, they decided to create a centralized great park instead of many small parks for New York City, and to make the overall design of the park to be naturalistic or "picturesque" landscape to provide an opportunity for the people to escape from the stress of the city. They believed in the healing power of nature. The park has changed over time, yet the overall characteristic remains basically the same as the original design (Fig. 1.2).

In the early 1990s, I visited an exhibition of the design entries for the Korean Museum of Arts in Los Angeles. There were over 300 entries; many entries were from internationally known architectural firms. Every entry had excellent drawings, model and presentation. I was wondering how the judges could pick from all these marvelous designs. It seemed that it would be a very difficult decision to pick the winner, yet all the judges came up with a unanimous vote for the winner. The winner had made their task very easy. The winning design scheme outpaced all other entries at the city scale of the design: the design

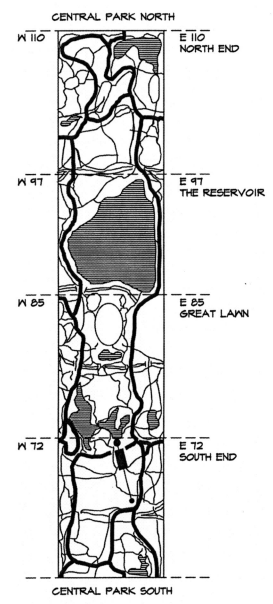

Fig. 1.2 The overall planting design of Central Park, New York was set to be Naturalistic at the city scale

concept came from Korean tradition; a huge bell covered by a classical pavilion was a center for traditional Korean community. The designer created a huge public space/plaza for the city, covered by a huge "roof of the city." The designer created a U shape space enclosed by multi-story building complex with a cover or huge "roof of the city," formed by upper building floors. Under the cover was an auditorium in an abstract shape to simulate the huge bell covered by a classical pavilion. This designer incorporated the Korean heritage in a very modern style, and created an important public space for at the city scale through his bold imagination. His creative concept at the city scale was the key to the success.

We can apply the same philosophy to planting design. Landscape designers probably need to catch every opportunity to create meaningful public space at the city scale. When we do planting design, we are not simply planting trees; we are also creating important public or private space. The overall layout of the planting design at the city scale is of paramount importance.

d. At plaza or neighborhood scale

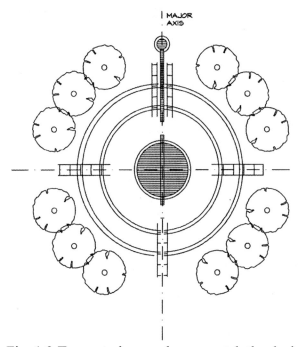

Fig. 1.3 Trees at plaza scale can match the design concept of the plaza

Plants can be arranged to reinforce the design concept of the plaza or neighborhood. For example, in a plaza with a circular fountain and radial pavement patterns, the trees can be arranged in a similar and circular pattern to reinforce the plaza's overall design concept (Fig. 1.3). In a residential neighborhood, a designer can create a very unique effect if he can put in a little thought at the plaza or neighborhood scale. For instance, if a designer places one tree in the front yard of each home along a residential street, this will create a tree-lined street. If all the trees are of the same or similar form, this street can be a very special street. Sometimes the street can even be named after the trees used (Maple St., Sycamore St., etc.) if it is in a new development area (Fig. 1.4). A new tract home development will offer designers this kind of opportunities to create some unique character at the plaza/neighborhood scale. This can usually be achieved by incorporating the planting design requirements in the covenant, condition and restrictions (CC and R) of the homeowner's associations (HOA). To avoid the pitfall of trees in an entire area or district of the city being wiped out by one kind of insect or disease, different species may be used in different streets. Even the same street can have two different species of similar forms and the two species may alter at every other tree. Trees used in streets may need to be long-lived, hardy, and not too slow of growth. They may need to be strong enough to withstand wind and storm, and not drop litter. They may need to be tolerant to smog, dust and gas, high branching with spread form, of a height and spread suitable to the street, have a tough and firm bark. They may also need to posses a compact and restricted root system or one capable of being restrained, and can survive with minimum food and water.[1]

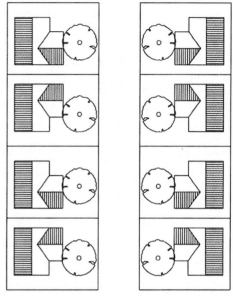

Fig. 1.4 Plant one tree in front of each home to form a very unique tree-lined street

e. At building scale

You may consider plants' relationship to a building. The scale, proportion and scale of plants close to a building probably need to be chosen according to the size, height and scale of the buildings. If a building has a large area of wall surface, it may appear to be too monotonous; plants can be used to soften the building elevation. Climbing plants (vines and other climbers) are often used to climb onto a large wall area to form a special composition, or climb along the colonnades or archway to soften a building's elevations. If a building's elevations appear to be too flat, high trees can be used to break the tedious skyline and create more interesting elevations. In the shade formed by canopies or other building elements, shade-loving plants can be placed. Trees placed close to or in front of the windows of buildings (especially multi-story buildings) should have very thin foliage to avoid blocking the view line of people inside the building (Fig 1.5). Trees with thick and huge tree canopies should never be

---

[1] Robinson, Florence Bell. *Planting Design.* Illinois: The Garrard Press, 1940. pp. 168-182.

placed in front of the windows of buildings. It is human nature to desire to look out of the windows of a building. Many people have complained about their view lines being blocked by trees right in front of their windows.

A TREE USED IN FRONT OF A WINDOW SHALL HAVE THIN FOLIAGE SO AS NOT TO BLOCK THE VIEW LINE

A PLANT THAT CAN BE VIEWED FROM ABOVE SHALL HAVE A NICE TOP VIEW

Fig. 1.5 Plants and view lines from a building

f. At detail scale

You can utilize many properties of plants. You can use plants to create sound effects, take advantage of the color and smell of plants, emphasize the beauty of lines formed by plants' branches. It is important to remember that most of the decorative plants probably need to be placed at a close viewing distance for people to see their decorative features. For example, decorative plants may be placed right next to the walkway to achieve maximum exposure. Decorative plants may also be placed along a waterfall to form a focus of the garden. Both the decorative plants and the waterfall can be placed at a close viewing distance next to a walkway.

For most average or even exceptional residential gardens, ground covers, perennials, annuals, hedges and shrubs can create important effects. They can provide many different colors, textures and create interest for the planting design. These smaller gardens are a celebration of small stuff and they can be exceptional also. I once talked with a well-known landscape architect and asked him what his secret to success was. He told me: "It is in details, God is in the details." This may be an overstatement, but it does show that details are very important to landscape and planting design. There will be a comprehensive discussion on planting design at the detail scale with Chinese gardens as case studies at the later portion of this book.

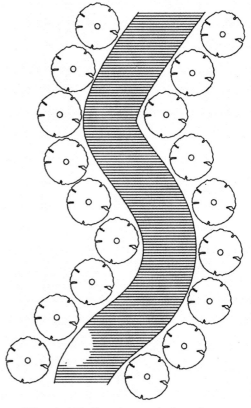

g. Follow existing shape

A very important rule of planting design is to follow the existing shape of the space, land, building and other design elements.

Fig. 1.6 Following existing shape-planting trees along the bank of a creek

Planting trees along the bank of a lake, a creek, outline of a building, border of a space or a site is a very effective way to achieve spatial effect (Fig. 1.6 and 1.7). At Getty

Museum, Los Angeles, the designer placed two rows of deciduous trees and some low-rise decorative plants along the bank of the creek leading to the Central Garden. These plants reinforce one of the main design features, the man-made creek. A walkway meanders through the creek and allows visitors to appreciate the low-rise decorative plants and the creek at a close distance and at a detail scale.

Fig. 1.7 Following existing shape-palm trees along a road

Rows of deciduous trees can be planted along a curved road and sidewalk. In the winter, the trees' branches provide gorgeous lines for both the pedestrian and the drivers who travel in their cars; in the summer, the leaves of the trees are fully grown and provide shade for the pedestrian.

3. Basic planting design principles

a. Plant materials

Relating to a specific purpose, all the plants in the world can be put into a system of classification or listing. For example, according to the scientific classification of Linnaeus, which is based on kinship, evolution and structure, plants can be classified into Division, Subdivision, Class, Subclass, Order, Family, Subfamily, Genus, Subgenus, Species, Subspecies, Variety and Form. Classifications of this kind are very helpful to indicate and identify plants accurately between different regions and countries, but they are not very useful in describing, analyzing and studying the form and habit of plants, and in expressing design ideas in planting design.

We adopt a more practical and useful system of classification here, and apply it to the plant materials in our discussion. This system is composed of common terminology and is used in most of the nurseries. Each plant is identified by a botanical name and a common name. The botanical name is composed of Genus and Species, and it is the Latin name of the plant, and is normally shown in italic font. The common name of a plant is the name commonly used in a region. Sometimes, the same common name refers to different plants in different regions. That is why planting plans always include the botanical name of a plant in addition to its common name so as to accurately identify a plant and avoid confusion. Landscape architects prepare planting plans as part of the legal contract documents between the owner and the landscape contractor. Planting plans have to be accurate.

This system of plant classification takes into account the size, appearance, form, habit, flowering seasons, colors and textures, etc. According to this system, plants can be divided into trees, shrubs, vines and climbers, ground covers, aquatics and sub-aquatics, bamboo, etc. Each kind of plants can be divided into groups by size: tall, medium, small, low, dwarf, etc. These groups can be further defined by some verbal description: deciduous, evergreen, broad-leaved, coniferous, flowering, autumn leaves, etc. Woody plants (trees and shrubs) can form the structure of a garden; herbaceous plants (annuals, perennials and climbing plants, etc) can decorate the structure of a garden.

b. The appearance of plants

"Form" and "habit" are terms often used in describing the appearance of plants, but what is the "form" and "habit" of a plant?

"Habit" is the growing direction of a plant, and "Form" is outline formed by leaves and branches of a plant.

With the help of the above definitions, we can classify the plants according to their appearance. For example, according to their habits, plants can be grouped into these types (Figure 1.8):

    a. Single-stemmed;
    b. Multi-stemmed;
    c. Up-ward;
    d. Downward (Weeping);
    e. Downward (Pendulous);

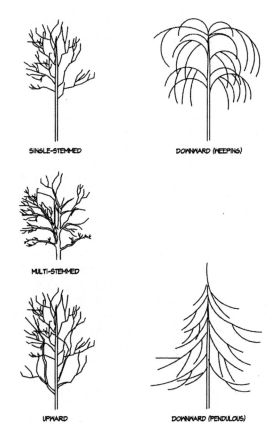

SINGLE-STEMMED   DOWNWARD (WEEPING)

MULTI-STEMMED

UPWARD   DOWNWARD (PENDULOUS)

Fig. 1.8 Habit of plants

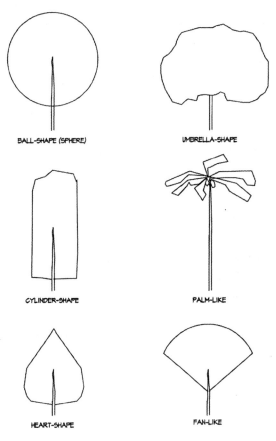

Fig. 1.9 Form of plants

Plants in Multi-stemmed and Downward (Weeping) types are usually found in Chinese and Japanese gardens.

According to form, plants can be put into these categories (Figure 1.9):

a. Ball-Shape (Sphere);
b. Cylinder-Shape;
c. Heart-Shape;
d. Umbrella-Shape;
e. Palm-like;
f. Fan-Shape;
g. Irregular;

Plants in Umbrella-Shape, Palm-like or irregular forms are commonly used in Chinese gardens.

In addition to form and habit, color and texture are two other important properties of plants. The distance between the viewer and plants also plays an important role: at a short distance, a viewer will notice more about the color and texture of a plant; at a middle distance, a viewer will notice more about the light and shadow or form of a plant; at a great distance, a viewer will notice more about the silhouette of a plant.

c. Color, texture and mass

You probably have learned about colors in art or drawing class before. Using colors in planting design is similar to using colors in drawings to some extent, but there are some significant differences between the two. For example, when you combine all different pigments together on a drawing, you'll get black, while when you combine all different colors of plant materials in field, you'll NOT get black, you'll probably get white or whitish color instead.

We can see the color of an object simply because of its ability to reflect light. For example, we can see a green leaf simply because it only reflects light in the green wavelength and absorbs light of other wavelengths. Light waves are subject to the physical laws of reflection and refraction. White is a combination of all the light waves of different lengths. Black is the complete absence of any light waves. You probably have learned about this experiment before: A ray of white light passing through a glass prism will be separate into light waves of different lengths, and these light waves form the colors of a spectrum: red, orange, yellow, green, blue and violet. These six colors are the fundamental colors. If these rays of a spectrum pass through another reversed glass prism, they'll become white again, even though it may not be pure white because of the refractions from the surrounding (Fig. 1.10). Colors have three qualities: hue (the name of a color), value (the light of a color), and chroma (the strength of a color). The colors of longer wavelengths, like red, orange and yellow, remind us of sun, fire, heat, etc., and are called warm colors. The colors of shorter wavelengths, like green, blue, violet, remind us of ice, water, sea, and shadows, etc., and are called cool colors. Warm colors can be distinguished at a distance, and appear to come toward us, and are also called advancing colors. Cool colors can be distinguished at a closer range and appear to retreat from us, and are also called receding colors.

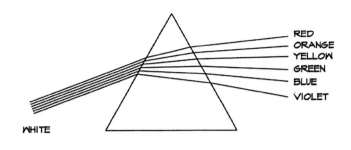

THE COMPOSITION OF WHITE LIGHT

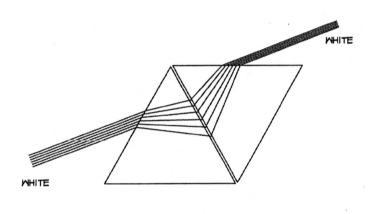

THE COMPOSITION OF WHITE LIGHT

Fig. 1.10 Light and color

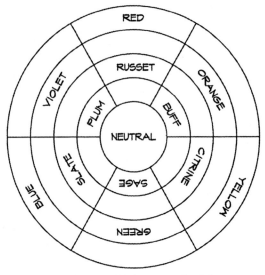

MIXING DIFFERENT COLORS

Red, yellow and blue are three primary colors. Mixing other colors cannot produce them, but they can produce all the other colors by proper mixing. Mixing the three primary colors can produce secondary colors (orange, green and violet). Mixing the secondary colors can produce tertiary colors (citrine, slate and russet). Mixing the tertiary colors can produce quaternary colors (sage, plum and buff)… Eventually, we can produce any color by proper mixing (Fig. 1.11). The more we mix, the more neutral the colors will be. We can arrange the colors of a spectrum into a color wheel. It can be as simple as a color wheel of the six fundamental colors (Fig. 1.11), or it can be a color wheel of hundreds of colors with nuances. We'll use the simplest color wheel for our discussion:

The pair of colors that oppose each other on the color wheel are called complementary colors, like blue and orange, red and green, yellow and violet. If we mixed the light rays of complementary colors, we'll get white light, but if we mix pigments of the complementary colors, we'll get black. This is because mixing light rays of different colors is an addition of light waves, while mixing pigment of different colors is a subtraction of light waves. For example, a red object reflects only red

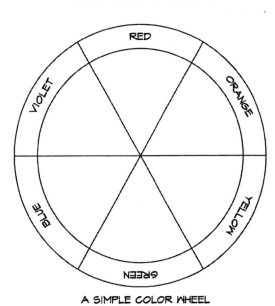

A SIMPLE COLOR WHEEL

Fig. 1.11 Color wheel

and orange light waves, a yellow objects reflects only yellow and orange light waves. When we mix red and yellow pigments together, the resulting pigment only reflects the common light waves: orange, and it'll appear to be orange pigment. When we mix pigments of complementary colors, they have no common light waves; the resulting pigment will NOT reflect any light waves and will appear to be black. Similarly, when we mixed pigments of all different colors, they have NO common light waves; the resulting pigment will NOT reflect any light waves and will appear to be black. When we draw a color plan, we are using pigment, but when we use plant materials in the field, we are using light reflected by plants of different colors. We need to pay attention to the differences between the two.

In planting design, the colors can be affected by the following factors: the smoothness and size of the leaves or flowers, reflections from the surroundings, the intensity of the light source and shadows over plants. Glossy leaves normally appear brighter than the less glossy ones. Smaller leaves typically appear stronger in color than larger leaves, even if they are actually of the same hue. Flowers or leaves of complementary colors can appear to be stronger and brighter when placed together. Plants placed in shadows will appear to be darker; this is similar to adding black or gray to a pigment. A strong light source will create stronger reflections and make the colors of plants stronger and brighter. In a garden, the colors of plants are constantly affected by the reflection and refraction light from the surrounding, and the ever-changing light density caused by cloud, fog or sun. The reflection and refraction light from the surroundings actually make the colors of plants less pure and easier to form a harmonious combination.

There are several ways to achieve harmony in color in landscape: use a dominant hue with variations in tones, use two complimentary colors, or use a full spectrum through graduation. Many gardens are dominant by green of different tones. In fall, the leaves of deciduous trees of a species in mass or group planting, such as *Liquidambar formosana* (Chinese Sweet Gum) can also form a dominant color. One way to study the color combinations of different plants is to sketch out the colors of the plants for the same area in different seasons. Through careful studies in this method, it is possible to achieve harmony combinations for all seasons.

When we consider color in planting design, we need to consider not only the interaction between different plants, but also the interaction between the plants and their surroundings, especially their background. For example, when we consider a plant in front of a red brick wall, we may need to decide if we want to use plants of similar colors or contrasting colors, including the colors of the plants' leaves, flowers, fruits and barks.

Local prevailing climate may also affect the use of colors in planting design. For example, England often has foggy and gray sky; the flowers used in England can be warmer than areas in Northern America that have a dominant blue sky for most of the year. The lack of intense sunlight in temperate climate zones makes the hues of plants more discordant than they would be under the harsh southerly sun. It may be a good design practice to use plants that have similar or close colors in temperate climate zones. For a southern climate zone, bright color flowers are affected by sunlight and shadows.

Their colors appear to be bleached to neutral under intense sun. Light color flowers appear even weaker in both full sun and in shadow. Shadows can cast a gray tone and calm strident tones and contrasting colors. Some warm pastels, like pink, yellow and peach color pastels can neutralize in shade and appear to be less noticeable. Most lavenders and violets disappear in shadow. Oranges can hold their tones in shade. Whites and blues can increase in intensity and luminance.

Colors of plants can be used to create illusion in distance and space. For a small garden, flowers of warm and advancing colors may be placed at the foreground and they'll appear to be closer than they actually are. Flowers of cool and receding colors may be placed in the back and they'll appear to be farther away than they actually are. This method may make the garden appear to be larger than its actually size.

Different colors, including the colors of plants can stimulate different emotional feelings in different people. Warm colors can arouse aspiring, warm, refreshing, passionate and exciting feelings. Cool colors can provoke retiring, cool, quite, calm, reserved, sooth and sometimes depress feelings.

Colors also have symbolism: Yellow is the color of gold and sun, and symbolizes wisdom and power. In many Eastern cultures golden yellow is the highest and most respectful royal color, and was only allowed to be used by the royal family in some Eastern countries in the past. Red is the color of fire and blood, it symbolizes courage, happiness and is the color used in wedding and birth ceremonies. Orange is the color of flame and autumn, and symbolizes light and knowledge. Violet symbolizes serious, solemn and feminine meanings. It is the color of the Magdalene in Christian art. Green is the color of most growing plants, and symbolizes abundance and fertility. Blue is the color of sky and symbolizes constancy, enduring and unchanging quality, and justice. Black and white are the colors of mourning in Eastern cultures, but white symbolizes truth and purity and is the color used in wedding ceremonies and baptisms in Western cultures.

Texture in planting design can be defined as the pattern formed by light and shadow of plants and surface quality of plants. It is determined by the size, surface quality and spacing of leaves, flowers, and branches. It can be coarse or fine, or rough or smooth. At a close distance, plants with large leaves appear to be coarse or rough, like *Acer palmatum* or *Hedera helix* (English Ivy). If the spacing between these leaves is larger, they will appear even rougher. Plants with smaller leaves appear to be fine texture, like a newly mowed lawn, or *Rosmarinus officinalis* (Rosemary). If the spacing between these leaves is smaller, their texture will appear to be even finer. The contrast formed by different textures of different plants can create a pleasing scene, like a nicely trimmed lawn next to *Hedera helix* (English Ivy) in a naturalistic and curly garden bed.

There is also a seasonal effect on the texture of plants. For example, deciduous trees have smaller, tender new leaves and may appear to have a finer texture than they are in summer when the leaves are fully-grown.

Uniformity can create harmony of textures. We may try to achieve a pleasing design effect by carefully studying and arranging the textures formed by different plants (Fig 1.12 and 1.13). Strive to achieve uniformity between different plants, and seek variations based on uniformity. Too much uniformity can create a stiff effect, while too many variations

Fig. 1.12 Lawn, low-rise decorative plants, shrubs and several pine trees soften the view of an iron fence

may create discords. The key is to achieve and maintain a subtle balance between the two.

There is also a scale relation that is linked to texture: Plants with coarse texture used in a small garden space will make the space even smaller. A very low hedge may require fine texture, while a higher hedge may require medium or even coarse texture.

In addition to color and texture, mass is another important factor in planting design. The

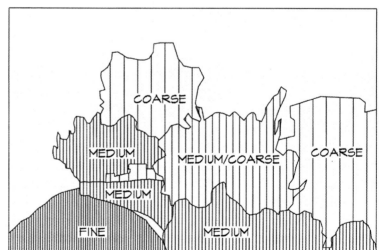

Fig. 1.13 Texture analysis in planting design-a texture analysis of Fig. 1.12

silhouette of a plant is the outline formed by branches and leaves, while mass can be considered as the three-dimensional quality of a plant, it is the "volume" formed by leaves and branches of a plant or a group of plants. A fine view in the distance may require the mass in the foreground to be relatively simple. When the distant view is not very attractive, the mass in the foreground may need to be more subtle and interesting. Masses of plants may be properly arranged to create harmony. The easiest way is the repetition of the plants of similar mass and form to create a simple and enjoyable scene. Plants that have too much difference in mass, such as a plant in umbrella shape and a plant in cylinder shape, may not create a harmonious scene when placed together.

Scale between one mass and another or one mass and the whole needs to be carefully considered. In a larger project, there is probably less danger of loss of scale than a smaller project. In larger projects, larger trees can combined with smaller trees to form individual pictures. Larger areas may also be separated into smaller areas with different themes. Larger trees and smaller trees can combine and blend to form a single mass. For a smaller garden or park, loss of scale can be very obvious and easy to notice. For example, a mature oak tree is probably too large for a 30 feet square courtyard.

Different masses formed by plants may form a balance: either asymmetrical or symmetrical. One easy way to achieve balance is to use a dominant mass in a group as focus or climax, and arrange other plants in some kind of sequence or balanced manner so that attention is directed toward or away from this dominant mass.

Mass of plants and buildings are the "solid" portion of a garden, while open space (lawn, low flower beds, etc.) is the "void" portion of a garden. Planting design may start from abstract studies of the overall composition of the "solid" and "void," of mass and open space, of the types of the pattern to be used: formal or naturalistic, or a combination of the two and the transition between the two. A garden may be composed of a large open space and a large mass. A few trees (normally more than three but fewer than nine) can be carefully placed in the vast open space to relieve the monotony. Similarly, a mass may require some open space or simply openings in its border to break its uniformity and create contrast. A detailed study of the color, texture and mass of the "solid" and "void" in plans, elevations, sections and perspectives and the overall pattern may be very helpful in planting design.

Color, texture, lines, form and mass of plants may need to be considered at the same time. At least one of the features of the plants probably needs to be similar or the same to maintain unity. At least one of the features of the plants probably needs to be different to create contrast or interest. A few species in a well thought out layout can be better than many kinds of different plants jumbled together. Repetition of similar or same form and lines can create simplicity. It can create a pattern that is used again and again, and ties the design into a unity.

Variation or contrast is introduced into a uniform planting design scene for two reasons: to create interest and prevent monotony and to create an accent. To prevent monotony, the contrast or change may need to be gradual. To create an accent, the change may need to be sudden. An accent in planting design is like an exclamation point in a paragraph, it attracts attention. It probably should not be used too often; otherwise, it may become less effective and even create confusion. This is similar to writing an article: properly used exclamation sentences can make the article more powerful, but too many exclamation points may make the article very confusing and lose its emphasis.

Some plants are humanized because of their lines, form, mass and habit. For example, Oak is called "monarch of the forest," Birch is called "lady of the woods." They are given personality and character because of their form and habit.[2]

In planting design, plants are not treated equally. They have different roles in the overall design and form a hierarchy. Their differences indicate their relative importance in the design. A visible and hierarchical order can assist you to express your design intent. There are several ways to demonstrate a plant or a group of plants to be significant to the whole layout: extraordinary size, distinctive form or a strategic location. In planting design, sometimes we can have more than one significant element or view. These other significant elements, views or scenes can be secondary to the dominant one, yet still be very distinguished. Again, we need to be cautious and try not to create too many "significant" elements, because "when everything is emphasized, nothing is emphasized."[3]

Datum is a term typically used in surveying or civil engineering. It is the base point or reference point for surveying other elements. We borrow this term and use it in planting design. A datum in planting design refers to a reference line, plane or volume that other elements can relate to. It can be a garden path or a sidewalk that links different plants together, or a lawn or a water surface that plants and other landscape elements can relate to, or the columns in a peristyle courtyard. An axis is a special case of datum; it is a straight line to which other elements are symmetrically arranged. A datum can also be a curved line, or a plane; it most likely needs to have continuity or regularity to be able to link various design elements together.

---

[2] Robinson, Florence Bell. *Planting Design.* Illinois: The Garrard Press, 1940. pp. 1-101.

[3] Ching, Frank D.K.. *Architecture: Form, Space, and Order.* John Wiley and Sons, 2nd edition, February 1996. p.338.

4. Plants and Human Being

a. "Looking through" or "blocking view"

Plants are very special design materials; some have dense foliage and some have very thin foliage; some are evergreen and some are deciduous. The characteristics of different plants have created great opportunities. You can use the branches of a tree to create a "frame" to allow people to "look through" this special "frame" to see the distant scenery. You can use the branches of a deciduous tree to create a special effect of "looking through" the tree to the sky. You can also use tall hedges or dense planting to block views to undesired elements, such as electrical equipment, transformers and truck-loading areas (Fig. 1.14). The eye level of an average human being is between 5 feet to 6 feet above ground. You may want to keep this and other basic human dimensions in mind for planting design.

b. Guiding or blocking movement

A designer can use plants to guide or block movement of human beings. For example, a hedge can block the movement across the hedge while encouraging movement along the hedge. A low hedge can block movement while allow viewing above the hedge. A low hedge can also act as "guard rail" to protect people from a dangerous slope (Fig. 1.14).

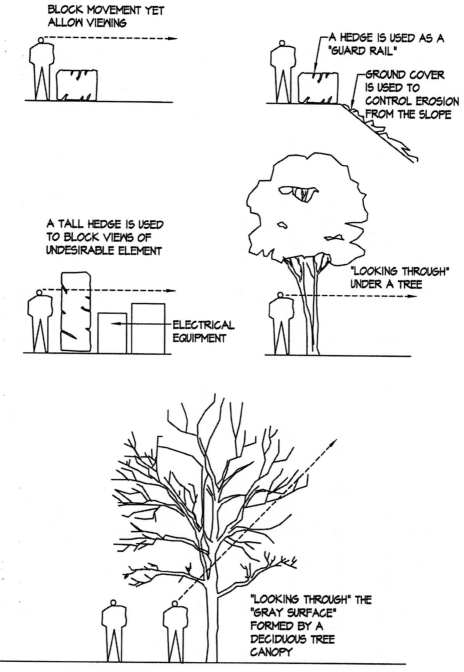

BLOCK MOVEMENT YET
ALLOW VIEWING

A HEDGE IS USED AS A
"GUARD RAIL"

GROUND COVER
IS USED TO
CONTROL EROSION
FROM THE SLOPE

A TALL HEDGE IS USED
TO BLOCK VIEWS OF
UNDESIRABLE ELEMENT

ELECTRICAL
EQUIPMENT

"LOOKING THROUGH"
UNDER A TREE

"LOOKING THROUGH" THE
"GRAY SURFACE"
FORMED BY A
DECIDUOUS TREE
CANOPY

Fig. 1.14 Plants and human being

c. Controlling the distance between trees to create different spatial feelings

Controlling the distance between trees can create different spatial feelings: placing trees at a distance larger than tree canopy will create an "open" feeling, while placing trees at a distance equal to tree canopy will create a "covered" and serene feeling (Fig. 1.15).

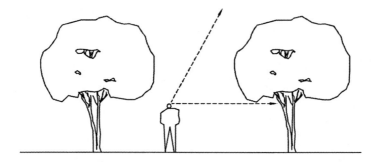

PLACING TREES AT A DISTANCE LARGER THAN TREE CANOPY WILL CREATE AN "OPEN" FEELING

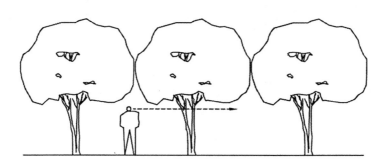

PLACING TREES AT A DISTANCE EQUAL TO TREE CANOPY WILL CREATE A "COVERED" AND SERENE FEELING

Fig. 1.15 Controlling the distance between trees to create different spatial feeling

5. Plants and Space

a. Dominance and focus

One huge tree or a few similar trees with a special characteristic can be used as the dominance or focus of a space. Landscape architects call this technique "Specimen." For example, a few large deciduous trees can be "casually" planted next to the entrance of the museum. The trees can attract visitors' attention and guide traffic toward the entrance. In winter, the deciduous tree branches form an enormous "sculpture". In a courtyard formed by several buildings, a very strange and graceful tree can be placed at the center of the courtyard and forms a "Specimen" or focus of the space. A gigantic evergreen tree is often used to dominate a lawn area. Plants with unique forms are also used to signify a building entrance.

At a city park, a large Ficus tree can be planted next to the playground; it can dominate the space and provides shade and resting area for children. It could achieve a better effect if benches or other seating furniture were placed under the tree canopy. One easy way to create a seating area is to raise the planter to about 16" high and 16" wide with smooth top finish, and the planter itself can become the benches.

b. "Gray surface" and "gray space"

Gray is the color between black and white. Similarly, a "Gray Surface" is the surface that sits between complete separation and connection. A "Gray Space" is the space that is between interior space and exterior space. It can also be the transitional space. Because of their many properties, plants can form very unique surfaces and spaces. By choosing plants with different density in leaves and branches, we can control the density of the "Gray Surfaces" formed by plants, thus creating different "Gray Spaces" that are separated and yet connected. "Gray Spaces" can make a garden more interesting. A very common "Gray Space" is the space formed by a tree canopy. This space is neither a completely exterior space nor a completely interior space. It is a space between the interior and exterior spaces: the tree canopy provides shade and protection from rains for people below, yet it allows sun to penetrate between the leaves and branches and winds to pass through. A good designer should encourage people to stay in and fully utilize this kind of "Gray Space." Research has shown that people tend to stay longer in places where they can sit down, so you may want to provide sitting areas in "Gray Spaces" to encourage people to stay and to create more activities (Fig. 1.16).

c. Bottom surface

Lawns, ground covers, low-rise plants, water, floating plants and paving normally form the bottom surface of a garden space. A lawn in public areas should be able to stand heavy traffic. Ground covers are very effective in dust and erosion control. Low-rise decorative plants can be placed at building entries and along the walking path to create accent for landscaping. A simple rule of thumb in designing the bottom surface of a garden is to ensure complete irrigation and plant coverage for all soil areas. You may want to avoid loose and exposed soil areas to minimize dust and erosion. The exposed soil area may also be covered with rocks or decomposed granite, as in many Eastern and desert examples.

At Las Vegas, Nevada, USA, large areas of lawn form the bottom surface of an urban plaza at the intersection of two major streets, surrounded by New York/New York Hotel and Casino, MGM Hotel and Casino, Tropicana Hotel and Casino, Excalibur Hotel and Casino. The lawn is designed to endure heavy traffic of many visitors and becomes an ideal place for visitors to take pictures of the famous casinos around the plaza. Most of the trees planted in this plaza are very low palm trees so as not to block the view of the well-designed casinos.

d. Side surface

Trees, hedges, shrubs, low-rise decorative plants, fences and climbing plants normally form the side surface of a garden. All these planting design elements can be combined to create multi-layer planting, to form an interesting side surface and to define a space. For example, lawn, low-rise decorative plants, shrubs and several pine trees can be used along the sidewalk to soften the view of the iron fence of a parking lot.

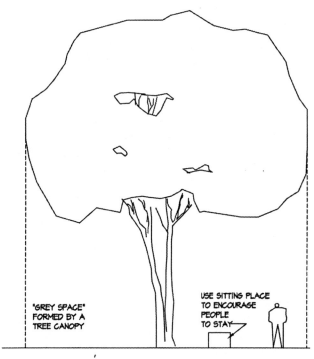

"GREY SPACE" FORMED BY A TREE CANOPY

USE SITTING PLACE TO ENCOURAGE PEOPLE TO STAY

Fig. 1.16 A gray space form by a tree canopy

A good example of using plants to form the side surface and to define a space is the planting design for a lake in a residential area in a subtropical climate. The overall planting design for the lake is naturalistic. To the west of the lake, the designer uses naturally-scattered deciduous trees along the lake to from a gray side surface; in winter, the beautiful lines formed by the branches of the deciduous trees is breath-taking (Fig. 1.17). To the north of the lake, a medium street terminates at the lake and splits into two streets. The designer intentionally uses very few trees along the north side of the lake to allow a splendid view of lake for people who travel toward the lake. To the east of the lake, the two-story-high homes and loosely planted trees form the side surface. To the south of the Lake, very tall evergreen trees are densely planted to define and enclose the space yet allow the view to the lake below the tree canopies.

Fig. 1.17 Side surfaces formed by plants-the west and north sides of a lake

At a city park in southern California, the space around a lake is almost completely defined by side surfaces formed by trees: To the north of the lake, several very tall Eucalyptus trees separate the lake from a children's Playground and provide shade for the resting area; To the east of the lake, smaller and lower trees are planted to match the size and mass of the youth center building and partially concealed the building; To the south of the lake, smaller trees are planted to provide shade for the picnic area and taller Eucalyptus trees are planted farther away to provide a second layer of planting; To the west of the lake, a combination of tall Eucalyptus trees and lower trees are planted to separate the lake from the soccer fields. Only trees and lawn are used in the planting design, no shrubs are used here. This is probably because this is a public park and belongs to the city. In many urban or suburban public parks, city police departments do not allow the use of shrubs because they can block the view of a police officer and create some dangerous hidden areas or spaces. A designer should always find out the city requirements at the beginning of a project so as not to waste a lot of time to design something that does not comply with public agency criteria.

27

Sometimes, bottom surface and side surfaces of a garden can be both formed by plants. For example, densely planted bamboos, palms and various other plants may surround a large lawn. The lawn forms the bottom surface for people to walk or rest on. The densely planted trees form the side surfaces and separate the lawn area with the rest of the garden.

Many similar cases can also be found in English Style Gardens: large lawn areas, surrounded by densely planted trees.

Along a street, English Ivy can be used to cover and conceal a concrete masonry unit (CMU) wall. A CMU wall is often used to block the noise and the view of pedestrians to the backyard of the homes. But the wall can be very unattractive if exposed. The English Ivy can completely cover the wall and turn it into a green wall.

A special kind of side surface is Espaliers: it is a fruit tree or an ornamental plant trained against wall and fence so that its branches grow in a flat plane.

e. Top surface

Trellis, climbing plants, tree canopies normally form the top surface of a garden space. These top surfaces provide shade for people and form a gray space below. In tropical and sub-tropical climate areas, trellis and climbing plants are often used to completely or partially cover a courtyard to provide a resting and retreat area for people in the summer.

At many lawn areas, top surfaces formed by evergreen tree canopies create perfect gray space or resting areas for visitors. At some gardens, decorative vines climbed up the side and top of the trellis and form a unique top surface and side surface.

f. Layers and depth in a space

Plants are often used to create layers and depth in a space. Plants can be use to form three layers of space:

a) The close layer: this is up to a distance of about 50 feet from the viewers. Plants at this layer, such as the hanging branches and leaves of a tree canopy, can be used to form a picture frame. The viewers can observe many details of plants, like smell, flowers, textures, etc. at this layer.

b) The medium-distance layer: this is the layer of plants placed between about 50 feet to about 300 feet. Plants at this layers can be use to soften building elevations, to improve the environment of a neighborhood, etc.

c) The distant layer: this is the layer of plants placed at about 300 feet and beyond. Plants at this layer normally form the background of a space. They need to be tall and visible from a distance.

Within each layer, you can use plants to create sub-layers. These different layers and sub-layers of plants can increase the depth of a space.

g. Organization of spaces

Spaces formed by plants have several basic relationships (Fig. 1.18): Space within a space, interlocking spaces, adjacent spaces and spaces linked by a common space. For the concept of space within a space to be perceived, a clear difference between the space sizes may be needed. Two interlocking spaces can retain their identities, while the interlocking portion of the space can have different roles. It can be equally shared by each space, or merge with one of the space, or develop into an independent entity. Two adjacent spaces can have different degree of visual and spatial connection, depending on the surface that separated them. They can be completely separate, or connected through openings, or partially separated by a free standing surface, or separated by a loose, net-like surface formed by plants. Adjacent spaces that are not completely separated can form some kind of "flowing spaces." Two spaces linked by a common space can have different spatial relationship, depending on the properties of the common space. The common space can be different from the two spaces in form, can be a long "corridor" to link two remote spaces, can be a smaller transitional space, and can be a large and dominant space that organize the spaces around it, or it can be "left-over" space solely determined by the spaces that are being linked. The common space can also be the same size and form of the two spaces, and form a series of space in linear sequence.

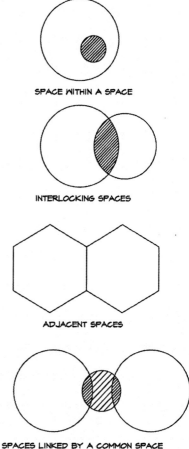

SPACE WITHIN A SPACE

INTERLOCKING SPACES

ADJACENT SPACES

SPACES LINKED BY A COMMON SPACE

Fig. 1.18 Basic spatial relationships

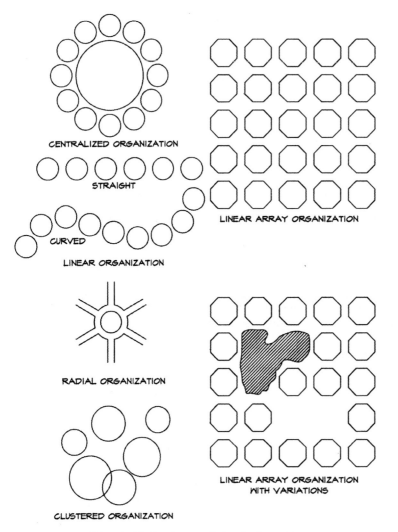

CENTRALIZED ORGANIZATION

STRAIGHT

CURVED

LINEAR ORGANIZATION

RADIAL ORGANIZATION

CLUSTERED ORGANIZATION

LINEAR ARRAY ORGANIZATION

LINEAR ARRAY ORGANIZATION
WITH VARIATIONS

Fig. 1.19 Basic spatial relationships

There are several ways to organize spaces (Fig. 1.19): Centralized organization, linear organization, radial organization, clustered organization, and linear array organization. A centralized organization typically has a large, dominant space surrounded by a number of smaller, secondary spaces. Furthermore, a large tree can be placed at the center of the dominant space to form a focus as we have discussed earlier. The central space can be regular in form. The secondary space can have the same form and size to create a regular, symmetrical organization. They can also have different forms to adapt to the site condition or functional needs. A linear organization is a series of spaces organized along a line, either a straight line or a curved line. It can also be broken into different segments. The spaces in a linear organization can be linked directly with each other or they can be linked by a long, linear space or corridor. Each space along the sequence can have an exterior exposure. The importance of a space in the linear organization can be achieved through a distinct form or a strategic location. A linear organization can terminates at a dominant space, an elaborate entrance, a different space organization pattern, or amalgamated with site topography. A radial organization is the combination of both centralized and linear organization. It is a centralized space with a number of linear organizations radiating outwards. While a centralized organization encourages inwards movement and attention to the central space, a radial organization encourages both inwards and outwards movement. It not only brings attention to the centralized space, but also reaches out to the context with its linear arms. A clustered organization relies on the proximity of spaces. Spaces can be of the same size and form, or of different sizes and forms. Compared with others, it is a flexible organization pattern. The significance of a space can be achieved by a dominant size, special location, form or orientation within the organization. A linear array organization can be viewed as linear organizations developed in two different directions. A linear array organization is often composed of modular spaces of same form and size. These modular spaces can be added or subtracted from the overall organization to create variations. The distance between these modular spaces can change at one or both directions to adapt to environment or project needs. A linear array organization can be disrupted to accommodate a natural feature or create a special interest.[4]

h. Contrast of spaces

Contrast is one of the most commonly used techniques in art. In drawings and painting, in order to show an object to be white, we often exaggerate the darkness of the environment or simply place a black or dark color object next to it. In literature, such as a novel, in order to create a climax of joyful feeling, an author customarily placed some tragic or depressing events before the happy event to create a sharp contrast between the depression and the joy. Similarly, we can use the same technique in planting design. In order to show the grandness of a large space, we need to direct the visitors of a garden through a cozy and enclosed space formed by dense trees, shrubs and trellis first, and then lead them into a grand, wide open and bright space. Without the contrast of a small space, a large space may not feel grand no matter how large it actually is. This technique can also be repeated in a varied way to create a series of climaxes in spaces: enclosed and small space→wide, grand and open space→ relatively enclosed and small space again→relatively wide, grand and open space again, etc. Plants need to be placed and selected accordingly per the spatial design concept.

In addition to the contrast in size, the spaces formed by plants can have contrast in shape, orientation and the degree of openness. Like any other elements in a garden, spaces formed by plants also conform to the principles of simplicity, balance, scale, sequence, climax, contrast and unity. Sometimes, spaces in similar shape and scale can be repeated to create rhythm. Repetitive spaces can create unity, while contrasting spaces can create interest and

---

[4] Ching, Frank D.K. and Ching Francis D. *Architecture: Form, Space, and Order.* John Wiley and Sons, 2nd edition, February 1996. pp. 177-227.

variations. The key is to properly balance unity and contrast, repetitions and variations.

You can use some hints to suggest the existence of another space and attract the attention of garden visitor. The hints and suggestions are not signage. They can be some elements that are not so obvious: paths leading to another space, some accent color plants at the entrance to another space, or loose planting to make another space partially visible from the current space.

i. Sequence and climax

When a number of spaces are organized together, they can form space series. It is important to have a climax for a space series. It can demonstrate the main theme of the garden. To achieve a climax, we may need some smaller, cozy spaces to create the enclosed feeling, and then larger space to create an open feeling. The contrast between large and smaller space may need to be repeated several times, and finally we can enter the main space, or the climax through a very small space. The smaller space can make the dominant space larger and create a feeling of grandness. The preceding repetitions of spaces can be considered as the preparation for the climax. You may want to pay special attention to the beginning and end of the space series. You also need to make sure that the space series will work both ways: both coming and going. You may also want to add some smaller, transitional space between spaces to maintain the continuity of space series.

j. Transition

For formal gardens and planting design, the spaces close to the building are typically formal, and the spaces away from the building are less formal, and the spaces farther away from the building are even less formal. For examples, at French formal gardens, low clipped hedges and parterres form the spaces close to the chateau. Higher hedges and less formal plantings form the spaces away from the chateau. Trees planted along straight line form the spaces even further away. These trees are not trimmed and are even less formal; they frame the vista along the gently raised path to the distant horizon. The transitions of spaces are pretty masterful: from very formal to less formal, and then even less formal and then to the horizon.

6. Time as another dimension

In addition to the regular three dimensions of a space (width, height and depth), time is another dimension in space design. This is also true in planting design. Time's impact in planting design is achieved by studying and controlling people's movement in the gardens to show or block various views along the path. It can also be achieved through plants' seasonal changes, through the life cycle of plants and even through different light and shadow created by plants in different time of a day.

a. Moving through a garden

You may place yourself in the position of a garden visitor; contemplate the potential path a visitor may take and the views along the path when he moves through a garden. By carefully selecting and placing plants along the garden path, you can create attractive scenes and block undesired views.

One way to achieve good space sequences is: from a simple and large space to a smaller, even smaller, tiny or restrictive space, and back to larger and larger spaces and then back to smaller and smaller spaces. The key is when moving from a small space to a large one, you'll feel the small space smaller than it actually is, and the large space larger than it actually is. This is because of the contrast between the spaces. Moving from a larger space to a smaller space, you'll get a reversed contrast and effect.

b. Four seasons

Compared to other materials, plants have a distinct advantage: plants change with seasons; different plants will bloom in different seasons. Through a designer's selection and combination, a garden could have flowers blossom in turn in all four seasons. In the appendix of this book, we have a list of ornamentals frequently used in Chinese gardens. These ornamentals are listed by each of the four seasons; they have also been used in the U.S. and other countries. For example, one of the plants in this list is *Pyrus kawakamii* (Evergreen Pear); it has been used extensively in the U.S. For instance, along the sidewalk of a city in the U.S., several *Pyrus kawakamii* trees are casually planted. It is amazing to see how the entire *Pyrus kawakamii* tree can be filled with flowers in just a few days in spring (Fig. 1.20).

Deciduous trees have new leaves in spring, mature leaves in summer, falling leaves in fall and no

Fig. 1.20 Four seasons- the entire Pyrus kawakamii tree is filled with flowers in spring

leaves in winter. It is astounding to see that one deciduous tree can have four different seasonal aesthetic effects in a garden. For example, at Grand Canyon National Park (the Grand Canyon), Arizona, snow covered branches of a deciduous tree becomes a "live sculpture" and create more interest at the observation area for tourists. Snow on a pine tree becomes "flowers" for the tree.

c. Different time in a day

In different time of a day, plants experience different forces of nature: frost, dew, sun, wind, fog, and rain. You may study the site carefully and try to understand all these natural forces and their impact on the site, and incorporate these factors in the planting design process. For example, sun can create light and shadow; the patterns formed by sun and shadow can create interest in a garden; shade-loving plants can be placed in the shadow or shade area to avoid damage to the plants from the sun.

d. The life cycle of a plant

A plant has its own life cycle, its seed will sprout, and then grow from small to large, from young to mature and eventually will die after many years. Because most of the plants used in a garden came from nurseries, they are not fully-grown yet. Your planting design concept may not be completely realized until the plants grow up. This can take 10 years or more. You can choose proper combination of the size and species of plants to achieve both short-term and long-term design effects. In some special occasions or some special projects, such as the grand opening of a major casino or shopping center, it may be necessary to achieve some "instant" landscape effect. We can achieve this effect by using appropriate plants, such as a certain number of palm trees.

Sufficient space shall be provided to accommodate the final fully-grown sizes of plants.

7. Plants and buildings

Plants can be used to provide shade for buildings so at to reduce the temperature of building walls and roofs and to save energy and air-conditioning cost in the summer time.

a. To the east of buildings

To the east of the buildings, we can plant tall trees with dense canopies so as to block sunlight at a high angle, while not blocking the view of sunrise. In the early morning hours, when the sun is rising at a low angle, the sunlight is still fairly gentle; there is no need to block it. In late morning hours, the sun is at a high angle and the sunlight is very strong and produces a great amount of heat, tall trees with dense canopies can block the strong sunlight at a high angle (Fig 1.21, Fig. 1.22).

b. To the south of buildings

In the Northern Hemisphere, we probably would plant tall and high crown deciduous trees to the south of buildings. This is because that the sunlight is at a high angle in the summer, while at a low angle in the winter. Deciduous trees have full foliage and can block high-angle sunlight to reduce heat in the buildings in the summer. They have no leaves in the winter and can allow sunlight to penetrate through the branches and south-facing windows and enter rooms to raise room temperature at a low angle.

A good designer should also consider the dominant wind direction of the areas that he works in. He should incorporate this into his overall planting design concept. For examples, in most Asian countries in the Northern Hemisphere, the dominant wind comes from the southeast in the summer, while the dominant summer wind direction is from the southwest in West Coast of America. The overall planting layout shall not block the dominant summer wind of a site to the buildings.

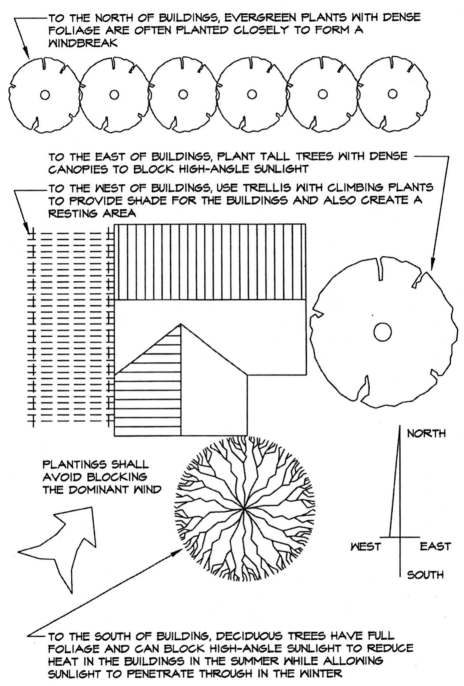

TO THE NORTH OF BUILDINGS, EVERGREEN PLANTS WITH DENSE FOLIAGE ARE OFTEN PLANTED CLOSELY TO FORM A WINDBREAK

TO THE EAST OF BUILDINGS, PLANT TALL TREES WITH DENSE CANOPIES TO BLOCK HIGH-ANGLE SUNLIGHT

TO THE WEST OF BUILDINGS, USE TRELLIS WITH CLIMBING PLANTS TO PROVIDE SHADE FOR THE BUILDINGS AND ALSO CREATE A RESTING AREA

PLANTINGS SHALL AVOID BLOCKING THE DOMINANT WIND

NORTH

WEST   EAST

SOUTH

TO THE SOUTH OF BUILDING, DECIDUOUS TREES HAVE FULL FOLIAGE AND CAN BLOCK HIGH-ANGLE SUNLIGHT TO REDUCE HEAT IN THE BUILDINGS IN THE SUMMER WHILE ALLOWING SUNLIGHT TO PENETRATE THROUGH IN THE WINTER

Fig. 1.21 Plants and buildings (plan view)

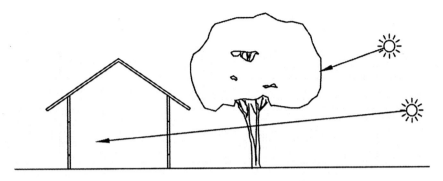

TO THE EAST OF BUILDINGS, PLANT TALL TREES WITH DENSE
CANOPIES TO BLOCK HIGH-ANGLE SUNLIGHT

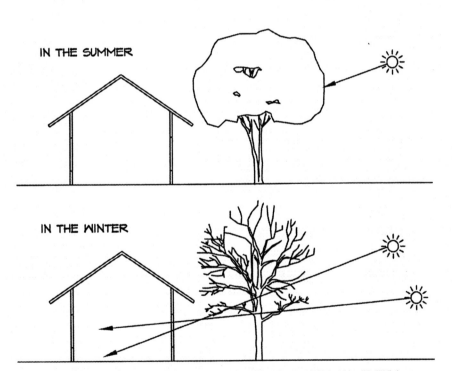

IN THE SUMMER

IN THE WINTER

TO THE SOUTH OF BUILDING, DECIDUOUS TREES HAVE FULL
FOLIAGE AND CAN BLOCK HIGH-ANGLE SUNLIGHT TO REDUCE
HEAT IN THE BUILDINGS IN THE SUMMER WHILE ALLOWING
SUNLIGHT TO PENETRATE THROUGH IN THE WINTER

Fig. 1.22 Plants and buildings (section views)

c. To the west of buildings

Westerly sunlight is one of the major reasons that buildings over-heat. To the west of Buildings, plantings should be able to block the afternoon sunlight. One commonly used technique is to use a trellis with climbing plants to provide shade for the buildings and also create a resting area under the trellis in the summer time. Climbing plants are also used to climb up vertical trellis or fences, which is very effective in blocking low-angle late afternoon sunlight.

d. To the north of buildings

Chilly north wind in the winter can significantly increase the heating energy cost. Evergreen plants with dense foliage, such as cypress trees are often planted closely to the north of buildings to form windbreaks.

e. Rooftop gardens

One of the Seven Wonders of the World, the Hanging Gardens of Babylon may be one of the earliest rooftop gardens. Waterproofing is the biggest challenge for rooftop gardens. To prevent damage to the roof and the waterproofing system, plants used in rooftop gardens shall have shallow roots and modest size, and are often placed in planting pots or planters. Climbing plants and trellis are also excellent choices for rooftop gardens. One of the recent examples for rooftop gardens is located at the pool area for Venetian Hotel and Casino in Las Vegas. It is a rooftop garden with a health and fitness center and a wedding chapel.

f. Plants and building elevations

As we have mentioned earlier in this chapter, plants can be used to break a monotonous wall surface and to create an interesting skyline. Plants can also be used to soften building elevations and even block part of a building elevation and create a "green wall."

When laying out the plants around a building, you may start with a floor plan and first find out the available planting areas, and then study the building elevations and decide the plants' heights, forms and habit in relation to the building elevations. You may also do a simple view line study in sections or elevations to further study the relationship between the plants and the building. You may find out that you need to go back to step one and add a planting area in plan to form a better composition in elevations. Perspective views and bird's eye views can also be used to assist your thoughts or present your ideas to clients. You may also need to imagine yourself as a user or an owner and the potential views you may encounter as you walk through the garden either toward or away from the building. Some designers prefer to start the planting design from elevations, which is another way of doing planting design. I am sure there are other ways or sequences to do planting design. It is just a matter of preference, and does not necessarily mean one way is better than the other. The important thing is that you know what you are doing and understand the relationship between the building and plants. I prefer paying more attention to planting plans because they are the drawings that actually tell a contractor what to do, and can convey most information. They are very easy to draw and can convey your ideas quickly. They can be used in schematic design stage, design development stage and the construction document stage. You can even use the same planting plan for all three stages of the project, and just change the level of details and notes accordingly. This way, you do not have to draw your drawings three times, and you can save a lot of time and energy and can be very efficient. The important thing is when you draw planting plans you need to know what the plants look like in elevations and in the field. Please note that people normally do not experience a landscape in plan view, unless from an upper floor of a multi-story building or high viewing terraces. That is why some design schemes look very good in plans, but may appear to be average or poor after the garden is built. ONLY considering the plants in plan view is a frequently failure of landscape architects. To alleviate this problem, elevations and sections can be used as tools to assist your thinking and understanding the major relationship between plants and building. You may want to pay more attention to volumes and planes and other major design elements, instead of spending too much time to details. Pretty and detailed elevations or perspective drawings may help you to sell your ideas to your clients, but the most important thing is that you know how to achieve a good end result, i.e., the result when the garden is built and planting is completed, including both the short-term and long-term effects. Some planting design rendered in pretty elevations or perspective drawings may turn out to be average or even poor planting design also. This may be because when drawing elevations, you can cheat by drawing the plants in the way that you want, or you may have a good training in drawing and can present an average design better than it actually is. To avoid this, you may want to pay more attention to the habit and forms of plants and realize the fact that we CANNOT completely control the plants: they are living things and they'll grow, and the design effect will change as they grow. You may also want to pay more attention to the principles and try to control the frame work of your planting design and try not to pay too much attention to details of specific plants, since you know you probably cannot completely control them anyway.

When considering the planting design around a building, we need to pay special attention to the building's entrance, and then windows or other openings. Simplicity, balance, good scale, graduation and climax may be the keys to success. A desire to use many plants may be detrimental to planting design. Good planting design is different from a collection of plants. A few well-chosen species may be better than jamming many plants in a garden. Too many different species of plants can cause confusion and chaos. Simplicity can create beauty. For example, a small residential garden can have a fine texture lawn with flowerbeds along the border. The fine texture of the lawn compared with the coarse texture of the flowers and leaves can create interest and a very simple but beautiful garden. It does not really matter which specific plant to use, it does matter how each plant is used. If we know what we want in a plant, we can easily pick a plant or substitute it with another plant to achieve the desired effect. We are not very concerned about the rarity of plants, but rather the effects of plants in our composition. We pay more attention to simplicity, balance, scale, sequence, graduation and climax.

One way to handle the relationship between building elevations and plants is to analyze the planes and volumes of the building. You may start from analyzing the rooflines first: does it need to be softened or repeated? Use big trees behind the building to make the rooflines disappear or use some high trees to break the monotonous rooflines? In some simple, classical buildings, they might need only lawn and trees, but no shrubs. In building with plain, simple and large area of walls, the silhouette or the shadow of plants should be fully utilized. Sometimes, vines or other climbing plants may be used to age the building. At the entrance of buildings, we may not want to use too many plants. We'd rather the entrance appear to be wide than narrow. We may want to use plants to create balance for a less than perfect building. The building entrance is often the imaginary axis for a symmetrical or an asymmetrical balance (Fig. 1.23). For a large building, we may want to use large plants to create a transition space between human scale and the huge building scale; For a tall building, we may want to use rounded trees within its façade, tall trees around them, and rounded and spread trees to make the building appear to be wider; For a low and flat building, we may want to use tall trees to break the horizontal lines, and trees with spread form around it to encroach on its edge and reduce its width; For a house with a chimney, we may want to use tall trees with dense foliage behind it to make it less noticeable. For a building with a triangular gable roof, we may use rounded trees of different heights to repeat the rhythm of the roof outline.

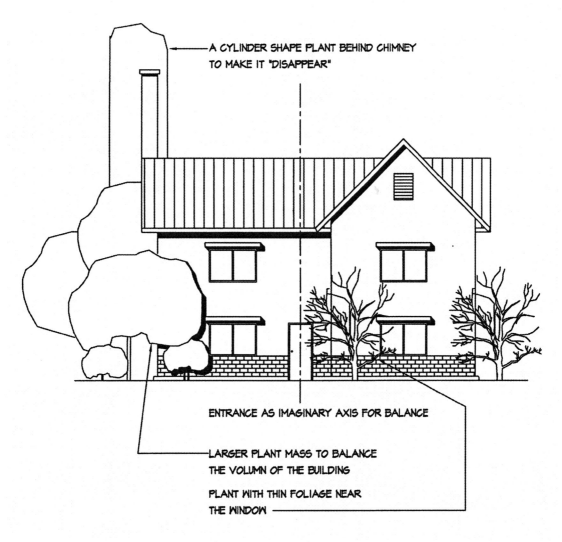

A CYLINDER SHAPE PLANT BEHIND CHIMNEY
TO MAKE IT "DISAPPEAR"

ENTRANCE AS IMAGINARY AXIS FOR BALANCE

LARGER PLANT MASS TO BALANCE
THE VOLUMN OF THE BUILDING

PLANT WITH THIN FOLIAGE NEAR
THE WINDOW

Fig. 1.23 Elevation study

In addition to considering the composition in elevations, you may want to leave enough distance between the trees and a building. For example, it is probably not a very good idea to plant a Ficus tree within five feet of the building. The strong roots of the Ficus tree may damage the building foundation and underground plumbing lines. It may not be a very good idea to place a clipped hedge along a building wall. It can create an ideal breeding place for insects.

g. Concealing and revealing

Plants can be used to conceal undesirable building elements while revealing the desired features. You may consider plants and building as one entity, and reveal attractive building features and blocking some functional, but not so pretty features. This principle can be used to handle practical, functional needs also. For example, it is absolute imperative to reveal the signage for a commercial tenant or owner of a shopping center or a major commercial building. That is one of the reasons that palm trees have become one of the favorite choices for shopping centers or casinos. For commercial buildings, some accessory equipment or building elements, such as a loading dock, electrical switchgears and transformers and double check valves require concealing. Dense evergreen trees/shrubs or hedges are often used in these situations.

Building codes also require the address of a building to be readily visible so that emergency vehicles and personnel can recognize and access the building easily. Plants should never block the address of a building.

8. Planting Plans in Landscape Practice

a. Planting presentation drawings

For most of the landscape architect's offices, planting presentation drawings are only 10% to 20% of the workload. 80% to 90% of the planting design work is handled through planting plans in construction drawing stage. Planting presentation drawings can be preliminary planting plans, except that they are normally color renderings and shadows of plants are often shown to create a three-dimensional graphic effect (Fig. 1.24). The key for a successful landscape planting presentation drawing is to select good colors, especially a few good green colors for plants. Each landscape office normally has a color palette for the colors that the office frequently uses for landscape planting presentation drawings.

b. Planting plans

For planting plans, graphic symbols and legends are normally simplified to communicate the design intent to the contractors in a most efficient way. There are two ways to organize and lay out planting plans:

c. Type I layout (Fig. 1.25)

All plants are shown on the plants, same kind of plants are linked together with straight lines and then called out directly. A plant's botanical name, common name, and size and quantities are called out for each group of plants. If one plant has been used in different areas of a project, then this plant may be called out more than once in the same planting plan. Normally, the call-out line connect to the end of a string of plants, and the connecting line between plants is straight within the group and curved when crossing another connecting line. In the example we show in Fig. 1.25, we use some curved connecting lines within the group. This is because the layout of the planting plan is circular; using curved connecting lines will reduce the overlapping and crossing of various lines and make the planting plan easier to read. We have made an exception to the rules here for clarity.

A plant list/schedule is also shown on the sheet, with the total number of each plant used shown on the list/schedule. This method was very commonly used in Landscape Architects' offices before Computer Aided Design and Drafting (CADD) became extensively used in Landscape Architecture and other design fields. The advantage of this method is that it is very straightforward: the name of the plant is right there next to the graphic symbols. It is easy to draw by hand: the graphic symbols do not need to be drawn exactly the same for the same plant, since they are linked together by straight lines. The disadvantage is that if the drawings need to be revised, often more than one locations need to be revised, since each plant has probably been called out several times in different areas of the project. If one or several groups of plants are missed in the revisions, conflicts and mistakes will occur. It is also more tedious and time-consuming to revise.

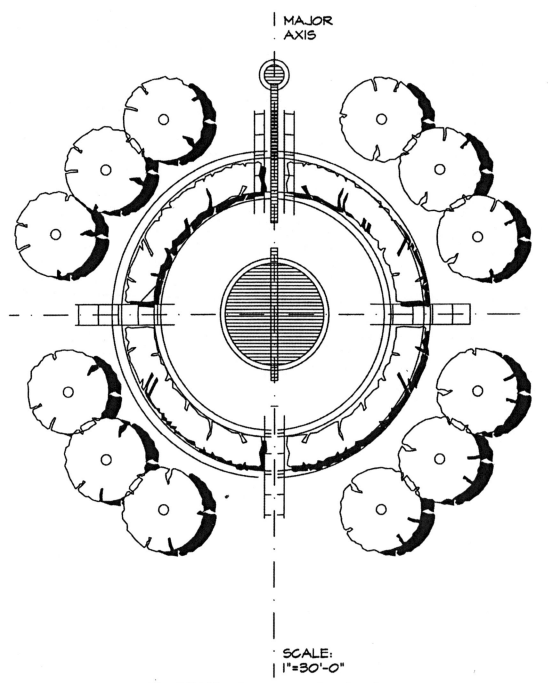

Fig. 1.24 Planting presentation drawings

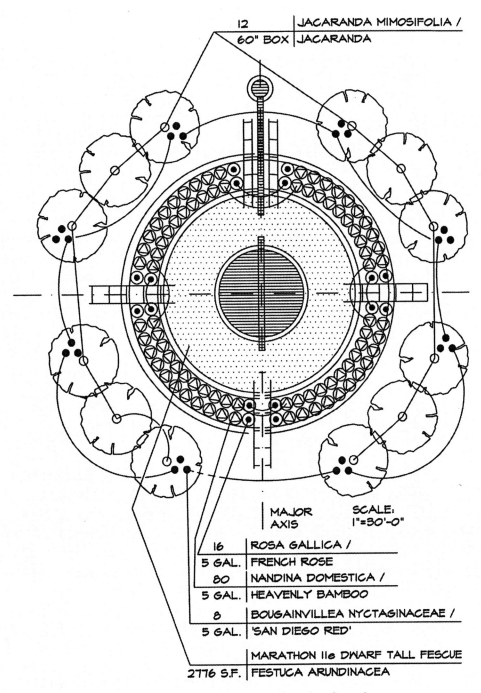

12 | JACARANDA MIMOSIFOLIA /
60" BOX | JACARANDA

MAJOR AXIS

SCALE: 1"=30'-0"

16	ROSA GALLICA /
5 GAL.	FRENCH ROSE
80	NANDINA DOMESTICA /
5 GAL.	HEAVENLY BAMBOO
8	BOUGAINVILLEA NYCTAGINACEAE /
5 GAL.	'SAN DIEGO RED'
	MARATHON IIe DWARF TALL FESCUE
2776 S.F.	FESTUCA ARUNDINACEA

Fig. 1.25 Type I layout for planting plan

d. Type II layout

The other way is to use graphic symbols to represent plants, each kind of symbol represent a different kind of plant (Fig. 1.26). There is a planting legend that explains what each graphic symbol means (Fig. 1.27). Each graphic symbol is followed by the plant's botanical name/common name, size (size of the plant's container when came from plant nursery. This is the way nurseries size and sell their plants. It is widely used in the Landscape Architecture Practice), distance between plants (a designer should decide the proper distance between plants based on the final sizes of the plants) and quantities used. Plants are grouped as trees, shrubs, ground covers, lawn, vines, container or pot planting, etc. The advantage of this layout is that each plant is called out only once at the planting legend. If revisions are needed, a designer can keep the graphic symbol and simply change the plant name in the planting legend. The key is that the graphic symbols for the same plant need to look exact the same at different areas of the project. The application of CADD has made this a very easy task. This type of layout is becoming very popular as the use of CADD is becoming more and more common. The biggest advantage of this layout is the saving of time in revisions, especially when the plants are changed, since you only need to change the plant call-out once at the planting legend. Any one who has worked in a landscape architect's office would know revisions are very common for various reasons: owner's review comments, plan check corrections, availability of the plants specified, etc.

For both Type I and Type II planting plan layouts, common sizes for trees are 15 gallon (gal.), 24" box, 36" box, 48" box, and 60" box. Shrub Sizes are often called out as 1 gal. at 24" On Center (O.C.), 5 gal. at 18" O.C, 5 gal. at 24" O.C, 5 gal. at 30" O.C. or 5 gal. at 36" O.C., etc. Ground covers are called out as 4" pot at 8" O.C., flats at 8" O.C., flats at 12" O.C., flats at 24" O.C., etc. Lawn is commonly called out as SOD (a very popular term for lawn in the U.S. Lawn is planted in the nurseries, and then harvested and cut out as 12" x 60" or 5 square foot flat pieces and then transported to project site and applied within a short time frame), and a designer customarily gives the total square footage of the lawn area for the project. Vines come in as 1 gal., 5 gal., and 4" pot sizes.

Soil areas that are not surfaced by ground cover or lawn are customarily covered by 1" diameter broken bark wood mulch to a depth of 2".

e. Other elements in landscape construction documents

We'll briefly introduce other factors in landscape constructions documents here so that the less experienced designers or lay people can understand some basic elements of landscape practice.

PLANTING DESIGN ILLUSTRATED

Landscape construction documents are the legal documents prepared by the landscape architects. They are normally part of the binding contract documents between the owner and the contractor. Landscape construction documents include landscape construction drawings and landscape specifications. Landscape specifications cover quality and workmanship of landscape construction. It can be a separate specification book or can be set up as one or a few sheets within the construction drawing set. Landscape construction drawings cover location, size, quantity and color of landscape elements. They are composed of planting plans (which we discussed in detail in this book), irrigation plans, some detail sheets and hardscape plans if applicable. Irrigation plans are normally done by outside consultants in most landscape architects' offices. Important things to check in irrigation plans are:

a) "Head to Head" coverage: water from one irrigation sprinkler head shall always cover the adjacent irrigation sprinkler head to ensure even coverage (Fig. 1.28);

b) "Zero run off": make sure water from the sprinkler heads will not sprinkler onto or run off to adjacent properties;

c) Each sprinkler head shall have enough water pressure to operate at the design sprinkler radius;

d) It may be a good idea to over size the irrigation line, because one may have to add more sprinkler heads and extension lines at a later addition to the original landscape project.

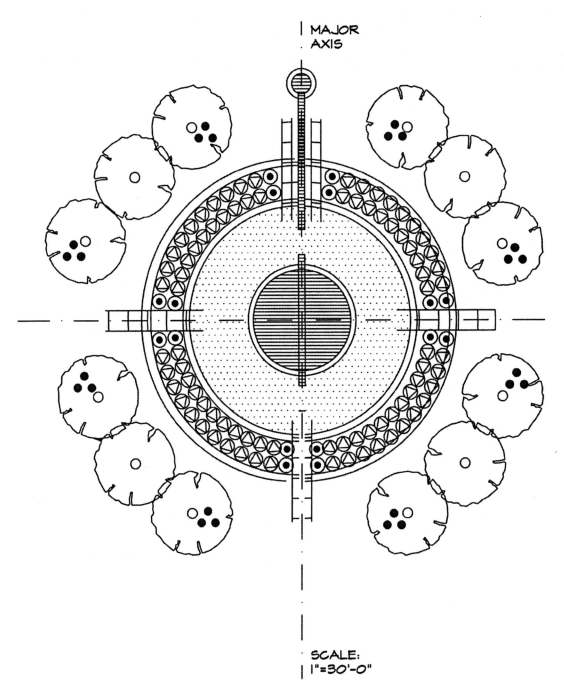

Fig. 1.26 Type II layout for planting plan

PLANTING LEGEND

SYMBOL	BOTANICAL / COMMON NAME	SIZE	QUANTITY	DETAIL
TREES				
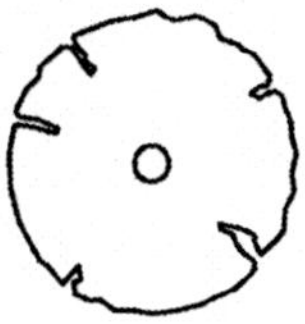	JACARANDA MIMOSIFOLIA / JACARANDA	60" BOX	12	-
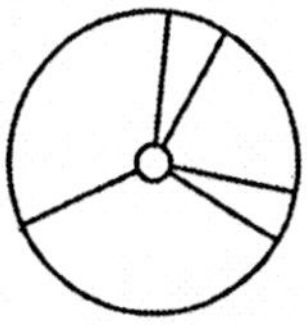	MAGNOLIA GRANDFLORA SOUTHERN MAGNOLIA	15 GAL.	48	-
	LIQUIDAMBER STYRACIFLUA AMERICAN SWEET GUM	36" BOX	18	-
SHRUBS				
⊛	JASMINUM OLEACEAE / JASMINE	1 GAL. AT 18" O.C.	76	-
▽	NANDINA DOMESTICA / HEAVENLY BAMBOO	5 GAL. AT 36" O.C.	PER PLAN	-
◉	ROSA GALLICA / FRENCH ROSE	5 GAL. AT 24" O.C.	PER PLAN	-
GROUND COVERS				
	HEDERA HELIX / ENGLISH IVY	FLAT AT 12" O.C.	PER PLAN	-
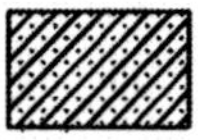	VINCA MINOR / DWARF PERIWINKLE	4" POT AT 8" O.C.	18	-
LAWN				
	MARATHON IIe DWARF TALL FESCUE FESTUCA ARUNDINACEA		2776 S.F.	-
VINES				
	BOUGAINVILLEA NYCTAGINACEAE / 'SAN DIEGO RED'	5 GAL.	8	-

Fig. 1.27 Sample planting legend

LEGEND:

⚐ 1/4 CIRCLE SPRINKLER HEAD

⚔ 1/2 CIRCLE SPRINKLER HEAD

⚑ 3/4 CIRCLE SPRINKLER HEAD

⊙ FULL CIRCLE SPRINKLER HEAD

SCALE:
I"=30'-0"

Fig. 1.28 "Head to head" coverage in irrigation design

Landscape details are pretty much standard at each region and most office have a set of standard details to choose from to set up the detail sheets. Important things to consider are to coordinate the detail with landscape planting plans and irrigation plans and make sure each detail is called out properly on the plans and modified if necessary per project conditions.

f. Plant identification, plant list and office library

Most landscape architects and landscape offices have their most frequently used plant list and catalogs from nurseries set up in their office library. These lists and catalogs normally are adapted to the local conditions and can be very helpful for projects, especially for fast-track projects.

Plant materials are the vocabularies for planting design and they are heavily affected by the local climate, weather and soils conditions. There are plants commonly used in many different areas, but there are also many plants that are unique to a certain area.

Even a very experienced landscape architect will have to learn plant materials and plant identification if he is relocated to a new area. Plant materials are very important, but they are not the focus of this book: First of all, this book focuses on the planting design principles and concepts, or the "grammar" and main ideas of planting design, which are the universal truth that can be used in different areas. Second of all, many books on plant identification and on plant materials for different climate zones have already been published and available. They can be very helpful for beginners in planting design or landscape architects who have been relocated to a new area. See annotated bibliography at the end of this book for a list of books in this subject. Many colleges and universities also offer inexpensive courses on plant materials and plant identification. Students can take pictures of plants in class to assist them in their studies. Frequent visits to botanical gardens and nurseries are also effective ways to learn about plant materials and plant identification. The knowledge of plant materials and the skill of plant identification can only be obtained by each individual's long-term studies and accumulation. This is an area each individual needs to work on. It requires not only knowledge from books, but also actual field visits and practice.

9. Functional and Ecological Considerations

Planting design often takes into account functional and ecological factors. Functional requirements generally come from the owner(s) and the users of the project. You can communicate with the owner(s) and the users and also visit the site to make personal observation to enlist all the functional needs. Many governing agencies have special landscape provisions. For examples, some cities require a minimum distance between trees along the streets so as not to block view of motorists to ensure pedestrian's safety, other cities may require a minimum percentage of planting coverage for a project site or a minimum ratio between trees and number of parking spaces. You may want to contact governing agencies (planning, public works, zoning or building department, etc.) and obtain all relevant provisions at the beginning of the landscape project and conform to them. This simple step can avoid major revisions at a later stage of planting design.

Ecology has been a major concern in the past decades. In planting design, this means you may choose plants that can adapt to the local climate and soil conditions and will not cause negative effects to existing local plant communities. This does NOT mean that we are excluding the use of non-native plants. Throughout history, many civilizations have successfully used and domesticated non-native plants in gardens, and non-native plants have achieved great landscape effects in the U.S. and many other countries. We just need to choose plants more carefully and keep ecology in mind.

Main ecological factors include sunlight, air, water, soil and temperature. Soil provides necessary "food" (minerals) for plants. The topsoil or surface soil often contains humus (organic decay) that can be very beneficial to the growth of plants. Many landscape architects would specify in their plan notes or specifications for the contractors to store and preserve the top 6" to 18" of surface soil or topsoil in the project site. The topsoil can be reapplied to the surface of the site after grading is finished. This is a good way to preserve and use the native topsoil of a site, which can contain many minerals and humus. There two common processes to improve soil: cultivation and fertilization. Cultivation is a mechanical process that stirs the soil. It improves the aeration, drainage of soils, conserves moisture and warm up soil. Fertilization increases the nutrients content and porosity of soil; it corrects ph value (alkalinity or acidity) and adds a specific mineral. Too much fertilizer can increase the acids in the soil and can be detrimental. Mulches over soil surface can retain moisture and reduce the range of soil temperature changes. Sunlight, water, temperature and wind also play important roles in plant life. Different plants have different needs for them.[5]

---

[5] Robinson, Florence Bell. *Planting Design.* Illinois: The Garrard Press, 1940. pp. 105-122.

CHAPTER 2
PLANTING DESIGN IN FORMAL GARDENS

In this chapter, we'll discuss historical development and major trends as well as planting design principles, concepts and common patterns in formal gardens. We'll use them to analyze some famous examples, to make some practical case studies, and try to uncover the underlying major principles and fundamental concepts of planting design in formal gardens (Fig 2.1).

1. Historical Development and Major Trends

It is believed that between 8,000 to 10,000 years ago, man changed from nomad hunters to settled agriculturists and started systematic cultivation of certain form of plants and the domestication of animals on the Anatolian plateau and the foothills to the east of the Mesopotamian plain.[6] Later he came down to the delta of the Euphrates and Tigris. Many early gardens came from agriculture and started with basic and practical needs. They were probably in geometric layout for efficient irrigation. The Western formal landscaping and planting design originated in the regions of Middle East, Mesopotamia, Egypt and Persia. Almost every civilization started at regions where water was readily available; often these regions were close to one or more rivers. Between 4000 BC and 3000BC, Sumerians constructed canals for irrigation at the alluvial plains of Euphrates and Tigris delta, "the fertile crescent." Within a few centuries, they developed luxuriant hunting parks with complicated water systems.[7] The hunting parks were probably laid out in formal patterns. They also built mounds and planted them with trees to provide new homes for their forest gods. These trees were probably planted in formal pattern. These mounds were built layer by layer and rose up toward the sky to formed ziggurats, man-made mountains like stepped

---

[6] Morris, A.E.J. *History of Urban Form: Before the Industrial Revolutions. England: Longman Scientific and Technical,* Longman Group UK Limited, 1979. Reprinted 1990. p3.

[7] Hobhouse, Penelope. *The Story of Gardening.* DK Publishing, 1st edition, November 1, 2002. p.19.

pyramids.[8] The plant materials were probably oak, plane tree, box, cedar, cypress, poplar, willow and date palm, etc. One example was the Ziggurat of UR: it was an artificial "Hill of Heaven" dedicated to Nanna, the moon god and recalling the home of the Sumerian ancestor's mountain gods. It was a sixty-eight-foot-high stepped pyramid with four main layers, built on a ten-foot-high terrace. There was a huge stair leading to the main entrance in the front and one stair at each side. The terrace seems to have been planted with trees. The outer walls were painted with different colors: the lowest layer black, the uppermost red, the shrine was covered with blue-glazed tiles, topped by a gilded dome. These colors were used to symbolize the dark underworld, the habitat earth, the heavens and the sun.

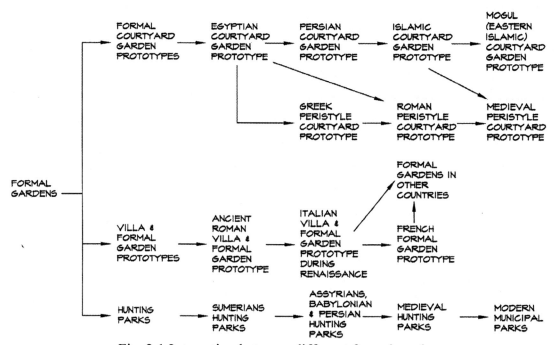

Fig. 2.1 Interaction between different formal gardens

Egyptians probably created the world's first ornamental gardens (Fig 2.2). These walled gardens were shown on tomb paintings discovered in the 19th century. Most of them were built between 3000 BC and 1000BC. Because the region is generally dry and some areas are actually deserts, a good-size pool was necessary to maintain the garden

[8] Loxton, Howard (Editor). *The Garden: A Celebration.* David Bateman Ltd., 1991. p.12

in all seasons. The pool was either rectangle or square; it gradually became the center of the gardens. It was typically located in the front of the house to provide an enjoyable view for the residents. Fish were stocked in it and water lilies were grown in it. Rows of trees were planted in neat straight lines along the reservoir to provide shade and fruits. They were typically date palm, fig, pomegranates or sycamore fig (*Ficus sycomorus*). Grape vines climbed onto the trellis to provide more shade and fruits and winemaking materials. Garden beds with vegetables and flowers filled the rest of the space. The mud garden walls protected the garden from the flood of the Nile and blocked some of the sun's heat. Trees and trellis provided shade. Water in the pool evaporated, cooled and refreshed the air. It also provided psychological cooling effect to the residents. The gardens were oasis in the desert and "paradise" on earth. They were often divided into formal and symmetrical pattern by irrigation channels. The formal planting pattern was determined by the practical need of efficient irrigation. This irrigation need might be the beginning of all formal gardens and planting design. The style of ornamental gardens eventually developed into a pure pleasure garden, but the basic pattern did not change: a formal pool with lilies and fish, decorative flowers along the bank and garden paths, and trees planted in straight lines to provide shade.[9] This was a very practical style for the dry Mediterranean regions and eventually spread to many areas, including Persia and India.

Since early times, walled hunting parks were developed in Assyria, Babylon and Persia. They were enclosed areas with some plants and stocked with animals for royal hunting sport. Persians called this kind of semi-natural parks "paradise," which simply meant an enclosed area at that time. The present meaning of paradise was not attached to this word until a later time.

The Assyrians conquered Egypt in the seventh century BC and took formal gardens and planting design back to Mesopotamia. Later Persians defeated Assyrians and conquered Egypt; they captured the idea of formal gardens and planting design and developed it into a new, exceptional form. They also took with them the Egyptian love for the blue water lily.

Persians copied Egyptian formal gardens and planting design idea and developed it to a new, advanced level. In some Persian gardens, they used cross canals to divide the garden area into four parts. At the intersection of the canals, a building or pool was placed. This four-part idea might have been the symbolism of a primitive concept of the world that was divided into four quarters. It was probably also the predecessor of the *Chahar-bagh* gardens of Islam (Fig 2.3), sacred expression of the Koran, a new sort of

---

[9] Kuck, Loraine E. *The World of Japanese Garden: From Chinese Origins to Modern Landscape Art.* Weatherhill, Inc., 1968. pp. 23-24.

paradise, a symbol of the heaven to come for Muslims. This style quickly spread around these areas and even to central Asia. Each quarter could be further divided to form more complicated patterns. At a sloped site, terraces were created and water would fall in cascades from one terrace to the next. When the water pressure was adequate, as from a pool at a higher level, rows of water jets were usually used along the centerline of the canal or its banks.

Persians had a much stronger interest in growing flowers than the Egyptians. They were among the first to cultivate flowers. Many of the common flowers in Europe were first brought from Persia. When contacts developed between Persia and China, significant exchanges of plants took place and many fruits and flowers now seem to have been native to both regions.

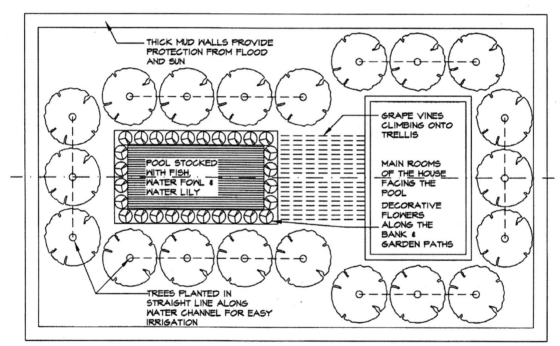

THICK MUD WALLS PROVIDE PROTECTION FROM FLOOD AND SUN

GRAPE VINES CLIMBING ONTO TRELLIS

POOL STOCKED WITH FISH, WATER FOWL & WATER LILY

MAIN ROOMS OF THE HOUSE FACING THE POOL

DECORATIVE FLOWERS ALONG THE BANK & GARDEN PATHS

TREES PLANTED IN STRAIGHT LINE ALONG WATER CHANNEL FOR EASY IRRIGATION

Fig. 2.2 Egyptian courtyard garden prototype

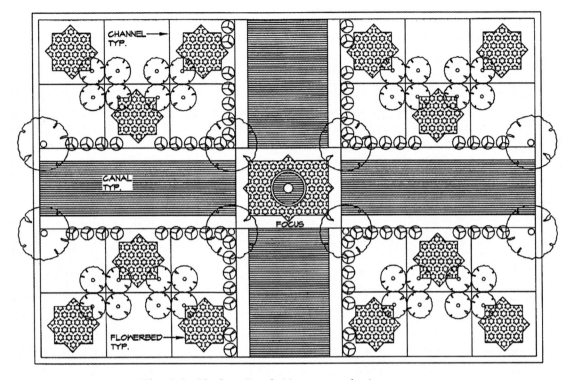

Fig. 2.3 *Chahar Bagh* (4-part garden) prototype

In the seventh century AD, the Muslim Arabs occupied Persia and carried back the Persian garden style to the Mediterranean. This garden style became the basic form of Islamic gardens. It then spread to Spain through North Africa and Sicily. The gardens of the Moorish Alhambra and *Generalife* in Granada have clear indications of their Persian origins: central axes and canals, water jets and flower beds. Many courtyard gardens in Mexico and the American southwest are their remote offspring.

Other areas of Europe had obtained the concept of the formal gardens and planting design via a different path. The conquest of Alexander the Great took the Greek Army to Egypt, Persia and beyond, and carried back the idea of the pleasure garden. They were impressed by the richness of the gardens they saw. In Greek colonies, extravagant gardens were created. In some areas, hanging terraces, flower-filled patios, statues, fountains and hydraulic toys were distinct features of the gardens. They also developed the peristyle courtyard gardens. Covered corridors with colonnades enclosed the courtyard. Pools and fountains were placed at the axis of the courtyard, which was also the axis of the house. Residents had a direct view to the center of the garden from the house. Aromatic and colorful shrubs or other plants were arranged symmetrical to the axis. Paintings of gardens were used on the wall to provide an illusion of a larger garden space. Many of the elements of the peristyle gardens were similar to those of the Egyptian courtyard garden.

Romans took the concept of peristyle gardens from the Greeks and they also obtained formal gardens and planting design directly from Egypt. They added trimmed hedge and trees. When the Normans conquered Sicily and the crusading knights traveled to the Arabian world, they rediscovered the pleasure courtyard garden. They took the idea and many new plants back to Europe. The formal gardens and planting design was carried to medieval Europe in the cloister gardens. During the Renaissance, there was renewed interest in the ancient gardens in Rome. The peristyle survived in courtyard gardens. The country villa and its formal gardens also became a favorite pattern again. Italian designers developed this classical form and used it to create many good gardens, including Villa d'Este, Villa Pratolino, Villa Lante and Frascati.[10] The villa and formal garden were designed as one organic "whole." The inward-looking garden turned outwards to include the landscape and the world beyond. In 1494, Charles VIII of France captured Naples and he was seduced by the Italian style villa and garden at Poggio Reale. He considered it to be "an earthly paradise." Charles's army carried Italian paintings, sculpture and tapestries as well as craftsman back to France to decorate their own chateaux. The Italian principles were adapted to fit French climate and topography. Italian landscape was mostly cultivated plains, valleys, terraced and hills, while French topography was flatter and densely wooded. The flat French terrain made it impossible to use many of the water features that were used in the steep hillsides of Italy. The French developed the ideas of using moats as decorative canals and to drain marshy ground.[11] The French inherited the formal gardens and planting design from Italy and other countries, further developed them and created a climax for this garden style. Many famous formal gardens and planting designs were created in France: Versailles, Chantilly, Vaux-le-Vicomte, Saint-German-en-Laye, etc. Formal gardens almost became synonymous with the French garden style. The French formal gardens and planting design spread to Holland, England and many other European countries. Some English gardens were also modeled after the Italian philosophy and formal styles.

While the Near East and the Europe were developing and perfecting formal gardens and planting design, in the other side of the world, Chinese were quietly developing and perfecting the naturalistic gardens and planting design. Chinese gardens were developed

---

[10] Kuck, Loraine E. *The World of Japanese Garden: From Chinese Origins to Modern Landscape Art.* Weatherhill, Inc., 1968. pp. 23-25.

[11] Hobhouse, Penelope. *The Story of Gardening.* DK Publishing, 1st edition, November 1, 2002. pp. 121-161.

as early as 2800 BC, and almost certainly much earlier, but firm evidence is still to be found. We'll have a very comprehensive discussion of the naturalistic planting design with Chinese gardens as case studies in later part of this book. These two major styles of gardening and planting design had its own distinct origin and each went its own way. Because of no or little communication between them, there was no influence on each other until seventeenth century. It was not until the eighteenth century that the English Landscape Movement started and created the naturalistic gardens and planting design in Europe.

Formal landscaping and planting design has dominated the Near East and Europe for several thousand years. Why?

I think the reasons are probably as following:

First of all, these regions are generally dry and with a short rainy season. Formal planting design is very efficient in term of irrigation and satisfied the practical needs of these areas.

Secondly, the idea of paradise as a garden has a long history in the West, even before the Garden of Eden was presented in the Bible. What the paradise looks like, there is hardly specific description. The description of the Garden of Eden was not very specific either, yet it gave the garden designer some ideas. There are many religions in the West and Near East, but the dominant religions like Judaism, Protestantism, Catholicism and Islam are all monotheistic. Even though some of these main religions have fundamental differences, yet they also have major similarities, at least to the Eastern eyes: They all believe in ONLY ONE omnipresent GOD, even though they may not agree who the GOD is. Many chapters of the Bible are the same for Judaism, Protestantism and Catholicism. The Koran also adapted some chapters of the Bible. They all agree that GOD created everything, including light, air, earth, sky, water, human beings, animals and plants, everything happened for a reason and was part of a great plan, and there is NO coincidence. They all agree GOD gave human beings authority to rule over everything on earth. Since plants are part of creation, then they too should be arranged in a rational pattern in the gardens, and not in any random appearance. The trimming of plants into neat and tidy formal shapes and forms was acceptable. Formal gardens and planting design demonstrated rationality and fit with the monotheist ideas. It is probably because of the same reasons that many of the formal gardens have ONE main axis, ONE garden center, and ONE dominant theme. All these dominant religions considered water very important and symbolized life. They called water "living water." So, the garden center was frequently water or some kind of water feature. From the pool in Egyptian courtyard gardens to the main moat in Versailles, there were numerous examples. Water was scarce and valuable in these regions, and people loved to see water and water features; this might also be the reason that water was frequently the center of the gardens.

The Garden of Eden had a river that separated into four headwaters: Pishon, Gihon, Tigris and Euphrates. Four canals usually separated a formal garden. They might be the symbols for these four rivers. That might explain the popularity of this garden pattern.

Thirdly, the political system in these regions was dominated by monarchy for most of the past several thousand years. Formal gardens and planting design could create a formal and ceremonial feeling, and could demonstrate the power of monarchy. Monarchy also provided the financial support that was needed to create and maintain a grand formal garden. Flat topography in France made the composition and advantages of this garden style more obvious. That was probably why the climax of this garden style was achieved in France, a country ruled by monarchy and with relatively flat topography.

Fourthly, many talented garden designers had developed successful patterns, techniques and skills in formal gardens. These patterns, skills and techniques spread from one country to other countries through trade or wars. One good example is the spread of the pattern found in Egyptian gardens, with a pond in the center, canals for irrigation, trees planted in straight lines and flowerbeds in formal shapes. Another example: the mud mounds built by Sumerians and many early gardens might have inspired the high terraces in the formal gardens in France and other countries. Formal gardens and planting design were frequently designed to be look down from high terraces or windows of upper floors. This was also probably because many of the more complicated formal patterns were easier to see and understand from above. It was a very ancient idea that higher is better. This was almost universal in both the Western and Eastern gardens. In large-scale French gardens, high viewing terraces were frequently built for visitors to perceive the formal patterns of parterres and flowerbeds and knot gardens. Tall trees were placed at outer edges or used to frame a vista, and they were never placed close to buildings so as not to block views of the formal patterns of flowerbeds, parterre, etc.

Last but not least, formal gardens and planting design are often symmetrical, formal and balanced. After so many generations of development and trial and error, they have become mature. They are beautiful and loved by many people. Our task is to learn and inherit from the past, analyze and absorb the essence of traditional formal gardens and planting design, and use them for today's needs.

a. Plants and symbolism

Some plants used in the Western formal gardens and planting design had symbolic meaning, depending on the specific region and culture. Many of the plants grown in European gardens today came from Mediterranean countries. In ancient Egypt, trees had significant symbolic and religious meanings and they were dedicated to different gods: the doum palm to Thoth, the date Palm to Re and Min, the tamarisk to Osiris and the sycamore to Hathor. Trees were used to frame temple buildings to create sacred landscapes. In Greece and Persia, young men were made to plant trees and a particular grove could be considered sacred. Greek women would plant lettuce, fennel and other fast-growing plants for the annual festival of Adonis, to symbolize the short life of Aphrodite's lover, killed in a boar hunt. Large Roman and Renaissance gardens often included a sacred grove and pool as a popular feature.[12] Palms, pines and pomegranates were grown in orchards and had a certain symbolism because special rites often took place under them. The Date Palm (*Phoenix dactylifera*) has been cultivated for 6,000 to 8,000 years. It has been used in Egyptian gardens and is also a favorite in Islamic gardens. Phoenix, its generic name, came from the mythical bird that is believed to dwell in the Arabian Desert and reinvent itself through fire every 500 to 600 years. *Phoenix dactylifera* is called *nakhl* in Arab; it is mentioned 20 times in the Koran. *Nakhilstan* is the name of a date palm garden, and also means oasis.[13]

2. Basic Prototypes and Main Design Considerations

Based on our discussions above, we can summarize formal gardens and planting design into three major categories: Formal Courtyard Garden Prototype, Villa and Formal Garden Prototype as well as Hunting Parks. Let's summarize the major features and design consideration for each prototypes.

a. Formal courtyard garden prototype

One major line of development of formal gardens and planting design is the development of formal courtyard garden prototype. It started from Egyptian courtyard gardens, spread to Persian Gardens, then spread to Islamic Gardens, Mogul gardens and medieval courtyard gardens; it also spread directly from Egyptian courtyard gardens to peristyle courtyard gardens in Greece, then Rome, and then Renaissance Italy. Nature was NOT considered as desirable in early formal Egyptian courtyard gardens, but as harsh and damaging force. The garden was to be a paradise separated from the harsh nature outside. The thick garden walls were used to block out the heat and flood. This formal courtyard prototype eventually spread to some areas that are not so dry and have made some changes to adapt to the local condition. For example, in dry, desert climate, flowerbeds are often sunken for easy irrigation, while in wetter climate they are sometimes raised for easy drainage.

---

[12] Loxton, Howard (Editor). *The Garden: A Celebration*. David Bateman Ltd., 1991. p.15.
[13] Hobhouse, Penelope. *The Story of Gardening*. DK Publishing, 1st edition, November 1, 2002. pp. 26-29.

b. Egyptian courtyard garden prototype (Fig 2.2)

They are the predecessors of pleasure gardens. A garden is designed for the house behind and used to provided views and cool area for the main room. It is typically enclosed by very thick mud wall and has one or more square or rectangular pool(s) with fish and floating plants, such as the blue water lily. Rows of trees are planted in straight lines and vines climb onto the trellis to provide shade. Plant materials were typically Date Palm, Fig, Pomegranates or Sycamore Fig (*Ficus sycomorus*). Irrigation channels and straight paths divide the garden into formal shapes. Flower and vegetables fill the rest of the garden space. Today, this prototype is still very valuable for dry climate and desert areas.

c. Persian courtyard garden prototype

They were probably the direct offspring of the Egyptian Courtyard Gardens. They were designed for viewing from shady pavilions. They had shallow crossing irrigation channels, whose water was supplied by underground *quanats*, or huge subterranean tunnels. These tunnels brought waters from distant mountains. For larger gardens, they might have a central pool and a pavilion over it, and canals instead of shallow irrigation channels. Trees along these irrigation channels or canals were planted along straight lines. Flowerbeds were sunken below the path levels for easy irrigation and to provide better views. It seems that the Persians already noticed that flowerbeds in formal patterns looked better from a higher level. Flowerbeds were in formal shapes but the flowers were not trimmed and were allowed to flourish freely. Plants with rich scent were favored. Persian loved and used more flowers than Egyptian. Narcissi, tulips, lilac, jasmine, roses and orange trees were commonly used plants. Many of the plants were obtained from China in exchange for horses and grapes. Outside the garden wall, there might be a larger enclosed park. On a sloped site, the garden might be divided into terraces at different levels, but the basic prototype remained. Other plant materials used in the Persian gardens were *chenar* (oriental plane trees), cypresses, tough elm, straight ash, knotty pines, fragrant mastics, kingly oaks, sweet myrtles, maples, grapes, pomegranates, pomecitrons, lemons, pistachios, apples, pears, peaches, chestnuts, cherries, quinces, walnuts, apricots, plums, almonds, figs, dates and melons, etc.

d. Islamic garden prototype

They were adapted and developed directly from the Persian Courtyard Gardens, especially the *chahar bagh* gardens (Fig 2.3). According to Koran, paradise was conceived as an ideal garden with running water, flowers, spread fruit trees, birdsong and black-eye houris. The *chahar bagh* garden was a garden divided into four parts by irrigation channels or canals; at the intersection of the channels or canals, a fountain or building was often placed. At the intersection of the smaller canals, *chenars* (oriental plane trees) were planted. The cypresses planted in rows in a straight line along the main canals symbolized death and eternity, the fruit trees symbolized life and fertility. This Persian garden prototype matched the Koran description and became the basic prototype of Islamic Gardens in many countries, including Spain and India. Famous examples are the Alhambra, or *Al Qual'a al-Hambra* (the Red Castle) and the *Generalife* (Garden of the Architect) in Spain, including the *Patio de los Leones* (Court of Lions), a typical *chahar bagh* enclosed by highly decorative arcades. Plant materials were *chenar* (oriental plane trees), poplar, willow, and orchard. In this complex, the *Patio de la Riadh* shows some Moorish influence with the lotus-flower-shaped basin at each end of the canals. In 1958, excavation showed that the original flower and vegetable beds were well below the level of current paths. This was probably for easier irrigation and for the blossoms to be level with the paths. Compared with the introvert interior of Alhambra, the Generalife was more open to the outside and its composition was based on a view to Granada. Because of the extrovert nature of the design, some scholars interpreted the Generalife as the forerunner of the villa and formal garden prototype of Italian Renaissance.

Isfahan (City of Gardens), the capital city of the *Safavid* Dynasty from 1598 was laid out according to the principles of the Persian Courtyard prototype. The complete city plan was inspired by the traditional Persian gardens. It was a complex of gardens, palaces and mosques. On the main axis were the *Chahar Bagh,* a double avenue of *chenar* (oriental plane trees)*,* and a central canal and flowers beds that connected the palace gardens with the Shah's terraced country garden on the other side of the *Zaiandeh* River.

e. Mogul garden prototype

The nomadic Mongols created one of the largest Empires in the Eurasian continent under Genghis Khan in 13th century. It was the result of the Eastern expansion of Islam. One group of Mongols adopted the Muslim religion and conquered India. They created the Mogul (or Mughul) Empire. Mogul Garden Prototype was also based and developed from Persian Garden Prototype that was brought back by the Mongol conquerors. The main components were fruit trees, fountains, raised paths linked by avenue of trees, and one or more rectangular pools connected by water channels. A special feature of the Mogul gardens is the *Chadar,* or sloped water screen used instead of a cascade. It is set at an angle that will always catch the sun and its surface is often carved with fish scale or shell patterns to increase refraction and the sound created by water. Famous Mongol examples gardens were *Bagh-I-Wafa* (the Garden of Fidelity), the *Shalamar Bagh* (Garden of the Abode of Love), and the *Taj Mahal*. The *Bagh-I-Wafa* was a four-fold garden enclosed by walls and was planted with sugar canes, orange trees and pomegranates. The garden was divided into four parts by water channels. *Taj Mahal* was an incomparable wonder of the world. It was a classic *Chahar bagh* layout divided into four parts by canals. The white mausoleum was placed on a raised terrace. It was placed close to the river to receive the cool river breeze and to be visible from the boats and the opposite riverbank instead of the center of the garden. It was placed at the intersection of the central canal and its branches. The central canal reflected the white mausoleum and added to its beauty. It was originally decorated with star-shaped parterres and fruit trees, but they are now replaced with lawn and single trees.

f. Peristyle courtyard prototype (Fig. 2.4 and 2.5)

The ancient Greeks learned from the Egyptian formal courtyard gardens and developed them into the Peristyle Courtyard Garden prototype; this prototype was inherited and developed by the ancient Romans, and then by Italians during the Renaissance. In a Peristyle Courtyard Garden, the courtyard was enclosed by a covered corridor with colonnades on one or more sides; it was designed as part of the building complex as an outdoor green "room." The main garden axis was also the main building axis. Pools, water features, fountains, sculpture, and plants were placed symmetrically along the axis. Flowerbeds were often sunken for easy irrigation. Frescos or paintings of landscape scenes were often used on the walls of the courtyard to create an illusion of larger space. In the Greek peristyle courtyard garden, plant materials used might be mandrake plant (*Mandragora officinalis*), aristolochia, anemone, anagallis, *Acanthus mollis*, *Acanthus spinosus*, irises, lilies, sea daffodil *(Pancratium maritinum)*, date palm, Abyssinian rose (*Rosa x richardii*), the single dog rose (*R. canina*), the cabbage rose *(R. centifolia)*, the saffron crocus *(Crocus sativus)*, peach *(Prunus persica)*, lemon *(Citrus limon)*, *Angelica sylvestris*, etc. Plants were also the sources of inspiration for ancient Greek architectural elements: either *Acanthus mollis* or *Acanthus spinosus* were molded into the capitals for the Corinthian order. *Angelica sylvestris* was the model for the fluted columns.

In the Roman peristyle courtyard garden, plant materials used might be Madonna lilies *(Lilium candidum)*, date palm, chrysanthemum, fig, olives, pomegranates, quince, bay laurel, myrtle, ivy, strawberry trees, plane trees, citron *(Citrus medica)*, lemon *(Citrus limon)*, opium poppies *(Papaver somniferum)*, and white morning glories *(Calystegia sepium)*, etc.

g. Medieval European peristyle courtyard gardens

Some Medieval European Peristyle Courtyard Gardens also used the Islamic Garden Prototype. For example, at Arles, the cloister garden had a variation on the form of the *chahar bagh* layout: the garden was enclosed by arcades; it was divided into four parts by paths; each part was covered with lawn and some natural wild flowers. At the intersection of the paths was a circular flowerbed with colorful flowers in concentric circular patterns. Four trees were planted at the four corners of the courtyard (one tree at each corner). Medicinal herbs, vegetables and flowers were planted in the Medieval European Cloister gardens. Flowers were cut for the altar. Lily of the valley, periwinkle, peony, hollyhock, violet, rose, strawberry, cowslip, wallflower, daisy, borage, iris, and cherry trees were some of the plant materials used in the Medieval Cloister Gardens. These gardens were often associated with the Virgin Mary. The Madonna lily and rosebud were use to symbolize purity.

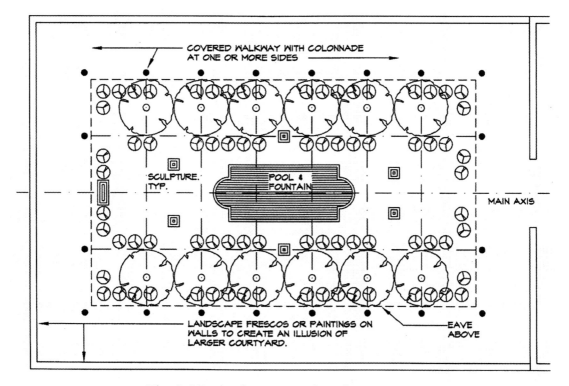

Fig. 2.4 Peristyle courtyard garden prototype

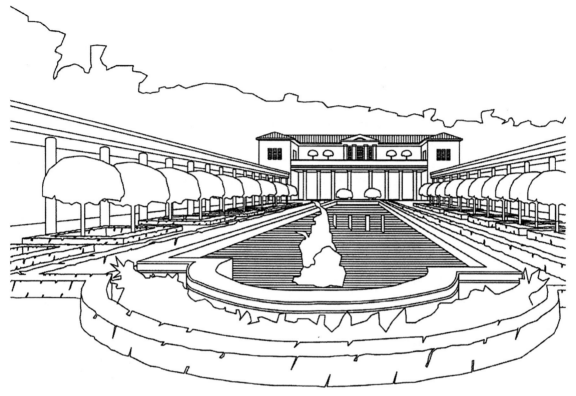

Fig. 2.5 Symmetric plant layout at a peristyle courtyard garden

In Medieval Europe, public gardens were also created in the city, and they were often meadows planted with trees. The noble and the rich who had land created pleasure gardens and kitchen garden, and they were often enclosed and were in a formal shape. Fish were stocked in ponds to supply the kitchen. Mazes were also created. They were sometimes marked on the pavement of the church or cut on turf outside. Pilgrims could follow its pattern on the knees as a symbolic journey for those who could not go to Jerusalem.

Elements of a medieval garden were: alley or tunnel of fruit trees, vines or roses trained on wooden frames; estrade (living topiary); flower mead (an idealized meadow of flowers); a fountain placed in the center of a small enclosed garden; gloriette (pavilion) placed at the center of the garden to mark the intersection of paths or avenues; raised bed; trellis work of fences or arboreal trees for roses to grow on; turf bench; viridarium (a plantation of trees)[14].

---

[14] Hobhouse, Penelope. *The Story of Gardening.* DK Publishing, 1st edition, November 1, 2002. pp. 98-117.

h. Villa and formal garden prototype

This category of formal gardens had a closer relation with nature compared with the formal courtyard garden prototypes. Villa and Formal Garden prototype was developed at least as early as ancient Rome, but it was not in the mainstream of garden design. Not until the Renaissance did this Villa and Formal Garden prototype acquired major attention and became very popular in Italy and some other countries, and eventually influenced and helped to create the French Formal Gardens.

i. Ancient Roman villa and formal garden prototype

Ancient Romans first developed this prototype. Wealthy Romans created formal gardens at their country villas. These gardens might have been inspired by the sacred groves in Greece and Greek gardens. They might have aviaries, fishponds and lakes, hillside terraces, natural-looking glades and formal garden beds and planting, as well as a hippodrome for exercise on horseback. Pliny the Younger had two villas. One was a seaside villa at Laurentium, 17 miles from Rome. In the house, a summer dining room faced the sea and one winter dining room faced the garden. The garden was a formal garden, with straight and controlled paths connect different points of interest. Plant materials were box, rosemary (used instead of box where salty sea wind was present and box would wither), mulberry, fig trees, scented violets in flowerbeds, and vines climbing onto a trellis. Pliny the Younger insisted on a close interaction between the villa and the garden and designed them as one unity.

The other villa was his Tuscan estate, located on a gentle slope. It had fine views on all sides. Pliny the Younger wrote to Domitus Apollinaris: "… my house, although built at the foot of a hill, has a view as if it stood upon higher up. The rise of the ground is so gradual and easy that you find yourself on the top almost before you feel yourself climbing." Behind it at a distance, is the Apennine mountain range. If you looked down from the villa, the countryside below appears "not as real land but as an exquisite painting." The garden demonstrated some important formal garden design principles: The house and garden were designed as one entity, they shared the main axis; both cross axes and diagonal axes were used; these axes radiated from the points of the interest (fountains, sculpture, etc.) and these different points of interest and views were connected by straight and controlled paths; the formal garden was designed to be viewed from the main rooms of the house. Pliny the Younger probably realized that the formal garden elements and planting design would look best from a higher advantage point. He placed the villa at a higher advantage point so that he could look down at the formal gardens at various levels of terraces and slopes (Fig 2.6). From the main entrance, looking down to the south, he could see terraces decorated with figures and bound by a box hedge. A slope down to the lawn of Acanthus was embellished with box cut in animal shapes and was enclosed by clipped hedges. The next space was an area for exercising decorated with more trimmed shrubs and topiary figures, adjacent to a grand dining room with an outdoor terrace and a view of meadows, garden and woods. The design also emphasized shade, cooling fountains and topiary. In his writing, Pliny the Younger described a very large hippodrome that is encompassed on every side with plane trees, ivy climbing around the trunk and branches, proliferating from tree to tree and connecting them. Between each plane tree and the next are planted box trees and behind these bay trees. At the further end, this plantation changes into a semi-circle which, being set round and sheltered cypress trees while the inward circular walks are filled with fragrance of roses and correct, by a very pleasing contrast, the coolness of the shade with the warmth of the sun. Having passed through these meandering alleys, you enter a straight walk, which breaks out into a variety of others, divided by a box hedge. In one place you have a meadow, in another the box is cut into a thousand different forms while here and there little obelisks rise, intermixed alternately with fruit trees: when, on a sudden, in the midst of this elegant regularity, you are surprised with a simulation of the negligent beauties of rural nature, in the center of which lies a spot surrounded with a knot of dwarf plane trees. Beyond these is a walk planted with the smooth and twining Acanthus, where the trees are also cut into a variety of names and shapes to form topiary.[15] There were a number of marble seats for visitors to rest from walking, each close to a little fountain.

j. Italian villa and formal garden prototype during the Renaissance

During the Renaissance, Italian humanist and architect *Leon Battisa Alberti* (1404-72) wrote *De re aedificatoria* in 1452 and this book was published 30 years later. He drew extensively from the writings of Pliny the Younger, sometimes almost copying the text verbatim, especially on how to locate villas and gardens: villas and their gardens should be located on hillside to obtain views, sun and wind. The slope should be gentle and visitors should hardly notice the ascent until they see the view as they arrive at the villa. Like Pliny the Younger, *Alberti* also recommended the use of scented evergreens and topiary, fountains, flowing water, statues, grottos and stone vases.

Many Formal Villa and Gardens were created in Italy during the Renaissance. They had some common features and obeyed some basic design principles: The formal gardens were designed for viewing from the main rooms of the villa. Since the designers probably realized that the formal gardens look best from above, they placed the villa at a higher

---

[15] Radice, Betty (Translator). *The Letters of the Younger Pliny*. Penguin Books., 1969. p.p.139-144.

location (typically the slope of a hill) and the villas were often built to be 3 or 4 stories high and placed on a terrace to make it even higher (Fig 2.6). The gardens were placed at various lower levels of terraces or slope. Lower flowerbed or parterres were placed closer to the villa and higher plants were placed farther away from the villa.

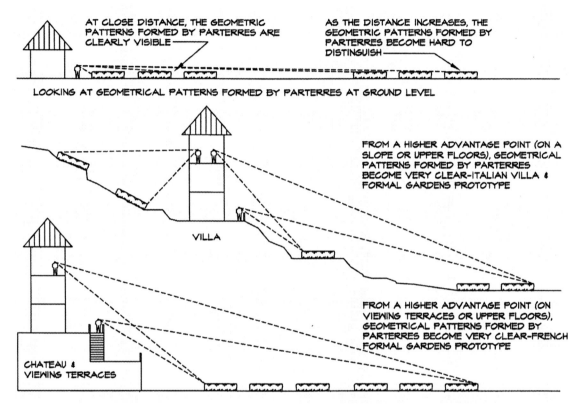

Fig. 2.6 Visual studies of formal gardens and planting design

The villa and the formal gardens were designed as one unity and shared the same main axis with pools, fountains, and obelisks; sculptures were arranged along the axis to form a series of different spaces. The villas and gardens were basically symmetrical to the main axis but some variations were allowed. The gardens were divided into regular, formal shapes by straight and controlled paths. The paths were framed either by cypress or clipped edge. Pavilions were placed at the intersections of paths. In additional to cross axes, diagonal axes were also used to linked various points of interest and create surprises for visitors. These diagonal axes also created the radial patterns of the paths. Early Villa and Formal Gardens followed the ancient Roman villa and formal garden prototype and the villas were placed at a very gentle slope, but in some later gardens, the slope became steeper and grand flights of steps were used. The designers took advantage of the slopes and differences in contour and created many water works and running streams. Water jets and fountains were used extensively. Famous examples included Villa *Medici* at *Pratolini,* Villa *Medici* at *Castello,* The *Pitti* Palace at Florence, Villa *d'Este* at *Tivoli,* Villa *Lante,* Villa *Torlonia* at *Frascati*, Villa *Garzoni* at *Collodi* and the *Isola Bella* in Lake *Maggiore.*

The Renaissance Villa and Forma Garden ideas spread to entire Europe, like other artistic ideas. *Alberti's* recommendations were not always applicable to northern Europe. Many Medieval courtyard garden features persisted in these areas, but many of these courtyard gardens became pleasure and entertainment gardens. *Desiderius Erasmus*, a Dutch philosopher, described an enclosed pleasure garden prototype based on Mannerist techniques, using the Christian symbolism: a gallery with marble pillars on three sides, an aviary, paintings of plants and animals along the walls and a library. In France, the idea of designing the chateau and the formal gardens as an unified "whole" started to emerge in late fifteenth century, but the nobles retained the defensive moats around the chateau and made the integration of the chateau and the formal gardens an uneasy task. At Burgundy, which was annexed by France in 1482, an Italian artist designed a rectangular formal gardens enclosed by raised viewing terraces. This idea was followed by French Architect *Philibert de l'Orme* at *Anet,* further north. The Italian-born Queen, *Catherine de Medici*, made elaborate additions to many gardens using the style of her homeland. French nobles and high churchmen also followed Italian ideas. However, because of the relatively flat northern plains, there were few sites that offered the slopes that were favored in Italy. The enclosed gardens were opened up for vistas and for greater display; however, successive terraces as seen in Italian gardens were rare. Italian style gardens also arrived at England via France.

k. French formal garden prototype

From the beginning of the seventeenth century, French gardens started to form their own style. They inherited the villa and formal garden prototype from Italy, but adapted it to the flat French topography. Instead of the successive terraces, they design the entire garden and the chateau as one entity on a pretty flat site. Since higher viewing points on the slope were rare or simply not available, the French created some man-made higher viewing points: the viewing terraces and rooms in the upper floors (Fig 2.6). The chateau was typically 3 or 4 stories high, and placed at a viewing terrace that was one or two stories high. It was placed at the main axis of the gardens and the gardens were designed for viewing from the higher points: the viewing terraces or the main rooms at the upper floor of the chateau. Parterres, flowerbeds, knots and lawns in formal forms were typically placed close to the chateau, and tall trees were placed at the outer edge of the gardens to enclose spaces and avoid blocking view to the parterres, flowerbeds and knots. Sometimes the patterns of the parterres were copied from other arts. For example, *compartiments de broderies* for the chateau at *Anet* was the first elaborate parterre at a much larger scale designed by *Etienne du Perac*, and the parterre pattern was the same as embroidery pattern. Colored earth instead of flowers was used between the box-hedge patterns. Instead of running water along the slope in Italian gardens, French designers used their large moats along the main axis or cross axes of the gardens. Fountains and water jets were still used.

In 1651, *Andre Mollet* published *Jardin de Plaisir*. He summarized the pattern for the French formal gardens in this book: from the main rooms of the house, there was an unblocked view of the parterre, and then parterres of turf and formal woods. A statue or fountain is placed at the end of almost every walk to create a vista. Grottos, aviaries, canals and other waterworks were other elements of the formal garden. He even suggested placing painted scenes at the end of walks to create more effective vistas. Again, the entire garden was designed for viewing from the main room of the house and the formal layout was to show man's control and ability and the power and authority of the owner.[16]

Versailles at France is one of the most famous illustrations of formal gardens and planting design (Fig 2.7). It was designed by *Andre Le Notre* and *Le Brun* in the seventeen century, and was originally a hunting park for the French king and subsequently enlarged and developed into the grand and glorious setting for the monarch, Louis XIV, the Sun King. Louis decided to use the Sun God, Apollo as the theme of symbolism for the garden. *Le Notre* and *Le Brun* were discovered by the King after they designed *Vaux-le-Vicomte* for *Nicolas Fouquet*. *Le Brun* was in charge of the symbolism and sculpture and *Le Notre* was in charge of the garden and planting design. *Le Notre's* design technique was to make the entire garden visible at a glance, so it must be relatively narrow so that a man's eyes do not have to turn from side to side. In order for the garden to be impressive and to show its grand scale, the garden must be long, so that a man can stand on the uppermost viewing terrace and look on and on. The main axis of the garden is also the main axis of the buildings; it ran from the center of the palace westwards to the setting sun. This made Louis the center of the design. The Apollo fountain was placed along this axis at the end of the canal. *Le Notre* used the radial pattern as the motif of the garden, and used the radial routes at both the main axis along the canal and the secondary axes of the smaller gardens. Fountains or statues were placed at the centers of the radial patterns. This way, a fountain or statue can served as vista for multiple paths or walks. Each smaller garden may have its unique characteristic, but it must be subordinate to the whole design concept. Three grand avenues connect the Versailles town to Place d'Armes and the palace. At the west side of

---

[16] Loxton, Howard (Editor). *The Garden: A Celebration*. David Bateman Ltd., 1991. pp.10-60.

the palace, high terraces make it possible for a visitor to see the entire garden at a glance and look at the main vista framed by trees and shrubs arranged in linear patterns and following the main axis of the palace. A number of low parterres and green lawn in various formal patterns have been placed close to the high viewing terrace. They can be looked down upon from the terraces and the upper floors of nearby buildings. Visitors can actually perceive geometric patterns formed by parterres and green lawn because they can look down at these patterns. Beyond that, paths and canals are framed by woodland. The canal was crossed by another channel linking a menagerie and Trianon. After the canals, the ground rises steeply and thicker woods leading to the horizon frame the paths. Overall, the Garden of Versailles was not built for pedestrians, but for visitors on a horse-drawn carriage.[17]

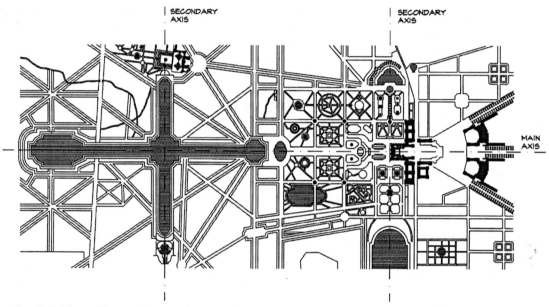

Fig. 2.7 Versailles at France is one of the most famous illustrations of formal planting design

A number of patterns we'll discuss have been use in the planting design of Versailles: Axis /Symmetry, Linear Array with Vista, Radial Pattern, Motif, Repetition and Rhythm, etc. Versailles is also a good example of the balance between unity and variations. Andre *Le Notre* used the cross axes to set up the basic pattern of the garden, yet he also used the

---

[17] Morris, A.E.J. History of Urban Form: Before the Industrial Revolutions. England: Longman Scientific and Technical, Longman Group UK Limited, 1979. Reprinted 1990. pp 174-178.

diagonal axes to break the pattern and create surprise, interest and climax. The smaller gardens are similar in size and most are in rectangular shapes, yet the patterns inside each garden are unique. Versailles is like an extremely well done symphony, with a very clear main theme, containing numerous variations. All these variations are unique and yet related and unified in some way to reinforce the main theme and create a harmonious overall planting design.

A good designer should be able to master all basic formal planting design patterns and use them flexibly.

Pierre L'Enfant, the planner and designer for Washington D.C., spent his childhood in Versailles. This probably had a significant impact on his concept for the overall design of Washington D.C. (Fig. 1.1), and explains the extensive use of diagonal axes, radial patterns and grand avenues in the planning and design of Washington D.C.

Now that we have discussed both Italian Formal Gardens and French Formal Gardens, lets do a comparative studies of these two garden styles to get a clear understanding of both.

Italian Formal Gardens were the 'rebirth' of Ancient Rome Villa and Formal Gardens created by their ancestors, while French Formal Gardens were direct decedents of Italian Formal Gardens.

In both styles, the formal gardens were designed for viewing from the main rooms in upper floors or viewing from high terraces. The villas or châteaux were always placed on the main axis of the gardens. It seems that the designers in both styles understood that the formal patterns formed by parterres, flowerbeds, lawn and canals in the formal gardens would look best from higher advantage points (bird's eye view), but they achieved this effect through different means. In Italian Formal gardens, the villas were often placed on the middle portion of a slope to raise the main view points, while French designers frequently placed the building (château) on a one or two story high viewing terraces to raise the main view points. This is probably because the Italian landforms contain more mountains, hills and slopes, while French landforms are pretty flat.

For the same reason, Italian Formal Gardens often used successive terraces connected by grand flights of steps, and water was often designed to be running down the slope in channels to show the refraction and beauty of moving water. French Formal Gardens would typically design the château and formal gardens as one entity on pretty much the same main base plain, except the château had a raised sub-base formed by viewing terraces. Water was placed in moats to create reflection to show the beauty of still water. Grand flights of steps were used in both styles to access the viewing terraces. Both styles used many water jets, water jokes and fountains.

Plants were handled in similar ways in both styles: they were either used as parterres, flowerbeds and lawns and placed close to the buildings (villas or châteaux) to form elaborate formal patterns, or used as trees arranged in straight lines or high clipped hedges along paths to frame and control views so as to form vistas or to divide the garden into different spaces for different functions. Taller trees or high clipped hedges were often placed at outer areas of the gardens and farther away from the buildings so as not to block the views to the formal patterns formed by parterres, flowerbeds, lawn and canals.

Both styles used paths along cross axes to divide gardens into different but symmetrical parts, and used diagonal axes and paths to link different points of interest and to break the regular patterns formed by cross axes or paths. There are three main advantages of using diagonal axes: the first is that they can link different points of interest in the shortest distance possible; the second is that they make it possible to create radial patterns from a single point of interest and link many paths to it so as to create the maximum use of one point of interest; the third is that they can create surprise and interest for those who reach the intersection of these diagonal and cross axes. One will discover many more views at the other end of the paths. These paths were either framed by low clipped hedges along the parterres or framed by tall trees planted in straight lines or high clipped hedges leading to different vistas.

l. Hunting Parks

As early as between 3000 BC to 2000 BC, Sumerians developed hunting parks with the domestication of horses. The pleasure landscape was combined with sports and need for food. The parks were laid out in formal planting design patterns and complicated irrigation system. Wild animals were placed in the parks, and the hunting box eventually evolved into landscape pleasure pavilions. Assyrians, Babylonians and Persians continued to develop hunting parks. Medieval kings and aristocrats also created Hunting Parks. These hunting parks may have inspired the development of English landscape parks and ultimately evolved into modern urban parks.

3. Formal Planting Design Principles, Concepts and Common Patterns

One important purpose of studying historical cases and trends is to summarize and generalize some useful principles and patterns that we can use in our landscape practice and planting design today. Let's analyze and try to summarize some of the specific principles, concepts, techniques and common patterns in formal gardens and planting design.

a. Parterres, flowerbeds and knots

Parterres, flowerbeds and knots are typically used in areas close to the houses, villas or chateaus. Parterres are flower or vegetable beds enclosed by clipped hedges. Plants and colored sands or soils can be used to form certain patterns, such as lions, dragons or geometric patterns. In Britain, these versions of parterres are called knots. For small gardens, parterres, flowerbeds and knots can be used and their patterns will be easily visible. For larger gardens, you need to consider how far a person can see at ground level. Raised viewing terraces or patios may be needed if large areas of parterres, flowerbeds and knots are used (Fig. 2.6). Parterres, flowerbeds and knots are typically designed for viewing from the main rooms of the buildings, such as villas and chateaux, etc. The patterns of the parterres, flowerbeds and knots can be viewed better from a higher vantage point, such as raised terraces, patios or main rooms of the upper floors. Patterns for carpet, drapery and embroidery were frequently copied and used in the design of parterres, flowerbeds and knots, as seen in some of the French formal gardens.

b. Proportion and scale

A basic principle in formal planting design is proportion and scale. Scale refers to the size of an object, while proportion refers to the ratio between an object and another object, or the ratio between a part and the whole. This includes the proportion and scale between plants, between plants and the overall garden, between plants and human beings, between plants and buildings, etc. You not only need to consider the proportion and scale between these elements in a plan view, but also consider them in elevation and three-dimensional views. Plant sizes need to be proper for the scale of the garden. Plants can also be used to break down the huge, inhuman scale of a huge building mass, and become the transitional elements between a building mass and human beings.

For example, in a plaza enclosed by several 6-story high buildings, we may use some trees that are at least three stories high and with large canopies and combine them with some lower shrubs, perennials, annuals and ground cover. These 3-story-high trees will be in good proportion to the buildings around them and their sizes (scale) are appropriate to the plaza. If we use the same kind of trees in a 10'x10' residential courtyard, the trees may be too large and out of proportion to the courtyard. In a small garden, we may want to use plants with smaller leaves and fine texture, instead of plants with large leaves and coarse texture. Plants with smaller leaves can create areas with smaller scale. Fine texture and pattern make the small garden appear larger. No matter how small a garden space is, we can probably find a small plant that fits into the space. It is important to choose the proper size and scale of plants for a garden space.

c. The "Golden Ratio"

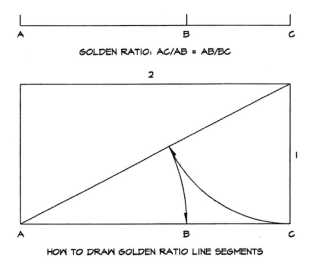

GOLDEN RATIO: AC/AB = AB/BC

2

HOW TO DRAW GOLDEN RATIO LINE SEGMENTS

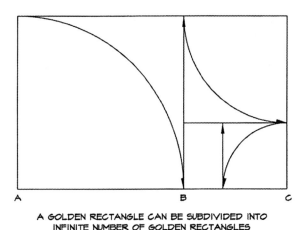

A GOLDEN RECTANGLE CAN BE SUBDIVIDED INTO
INFINITE NUMBER OF GOLDEN RECTANGLES

Fig. 2.8 The golden ratio

Ancient Greeks discovered at about 300 BC the proportion that is most pleasing to human eyes: the "Golden Ratio." What is the golden ratio? Take a line segment AC (Fig 2.8), and break it into two segments: AB and BC, if the ratio of AC/AB = ratio of AB/AC, then this ratio is called "golden ratio." It equals 1.61803 39887 49894 84820, or roughly 1.6. It is also called "phi", named after the Greek sculptor Phidias. Fig 2.8 also shows how to draw two line segments to form the "golden ratio." A rectangle with a length to height ratio equals the "golden ratio" is called a golden rectangle. It can be subdivided and form an infinite number of golden rectangles (Fig 2.8).

Hundreds of items that we use everyday have been made approximately per this ratio: 3"x 5" photos, the length and width of a TV screen, etc.

The "golden ratio" has been used extensively in architecture since ancient Greek times: the Parthenon in Athens, Greece is a good example. Its plan has many golden rectangles. The width to the height of the front elevation is roughly a golden rectangle, and the spaces between columns also form golden rectangles.

In formal planting design, the "Golden Ratio" can be used in dividing planting areas and laying out the planting plan (Fig 2.9). It can also be used in deciding where to place plants to create a good proportion in building elevations or garden views (Fig 2.9).

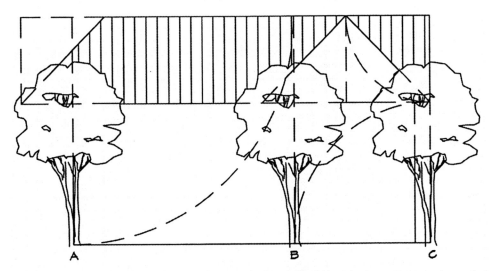

GOLDEN RATIO CAN BE USED TO LOCATE TREES IN
BUILDING ELEVATION

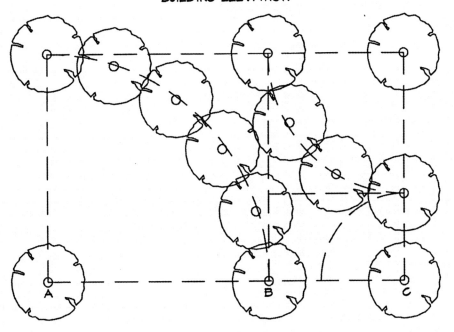

USING GOLDEN RATIO IN PLANTING PLAN

Fig. 2.9 Using the golden ratio in planting design

d. Axes and symmetry

The use of Axes and Symmetry is one of the most important techniques in architecture, formal planting design and other arts. Human bodies, leaves of plants and many other things we see everyday are symmetric. In architecture, the use of Axes and Symmetry has been seen in almost every civilization throughout history: the pyramids in Egypt, the Parthenon in Athens, Greece, the design and layout of the Forbidden City in Beijing, China, as well as the U.S. Capital Hill, Washington Monument, and Lincoln Memorial in Washington D.C., etc.

Axes and Symmetry are also broadly used in formal planting design. Sometimes multiple axes are used. In these cases, you need to differentiate which axis is the main axis and which axis is the secondary axis (Fig 2.10). At the "old" Getty Museum, Malibu, California, the overall architectural layout for the Museum and courtyard is symmetric and is more or less inspired by Peristyle Courtyard Prototype. The planting design also utilizes the same Axis of Symmetry for the building to create a symmetric layout: two rows of well-trimmed Ficus trees were symmetric and planted along the side of the courtyard. The hedges are also symmetric to the Main Axis. The hedges and rows of trees lead to the main Museum building at the end of the courtyard. This layout can also be viewed as two rows of trees in Linear Pattern with a "Vista", the main Museum building.

e. Linear pattern

One of most commonly used pattern in formal planting design is linear pattern (Fig 2.11). Plants of similar shape and size are planted at roughly equal distance in a straight line. It is one of the simplest and also one of the most powerful patterns. One tree may appear to be ordinary, but if a group of trees of the same species arranged in linear pattern, they'll appear to be very powerful. The avenue in traditional garden term is a special case of linear pattern; it is a group of trees in spread form arranged in linear pattern to form a cathedral effect. Linear Pattern encourages visitors' movements along a straight line and can create a great perspective view. It has been used widely. It can be used for groundcovers, shrubs, or trees. We have all seen lines of trees planted along the streets, roads and boulevards. In *Rio de Janiero,* Brazil, an avenue formed by two rows of Royal Palms generates a unique scene. At the Botanical Garden at Adelaide, South Australia, an avenue formed by two rows of indigenous Moreton Bay Figs *(Ficus macrophylla)* creates a grand "cathedral" effect. At an elementary school in California, tall Eucalyptus trees can be arranged in Linear Pattern to separate the school from the residential neighborhood. Another example is the deciduous trees planted along a street. In summer, they are filled with green leaves. In fall, their leaves will turn yellow and create a splendid view.

Tall palm trees in Linear Pattern often form an interesting skyline for tropical or subtropical cities and give visitors a sense of "Genius Loci."

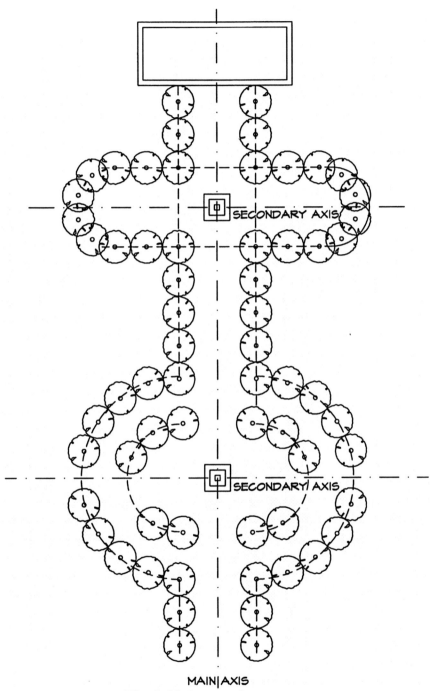

MAIN AXIS

Fig. 2.10 Axes and symmetry

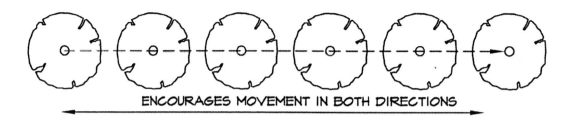

ENCOURAGES MOVEMENT IN BOTH DIRECTIONS

Fig. 2.11 Linear pattern

At new Getty Center, Los Angeles, Linear Pattern is used extensively to guide the movements of the visitors. The Getty Center is located next to the 405 freeway on a hilltop to the north of the City of Santa Monica. When visitors arrive, walking into the lower tram station from the parking structure at the bottom of the hill, they'll see a row of Jacaranda trees and a row of Crape Mytle trees. Both rows of trees are arranged in linear patterns to reinforce the direction of travel for the tram. As they travel up toward the hill in the tram, they'll see a row of trees following the curved path of the tram. At the arrival plaza of the Getty Center, four pine trees are planted in a square pattern. This can be view as a special case of linear pattern. Because all sides of a square are equal, this layout actually creates a resting area with serene feeling and encourages people to stay. Seating areas are designed under the shade of the pine trees. As visitors walk up 3 runs of huge outdoor steps, to the left, they'll see the North building, the East building and the museum entrance connected by nicely trim hedges, 3 rows of shrubs and a row of Crape Mytle trees, all arranged in linear patterns along the walkway. At the museum entrance, two large Sycamore trees form a live sculpture with their graceful branches. To the right, they'll see another row of trees in linear pattern, but the plant materials have been changed to Willow trees and the angle of the array has been tilted toward the entrance of the Central Garden. Along the outdoor stairs leading down to the Central Garden, another row of Crape Mytle trees are arranged in linear pattern, but this time, the trees are planted on terraces that step down toward the central garden. You can see the designer repeats the linear patterns many times to achieve unity, yet each time this pattern is repeated, there is some changes made to it to create variation. The balance between unity and variation is one of the secrets to the success of this garden. The linear pattern is the theme, and the changes in plant materials, number of plants, the contour and the direction of linear array are variations based on the unified theme.

f. Linear pattern with vista

Two rows of trees in Linear Pattern are often arranged along a path with a vista at the end. This pattern can create a great perspective view and has become very popular since the discovery of perspective drawing technique during the Renaissance. A Vista is a point of interest in a garden; it can be a fountain, a sculpture, a pavilion, a building entrance or a special garden feature, such as a unique tree (Fig 2.12). Sometime, double rows of trees are planted on each side of a main path, and one narrower and subordinate path is formed on each side of the main path. This is a technique used frequently in the past. For example, in French classical gardens designed by *Le Notre,* he liked to use the linear pattern with a Vista. He would build the path to gently slope up and create an illusion that the end of the path is the "horizon" to create an endless feeling; in this case, the Vista is the "horizon."

This pattern was also used in Stowe in Buckinghamshire: rows of large trees were planted in linear pattern on each side of the road and lead to a Vista, the gothic "temple."

Two rows of Jacaranda trees can be planted along the walkway from the parking lot to the main entrance of a building. Two rows of Carrot Wood trees may also be planted in a Linear Pattern at a wider distance from each other to accommodate for a gathering and waiting area for visitors. Rows of rose shrubs may be arranged in a Linear Pattern too to match the overall design concept. All the Linear Patterns formed by these trees and shrubs can be oriented toward "the Vista", the main entrance of a building.

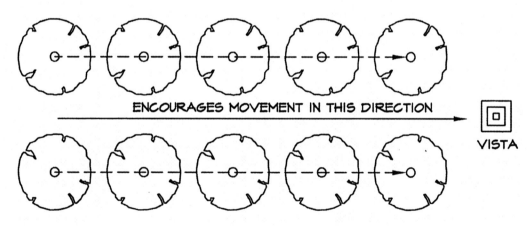

Fig. 2.12 Linear patterns with vista

g. Linear array

Linear array has been used in planting in almost every civilization. It was first used in agricultural planting. It has been used in the rice fields and cornfields in many Asian countries, in the pistachio fields in Central California, and in the orange groves in Southern California. It can be considered as more than two rows of plants arranged in Linear Pattern (Fig 2.13). This technique is ideal to cover a large planting area or to create a grove; it can be used for groundcover, shrubs or trees. You can create different feelings by increasing the size of tree canopy (Fig 2.14).

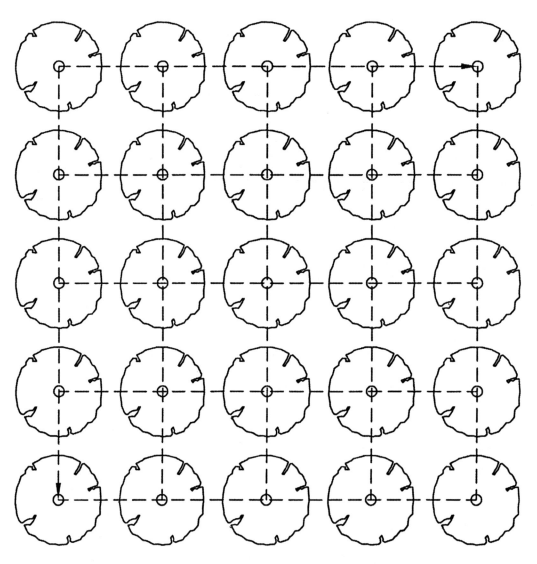

Fig. 2.13 Linear array

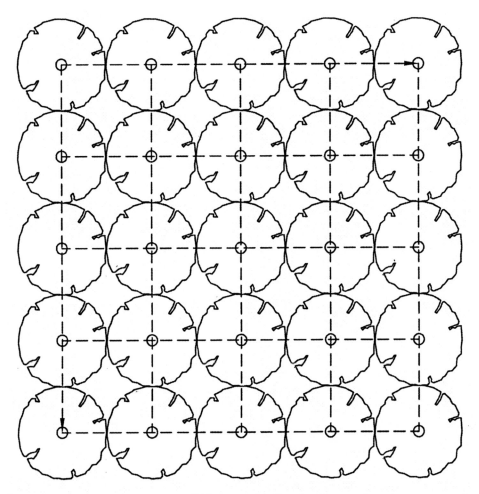

Fig. 2.14 Linear array-creates difference feeling by increasing the canopy size

At the *Patio de los Naranjos* (Court of the Oranges) in Spain, rows of orange trees were planted in the Linear Array pattern and filled the entire courtyard near Cordoba's Mosque (now the Cathedral). The rows of orange trees were aligned with the rows of columns inside the mosque. The design of the architectural interior and the outside courtyard was considered as one entity.

When the overall shape of the planting area formed by Linear Array is approximately a square, it creates a serene feeling. One example is the outdoor dining area at the U shape courtyard enclosed by the restaurant and café building of the Getty Center, Los Angeles. The deciduous trees are arranged in Linear Array pattern, and yet the center of the linear array pattern has been cut out to form a reversed U-shape to enclose the open side of the courtyard. The area enclosed by the building and the trees is roughly a square; this layout can create a serene feeling and encourage people to stay. In summer, the tree canopy is filled with leaves and can provide shade for the guests. In winter, when all the leaves fall, the scene is completely different from summer. Sunshine can penetrate through the branches and make the seating area warmer. At the 100-acre hillside area that surrounds the Getty Center, many of the trees and shrubs used are also arranged in linear array pattern, but the pattern is used on a slope condition this time.

When the overall shape of the planting area formed by Linear Array is approximately a rectangle, it encourages people's movement along the long side of the rectangle (Fig 2.15). At Luxor Hotel and Casino, Las Vegas, several rows of palm trees are planted in a Linear Array pattern along the sidewalk, and the overall shape of the planting area of the palm trees forms a rectangle. This pattern encourages visitors' movement along the long side of the rectangle, toward the building's main entrance. This directional guidance function will gradually diminish as the number of rows for trees in the short side of rectangle increase.

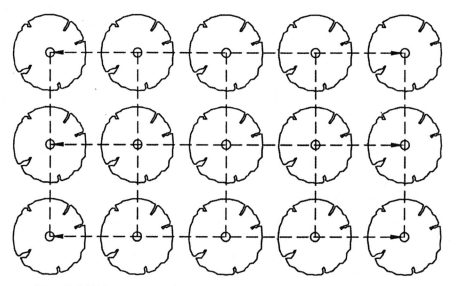

Fig. 2.15 Linear array in rectangle shape encourages people's movement along the long side of the rectangle

A variation of the Linear Array Pattern is the Triangular Array Pattern (Fig 2.16). Plants are arranged in equilateral triangle. This pattern is also very useful for a large planting area, and it can be used for groundcover, shrubs or trees.

h. Circular array

Circular array is arranging plants in a circular manner (Fig. 2.17). In this pattern, the center of the circle formed by the plants is also the focal point of the space. It is an ideal place to place a sculpture or fountain or other interesting garden features. This pattern can be used at the termination point of an axis.

At the garden at Hartwell House, Buckinghamshire, England, a number of flowerbeds were arranged in several layers of plants in circular array pattern. The concentric layers were arranged with the lower plants at the outer edge and taller plants at the center.

At Disneyland Theme Park (Disneyland), Anaheim, California, the sculpture of Walt Disney, the founder of Disneyland, is placed at the end of Main Street USA, right on one of the main axis of Disneyland formed by the Entrance, Main Street USA and Fantasyland. It is also surrounded by 6 evergreen trees that are arranged in Circular Pattern, and becomes the focus of the space and an important point of interest for the theme park.

At a community park in California, 6 deciduous trees are planted in a Circular Pattern around the sand play area. This layout is consistent with the form of the sand play area and the Circular shape concrete bench. The colorful slides become the focus of the Children's play area.

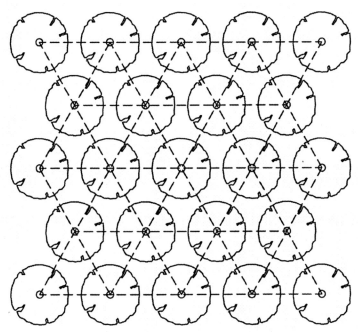

Fig. 2.16 Triangular array

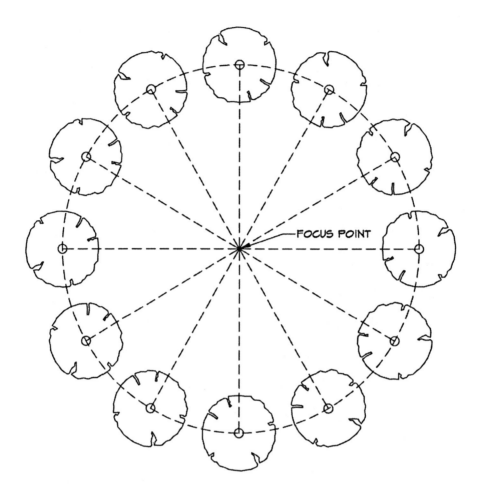

Fig. 2.17 Circular array

i. Repetition and rhythm

Repetition is repeating the same planting layout to create rhythm. In order to create rhythm, a layout or pattern needs to be repeated at least three times. If it is repeated less than three times, it can hardly create rhythm; if it is repeated too many times without changes or contrast, it'll become boring. Repetition creates unity, and contrast creates changes. The secret of a good design is to achieve the balance between repetition and contrasts, between unity and changes. Similar to Linear Pattern, this technique encourages movement along the repetition line (Fig 2.18). There is a saying in architecture: music is flowing architecture while architecture is solidified music. This saying is referring to the use of common principle of rhythm in both architecture and music. This principle can also be used in planting design. In music, many songs have a basic rhythm or theme, and it is repeated and sometimes changed to a higher or lower pitch, and different words are used when the same rhythm is repeated. This principle can be used in planting design: we can use the same pattern, say, linear array pattern, repeat it for different groups of plants in the planting design of a garden, but make some changes: change the plant materials, for example, change from ground cover to shrubs to trees, change from deciduous to evergreen trees; change the number of trees in each group, change the sizes of trees between groups and so on to create a harmonious and unified planting design with variations. It'll be very helpful if a designer has musical background.

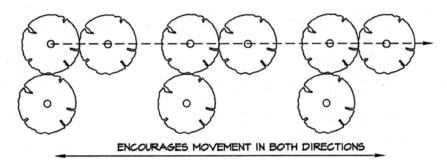

ENCOURAGES MOVEMENT IN BOTH DIRECTIONS

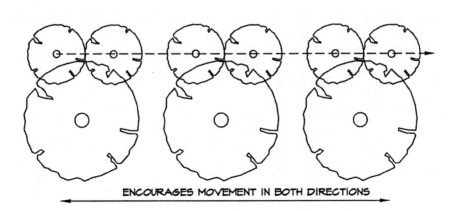

ENCOURAGES MOVEMENT IN BOTH DIRECTIONS

Fig. 2.18 Repetition and rhythm

j. Radial pattern

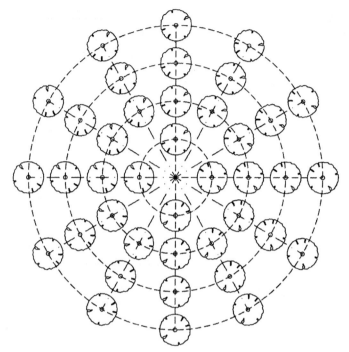

Fig. 2.19 Radial pattern – circle

Radial Pattern is to use radial axes to layout plants or a planting area. The focus point of the space in this pattern is the intersection of all the radial axes (Fig 2.19, Fig 2.20 and Fig 2.21).

At an Herb Garden, the planting area may be arranged in Radial Pattern. An iron sculpture of vegetable basket may be placed in the center point of the Radial Pattern and became the focus of the space to symbolize the theme of the Herb Garden.

Another famous example of using the Radial Pattern is Versailles, France. Please see detail discussions earlier.

k. Motif

Motif is the repetitive use of a form, shape or pattern in the same or different sizes. This technique has been used in architecture, hardscape design, graphic design, etc.; we can also use it in planting design. For examples, using various sizes of hexagon as motif can form a planting pattern (Fig 2.22). We can use any other forms or

Fig. 2.20 Radial pattern – ellipse shapes as motif to create a different pattern.

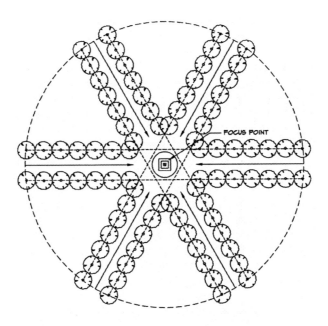

Fig. 2.21 Radial pattern - circle variation

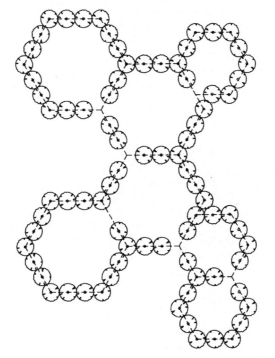

Fig. 2.22 Motif - hexagons as a case study

l. Progression and regression

Progression in planting design is to arrange plants according to their sizes, heights or masses, from small to big. Regression in planting design is just the reversed process of progress (Fig 2.23). It is to arrange plants according to their sizes, heights or masses, from big to small. This technique can be used in laying out planting plans, it can also be use to arrange plants in elevations.

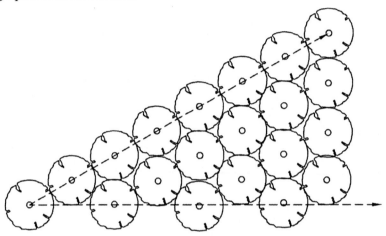

PROGRESSION

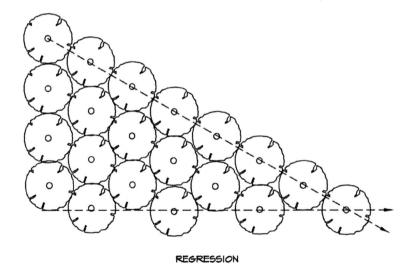

REGRESSION

Fig. 2.23 Progression and regression

m. Spiral pattern

We have all seen a spiral pattern in nature: whirlpool in a river or ocean, a cyclone or tornado, or the spiral lines of the shell of a snail. In architecture, one of the famous examples for the use of the spiral pattern is Guggenheim Museum in New York: the entire building's floors slope up in a spiral pattern. The stairs between floors have been eliminated.

Spiral Pattern in planting design is to arrange plants in a spiral shape; the center of the spiral pattern is the focus of the space (Fig 2.24).

n. Inspiration from architecture, graphic design, abstract painting, music and other arts

Many principles in arts are common. A good landscape designer should be able to acquire inspiration from architecture, graphic design, abstract painting, music and other arts. For example, French designers used the geometric patterns of a carpet

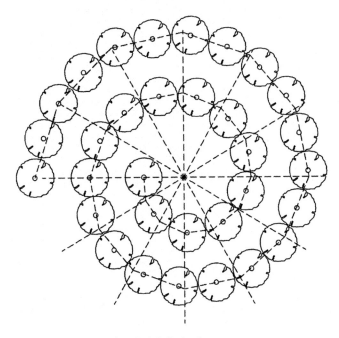

Fig. 2.24 Spiral pattern

in laying out the parterres in many famous formal French gardens. Similarly, some abstract painting patterns and some lattice window patterns can be used in formal planting design. We can use the same or similar patterns with a different kind of materials: plants. We can build a nicely trimmed hedge or ground cover in different colors with these patterns, or we can simply obtain inspiration from these patterns of other arts to create our own new patterns.

o. Extract abstract forms from nature

Nature is another important source of inspiration for planting design. The spiral pattern can be seen as the abstract form inspired by the whirlpool in a river or ocean, or a cyclone or tornado, or the spiral lines of the shell of a snail.

p. Flexible uses of patterns

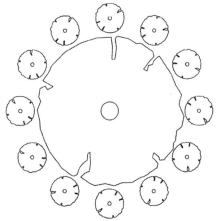

Fig. 2.25 Dominance and focus point and circular array

There is a Chinese saying: A master can lead an apprentice into the door (of each profession), but it is up to the individual to strive for his success. After we discuss the basic patterns for formal planting design, I encourage readers to experiment and try to master the basic patterns and use them flexibly according to their project's needs. We can use several examples to show the readers how to do that: Circular Array Pattern can enhance the dominance or focal point of a space (Fig. 2.25). A Radial Pattern can be cut into half and re-arranged (Fig. 2.26). It can be further cut into a half and two quarters, added to another half, re-sized and re-arranged again to form more complex patterns (Fig. 2.27).

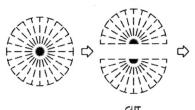 

CUT   REORGANIZATION

I'd suggest the use of some simple techniques like addition, subtraction, multiplication and division in developing new geometric patterns and layout for planting design. Addition is adding two or more basic patterns to form a new pattern. Subtraction is subtracting part of basic pattern to form a new pattern. Multiplication is repeating the same basic pattern a number of times to form a new group or pattern. Repetition as we have discussed earlier is one kind of multiplication. Division is dividing a basic

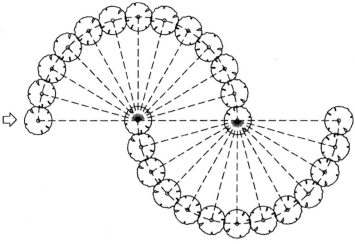

Fig. 2.26 Variation one of circular array

geometric pattern or form into equal parts to form new groups or patterns (Fig. 2.28).

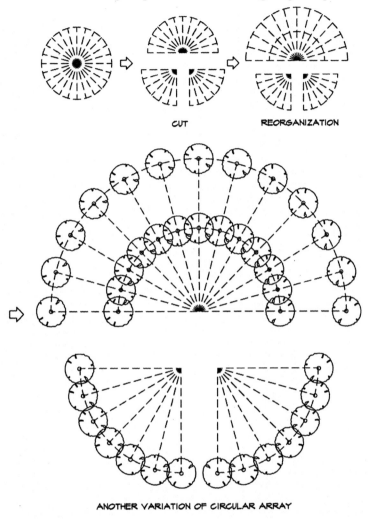

CUT

REORGANIZATION

ANOTHER VARIATION OF CIRCULAR ARRAY

Fig. 2.27 Flexible uses of patterns

Using the basic patterns and techniques that we have discussed previously, I have developed several schemes for formal gardens and planting design: Scheme One's center is a parterre garden created through the use of addition, subtraction and multiplication, enclosed by trees arranged in linear patterns (Fig. 2.29). The garden is arranged symmetrically to the main axis of the house. The focus of the garden is a fountain. This garden will look good from any angle. From the main room of the house, you can look at the parterres and the fountain, and trees at the front side of the garden frame the view to the distance.

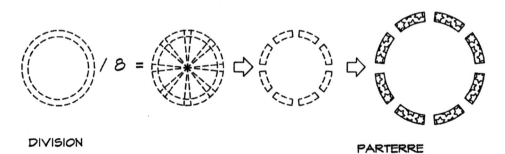

ADDITION

PARTERRE OR POOL

SUBTRACTION

PARTERRE

MULTIPLICATION

FLOWERBEDS & PATHS

DIVISION

PARTERRE

Fig. 2.28 Addition, subtraction, multiplication and division

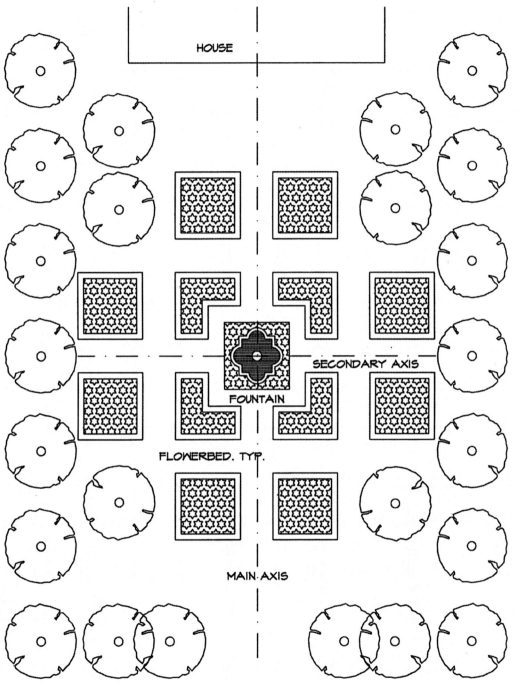

Fig. 2.29 Formal garden scheme one

Scheme Two uses the circular parterres as motif. Three circular parterres form three points of interest for the garden, each with fountain, sculpture or a pavilion at the center (Fig. 2.30). These three points of interest are linked together by trees in Linear Patterns. These trees also enclose the garden space and the multi-functional central lawn area. The geometric composition of the garden supplements the form and shape of the house.

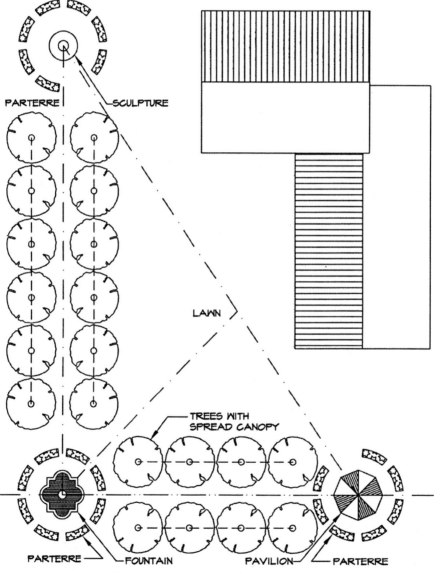

PARTERRE   SCULPTURE

LAWN

TREES WITH
SPREAD CANOPY

PARTERRE   FOUNTAIN   PAVILION   PARTERRE

Fig. 2.30 Formal garden scheme two

Scheme Three is a traditional knot garden enclosed by clipped straight hedges and trees in Linear Patterns (Fig. 2.31).

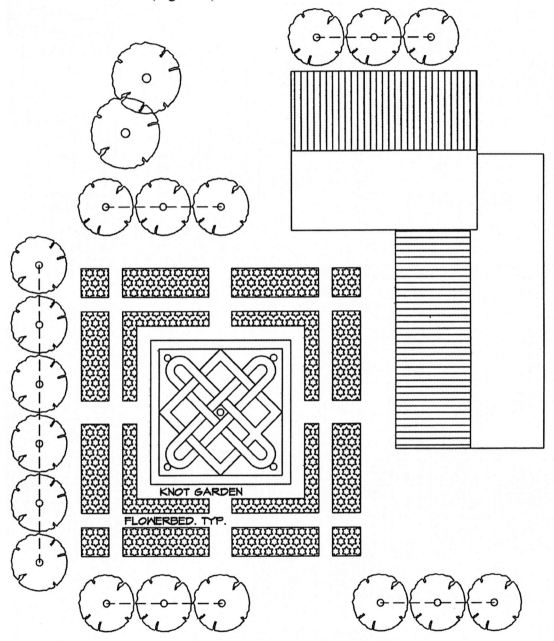

Fig. 2.31 Formal garden scheme three

Scheme Four has four square knot gardens at the center, enclosed by trees arranged in Circular Array Pattern. In many ancient civilizations, the square shape symbolizes the earth and the circular shape symbolizes the heavens. This garden's geometric forms relates to this ancient concept (Fig. 2.32).

KNOT GARDEN. TYP.

Fig. 2.32 Formal garden scheme four

Scheme Five focuses on the geometric shape formed by flowerbeds designed to be viewed from the higher viewing terrace and the main rooms of the house (Fig. 2.33). It uses smaller shrubs to form two controlled paths with a sculpture as vista for each path. Two fountains are placed along the main axis and at the intersection of paths. The house and the terrace have nice views into the flowerbeds/parterres framed by tress along the edge. Flowerbeds and trees form a semicircular shape at the end of the garden. A gap at the semi-circle formed by trees allows view to the distance. The raised viewing terraces and strictly- controlled paths in Italian and French Gardens inspire this scheme. A few seemly casually planted trees around the house break the overall regular and geometric patterns to create variations and interest.

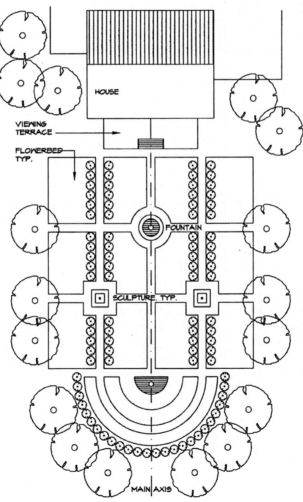

Fig. 2.33 Formal garden scheme five

Scheme Six is a more complicated scheme based on Scheme Five (Fig. 2.34). We use the same techniques and principles to create a flower garden and an herb or vegetable garden in a larger site. We also added a pool in front of the house to create reflection and cool air for the house, and psychological feelings of coolness. Inspired by Egyptian Courtyard Garden Prototypes, we can also add fish and lilies to the pool to create more interest. We can also simply use a swimming pool instead, depending on the owner's choice. Common paths link the flower garden and the vegetable garden to the pool area.

q. Forms and habit of plants as variables

Now that we have learned the patterns and principles of formal planting design, we can use the form and habit of plants as variables and create more varieties in planting design. The same planting pattern can create different effect if different plants are used (Fig 2.35 and 2.36).

4. Some Practical Case Studies

a. The Central Garden of Getty Center

At the Central Garden of Getty Center, Los Angeles, a number of techniques that we have discussed previously have been used: the entire Central Garden uses circular forms as a motif. This also reinforces the circular shapes used in the research institute building, the museum buildings and the auditorium. The entire garden is built on a pretty steep slope. If you start from the highest point, the north end of the garden, you'll see a circular half-bottle-shape void space carved into the north garden retaining wall. This "bottle" is about 12 feet high. Water slowly leaks from the top of the "bottle," flows down along the interior "bottle" wall and is the origin of a stream. The stream will lead you toward a walking path. This path is actually a handicap-access route that zigzags down the slope. It is a combination of straight and circular ramps. When you walk down the ramps, you actually cross the stream and two rows of trees along the stream several times. Your view lines will be turned to the left or the right toward the lawn area several times and you barely have a chance to look straight down the hill. Your eyes will be attracted to the low colorful decorative plants along the stream and the rocks that cover the stream. The stream has a lot of changes: it is sometime covered by plants, sometime covered by rocks and some other time passed through the bridge right under your feet. The lawns around the walking path are larger areas in the U-shape courtyard enclosed by the Research Institute Building, the Garden Terrace Café building and museum buildings. As you walk between the trees and past the bridges over the stream, you'll experience spatial sequence changes from large space to small one and then from small space to large one again. This spatial sequence will repeat a few times. Finally, you'll cross a longer bridge and the stream start to spread wider, and you'll hear the sounds of a waterfall. All a sudden, you'll see a huge circular shape garden in front of your eyes and the city view in the distance, you enter a huge space. This is the climax of the garden. You realize that the zigzag path you walked through was not only a handicap ramp, but was also used with the stream and the trees to direct your attention away from this main garden and is a means to build up this surprise for you. The stream that you have been crossing spreads wider and passes under a last bridge and then flows down along the main axis of this huge garden and becomes a waterfall. The transition from the naturalistically curved stream and the trees planted along the bank of the stream to the formal and symmetrical circular garden is very smooth and natural. On each side of the waterfall, decorative vines climb up the three circular artificial "trees" built of steel bars, which are placed at symmetric positions to enhance the main axis. Beside the waterfall, large areas were left empty as gathering places for the Central Garden. Since the Getty Center is located on the top of a mountain, it has splendid views to downtown Santa Monica and West Los Angeles, the Pacific Ocean, and the Hollywood Hills. On a clear and sunny day, if you stand at the gathering area next to the waterfall, you can see the view of entire downtown Santa Monica and Los Angeles and even the Pacific Ocean through the "frame" formed by the trees in partial Circular Array Pattern. The center of garden is an abstract circular configuration formed by decorative plants floating on water, embraced by 2 rows of deciduous trees in partial Circular Array Pattern. Circular shape cactuses are also used to reinforce the partial Circular Array Pattern formed by deciduous trees. These patterns were placed at about 15' below the ground level and make it very easy for you to perceive the patterns if you are standing at the ground nearby or looking down from the upper floors of adjacent buildings. Again, we notice the application of the principle that formal patterns look better from above in bird's eye view. Circular handicap-access ramps zigzag down again to connect walking paths around the Central Garden. As you walk along this path toward the center of the garden, sometimes the space you walk through become very narrow and enclosed by densely planted shrubs and vines, some other times, you'll have a more open view and you can see the decorative plants floating on water at the center of the garden. As you can see, plants and other garden elements have been used to create a series of interesting spaces along the garden path: change from larger space to smaller space, then larger space and smaller space again. As you walk back, you'll also experience an interesting reversed spatial sequence and you'll end up at a vista, the circular half-bottle-shape void space carved into the north garden retaining wall. The spatial sequences at the Center garden work well in both directions, both going and coming, both to and from the center of the garden.

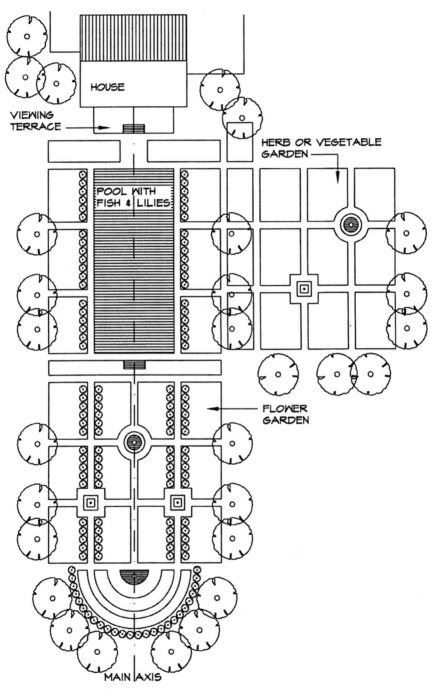

Fig. 2.34 Formal garden scheme six

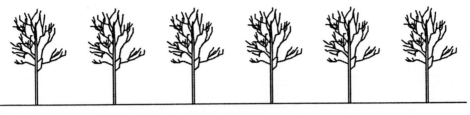

SINGLE-STEMMED TREES IN LINEAR PATTERN

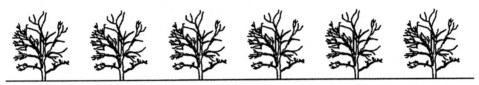

MULTI-STEMMED TREES IN LINEAR PATTERN

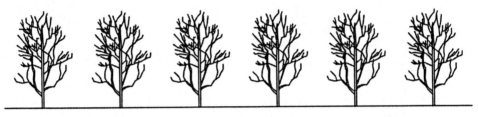

UPWARD TREES IN LINEAR PATTERN

DOWNWARD (WEEPING) TREES IN LINEAR PATTERN

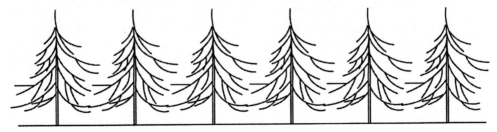

DOWNWARD (PENDULOUS) TREES IN LINEAR PATTERN

Fig. 2.35 Habit of plants as a variable

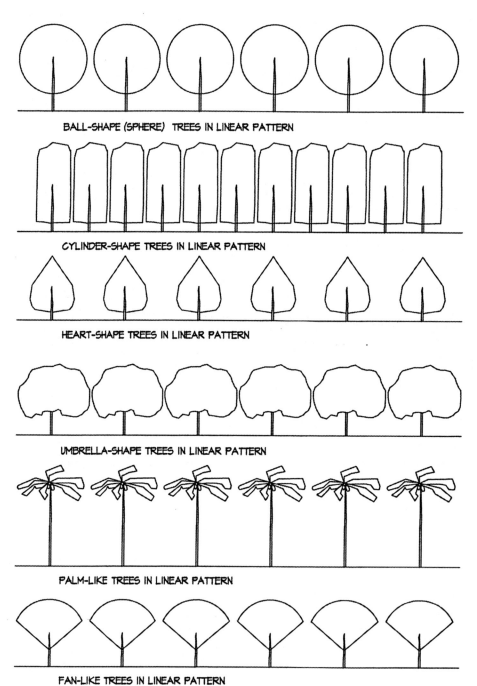

BALL-SHAPE (SPHERE) TREES IN LINEAR PATTERN

CYLINDER-SHAPE TREES IN LINEAR PATTERN

HEART-SHAPE TREES IN LINEAR PATTERN

UMBRELLA-SHAPE TREES IN LINEAR PATTERN

PALM-LIKE TREES IN LINEAR PATTERN

FAN-LIKE TREES IN LINEAR PATTERN

Fig. 2.36 Form of plants as a variable

In summer, when the deciduous trees are filled with leaves, the scene in the Central Garden looks completely different from that in winter.

b. A commercial plaza surrounded by mixed-use buildings

The next site we are going to discuss is a commercial plaza formed by a group of multi-story mixed-use buildings (Fig. 2.37). As we can see, the overall architectural layout is symmetric. There are one main axis and two minor axes. We can use symmetric layout in the overall planting design to match the original architectural design concept (Fig. 2.38). We use trees in Linear Pattern to encourage people's movement from the intersection to the plaza, and place two huge trees to create "Grey Space" next to the main building entrance. We'll use evergreen trees in Linear Pattern along the main axis; use trees in Circular Array Pattern to reinforce the fountain and "amphitheater" layout. We place low accent plants next to each of the building entrances in a symmetric manner to enhance the minor axes, and use 8-foot-high hedges to block undesired view of transformer. We'll use ground cover for erosion control at slope, and use low hedge (about 3'-6" high) as "guardrail" to protect people from the slope. We use deciduous or thin foliage trees along the outline of the building to allow "looking through" from the windows of the multi- story office buildings layout.

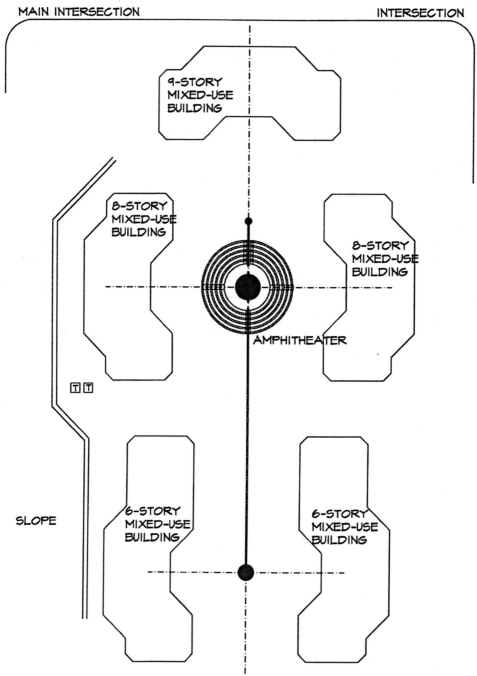

Fig. 2.37 A commercial plaza formed by office buildings

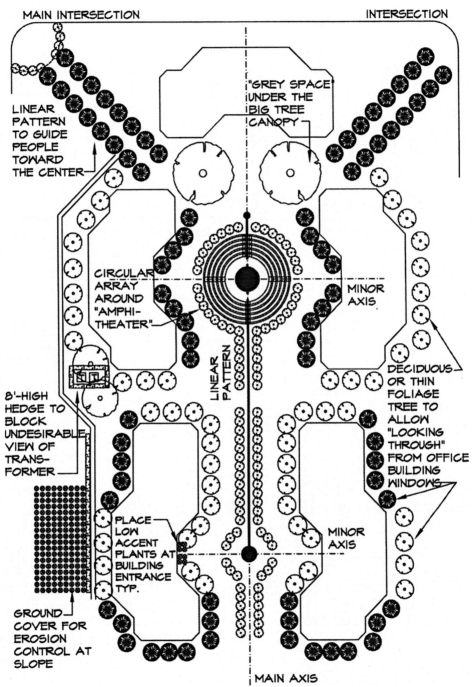

MAIN INTERSECTION

INTERSECTION

LINEAR
PATTERN
TO GUIDE
PEOPLE
TOWARD
THE CENTER

"GREY SPACE"
UNDER THE
BIG TREE
CANOPY

CIRCULAR
ARRAY
AROUND
"AMPHI-
THEATER"

MINOR
AXIS

LINEAR PATTERN

8'-HIGH
HEDGE TO
BLOCK
UNDESIRABLE
VIEW OF
TRANS-
FORMER

DECIDUOUS
OR THIN
FOLIAGE
TREE TO
ALLOW
"LOOKING
THROUGH"
FROM OFFICE
BUILDING
WINDOWS

MINOR
AXIS

PLACE
LOW
ACCENT
PLANTS AT
BUILDING
ENTRANCE
TYP.

GROUND
COVER FOR
EROSION
CONTROL AT
SLOPE

MAIN AXIS

Fig. 2.38 Planting design concept for a commercial plaza

If local climate is hot and humid and does not allow the placement of "amphitheater," we can use a raised platform instead. The spatial effect will be different: the "amphitheater" encourages people to look down towards the center of the "amphitheater," while a raised platform encourages people to look up towards the platform. In both cases, we can use the Circular Array Pattern to enhance the spatial effect layout.

c. Planting design for a typical parking lot

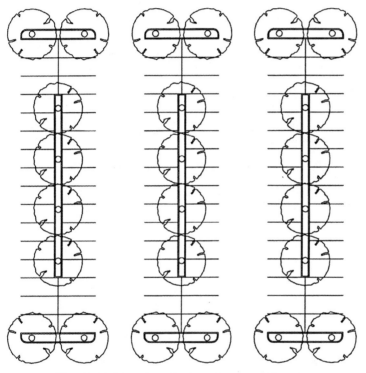

Let's discuss the planting design for a typical suburban parking lot. Let's assume that the city requires a ratio of one tree every 6 parking stalls, typical parking stall size is 9'x17', and minimum driving aisle width is 25'. There are three ways to layout planters: The first is to use a long strip planter between parking stalls. In this case, we use the long strip planter and make the parking stall next to planter 9'x17', and make the parking stalls without planter 9'x19'-6" (Fig 2.39). We need to use wheel stops

Fig. 2.39 Planting design for a parking lot

at parking stall adjacent to the trees to prevent cars from bumping into the trees. This way we can have a planter that is 5' wide and about 90' long. We'll use 4 trees in the strip planter and arrange them in a Linear Pattern, and we'll plant two trees at each end island. We have a total of 8 trees in every two rows of parking (32 stalls for every two rows of parking facing each other). This is one tree every 4 parking stalls and is more than the minimum number of trees required by the city (one tree every 6 parking stalls). We can also use about 3-foot-high hedge or shrub to block the view of parking cars, yet allow pedestrians to look between the tree canopies and the low hedge and also allow the motorists to see the pedestrian. Be sure to leave enough number of gaps in the shrubs to allow people to transverse them. We can repeat this layout in other parking rows and form some kind of Rhythm through Repetition (Fig 2.39). The second way is to use diamond shape planters and place them between parking stalls (Fig 2.40). The third way is to place planters between parking stalls and at the end of the parking rows and place trees in the center of the planters. This layout can prevent the cars from bumping into the trees and avoid the use of wheel stops. Roots of the trees use in parking lot planters will get compressed, we should pick a species that can take it. Shrubs and ground cover used in parking lot planter shall also be able to stand heavy traffic.

5. Underlying Major Principles and Fundamental Concepts of Planting Design in Formal Gardens

In order to have a better understanding of formal planting design and principles, let's analyze its underlying major principles and fundamental concepts.

a. Emphasis of man's ability to improve nature

The first fundamental concept in Formal

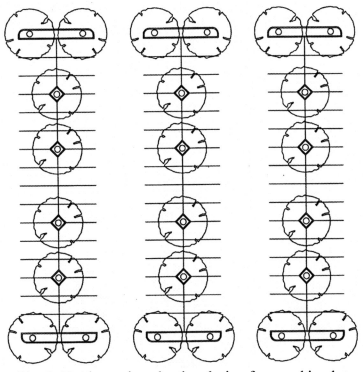

Fig. 2.40 Alternative planting design for a parking lot

Planting system is the emphasis of man's ability to improve nature. Formal planting design is one of the demonstrations of man's ability to improve nature. We have seen this demonstration in formal planting design in Versailles, France, the Mall in Washington D.C., the Court of the "old" Getty Museum in Malibu, CA, and many examples we have discussed in this Chapter.

b. Integration of garden and architecture as one entity

The second fundamental concept for Formal Planting system is the integration of garden and architecture as one entity. In this system, plants are treated in the same way as building components. Formal planting design use the same aesthetic principles and patterns as architecture, such as proportion and scale, "golden ratio", linear pattern, linear array, circular array, axis and symmetry, repetition and rhythm, radial pattern, motif, progression and regression, etc.

c. Emphasis of human wisdom and geometric beauty

The third fundamental concept in Formal Planting system is the emphasis of human wisdom and geometric beauty. This is consistent with the quest for geometric beauty in the overall Western Civilization since ancient Greece and Rome.

SECTION 2
NATURALISTIC PLANTING DESIGN WITH CHINESE GARDENS AS CASE STUDIES

Naturalistic planting design includes Chinese gardens, some American and European gardens, especially English naturalistic gardens, etc. In this section (Chapters 3, 4, 5, 6 and 7), we'll use Chinese gardens as case studies to discuss naturalistic planting design. This is for two reasons:

First of all, in order to do an in-depth and detailed discussion on naturalistic planting design, we have to focus on a style of garden to be able to explore cultural, symbolic, emotional and psychological aspects as well as the artistic conception of planting design. This is partly because that no comprehensive discussion has been done on naturalistic planting design so far. In order to solve the problem of the deficiency in discussion on naturalistic planting design, we have to start with one particular style of gardens. Once we have done a comprehensive discussion on this particular style of garden, we can use the same methodology to analyze other styles of naturalistic planting design. In fact, I have paid special attention to summarize the universal naturalistic planting design principles, methods and concepts from Chinese garden case studies. They can be used not only for planting design in Chinese gardens, but other naturalistic planting design as well. Many of the plants discussed in this Chapter have already been used in the U.S., Japan, England, Australia and many other countries also.

Secondly, Chinese Gardens have a long history and the author of this book has been educated in both the U.S. and China, and is fluent in both Chinese and English. It is possible for him to draw extensively from resources in both Chinese and English and initiate a comprehensive discussion on naturalistic planting design with Chinese gardens as case studies. Many of the raw materials used in this book about Chinese gardens are introduced to the English-speaking world for the first time and are enlightening and useful to the West. I also included a chapter on comparative studies of Chinese gardens and Japanese gardens and a chapter on comparative studies of Chinese gardens and English naturalistic gardens so that you can have a better understanding of these three major schools in the naturalistic gardens and planting design. Let's start by studying the natural, historical and cultural context of planting design in Chinese gardens.

CHAPTER 3
NATURAL, HISTORICAL AND CULTURAL CONTEXT OF PLANTING DESIGN IN CHINESE GARDENS

1. The natural landscape in China

To some extent, Chinese gardens are subjective interpretations of the natural landscape in China. Therefore, in order to understand planting design in Chinese gardens, it is necessary for us to get a general idea of the natural landscape of China.

a. Landforms

The general topography of China is higher in the West and lower in the East. Most of the mountain ranges in China run from west to east, and the landforms of China vary greatly: plains, basins, hilly regions, plateaus, mountains (Figure 3.1) and special kinds of landforms (loess land, karsts and glaciations).

b. Climate

The climate of China is controlled by three factors: monsoons, mountain ranges and cyclones. In winter, the monsoons are dry and cold, blowing from the continent to the Pacific Ocean; in summer, the monsoons are warm and moist, blowing from the Pacific Ocean to the continent. Thus, in most areas of China, there is more rainfall in summer than in winter.

The east-west running mountain ranges act as barriers to the rain-bearing winds from the South in summer and the cold winds from the North in winter. Thus, the climate is generally cold and arid in the northern and inland regions, and warm and humid in the southern and coastal areas in China. The coastal areas also have far more days of fog than inland areas. The areas with greatest number of days of fog are the southeast part of the Shangdong Peninsula and the mouth of Hangzhou Bay and islands along the coast. Cyclones usually cause abrupt weather changes like storms and typhoons.

Fig. 3.1 The natural landscape of China: A view in Huashan Mountain.

c. Hydrology

The general layout of the landforms of China-higher in the West and lower in the East-makes most of Chinese rivers flow form the West to the East and pour into the Pacific Ocean. The most famous of these rivers are the Yellow River (Huanghe River) and Yangtze River (Changjiang River, or Long River). Since the annual rainfall is higher in the southern and inland regions, south China has a greater number of rivers and the amount of runoff in these rivers is much greater than those in north China. For instance, the runoff of Yangtze River is twelve times as much as that of Yellow River.

The silt content of Chinese rivers varies greatly. A major reason is whether there is sufficient vegetation to prevent soil erosion in the regions through which the rivers flow. The Yellow River flows through the loess region, where erosion is severe. Its silt content (1,360.0 million metric tons per year[18]) is more than twice of that of Yangtze River. This makes flooding a constant problem for its surrounding regions and creates a battle that

---

[18] Chiao-min Hsieh (Jiaomin Xie), *Atlas of China* (San Francisco: McGraw–Hill Book Company, 1973), p.45.

has lasted for thousands of years between man and the Yellow River. The sediment keeps accumulating in the waterbed of the Yellow River, while people keep building the riverbank higher to prevent flooding. As a result, in some areas, the bottom of the Yellow River is much higher than the nearby villages.

d. Soils

As the result of several environmental factors (latitude, distance from the sea, the effect of high mountains, and changes in climate and vegetation), the soils in China can be put into two realms: the oceanic type, which is developed under relatively humid forest vegetation; and continental type, which is developed under the semi arid and arid climate conditions in the inland areas. Human activities also influence the soil types in China. In fact, the entire central and southern lowlands of China are occupied by highly modified paddy soils.

e. Vegetation

The diversity in topography, climate, hydrology and soils makes China a country that possesses the richest plant resources in the world. For example, the number of species of flowering plants and ferns in China is about 10 % of the described taxa of the world flora. That is about 30,000 species, including approximately 7,500 indigenous species of trees and shrubs alone. Chinese people successfully domesticated hundreds of wild plants in the past thousand years.[19]

There are three major reasons for the startling resources of plants in China: First of all, most of areas in China have not experienced cold climates in the geological past. While many species were wiped out in other part of the world, they survived and continued to develop in China. Secondly, the wet monsoon from the South brought moisture to the foothills of the Himalayas and made it a perfect growing place for many mountainous plants. Thirdly, the three floras of cold North, that of sub-tropical South, and that of the mountainous species commingled in this perfect environment for thousands of years.[20]

In general, the vegetation of China is characterized by two great natural plant formations: woodland in the east and south of China, and grassland-desert complex in the

---

[19] Sheng-ji Pei, *Botanical Gardens in China* (Hawaii: Harold L. Lyon Arboretum, University of Hawaii, 1984), p. 7.

[20] Maggie Keswick, *The Chinese Garden: History, Art and Architecture* (New York: Rizzoli International Publications, Inc., 1978), p.175.

west of China.[21]

From south to north, Chinese forest types change in such a latitudinal sequence: rainforest, evergreen broad-leaved forest, mixed forest, temperate deciduous broad-leaved forest, mixed northern hardwood forest, and boreal coniferous forest. From the upper parts to the lower slopes of the mountains, Chinese vegetation types also change in an altitudinal sequence: perpetual snow, alpine shrub and meadow, boreal coniferous forest of spruce and fir, deciduous broadleaf forest, evergreen broadleaf forest and, lastly, rainforest.

Since the northwest steppe-desert of China is arid and in the internal drainage region in the heartland of the Eurasian land mass, the vegetation in the regions demonstrates a concentric ring pattern, surrounding an immense desert, or a dried–up lake basin, or a salt lake. From the periphery to the innermost ring, the vegetation types in the concentric zones are: the transitional belt of mixed grass and woodland, a vast expanse of short and tall grass, steppe, alkaline-saline plant communities and desert scrub.[22]

2. The Chinese view of man, nature and gardens

In the Chinese view, man is the product of heaven and earth, or the universe. Nature normally refers to the parts of the world that are intact and beyond the influence of human beings, which should be precisely called "the first nature." Sometimes it also refers to the parts of world that have been reproduced or adjusted by man, but still retain their major properties and are still similar to their original state, which should be precisely called "the second nature." A Chinese garden can be defined as: in a sector of an area, man utilizes or transforms natural landforms, or creates artificial landforms, integrates them with literature, paintings, architecture, water, plants, or animals, so as to form a viewable, tourable, livable and naturalistic environment that is pleasing to both the eyes and the mind.[23]

Chinese gardens originated from nature, but they are higher than nature. Mountains, water and plants are essential factors of natural scenery, and they are also key elements in naturalistic gardens. Chinese gardeners never simply mimic the primitive state of these natural elements, but consciously transform, adjust, process and tailor them so as to reproduce or represent a concise, summarized and typified "second nature."

---

[21] Ibid., pp. 51-56.

[22] Hsieh (Xie), *Atlas of China*, pp. 51-54.

[23] Weichuan Zhou, *The History of Chinese Classical Gardens* (Beijing: Qing Hua University Press, 1990), p. 2.

3. The origin of planting design in Chinese gardens

The civilization of China crystallized in the Yellow River basin about five thousand years ago, and has evolved continuously ever since. Chinese gardens, as one aspect of Chinese civilization, also were born here.

The earliest garden in China was a garden of Chinese medicinal plants built around 2800 BC by Shennong, the Divine Husbandman. Shennong should probably not be taken as a specific person; he should be the representative of a period during which the nomadic Chinese people turned from herds towards a more stable agricultural economy. A classical lexicon on the classification of plants, *Shennong Ben Chao Jing (Shennong's Record of Plants)*, was issued in 2737 BC.[24] The cultivation of plants in China initiated from the purposes for food (rice, vegetables, fruit, etc.) and medicine, and the cultivation of plants for aesthetic appreciation developed gradually with the development of gardening.

Gardens for pleasure originated from the "You" and "Tai." The "You" was a special hunting park for the emperor and nobles. "Tai" was a kind of high-rise terrace built by the ancient emperors to symbolize celestial mountains and to access the deity. It was also used for meteorological observation and sightseeing.

The reason why classical planting design in Chinese gardens developed towards a naturalistic orientation from its very beginning is that it was influenced by these philosophies: the ideas of "man and nature in one," of the metaphor of moral integrity and nature, of deity.

Confucianism and Taoism are two major parallel schools of philosophy in ancient China. Even though Confucianism emphasizes rites, moral codes and other rigid and hierarchical concepts of social organization, and resulted in the axial, symmetrical, formal layouts of ancient Chinese architecture, yet Confucius (Konfuzi, or Konzi) did have his other side: he also promoted "Tianmingun" (the theory of destiny), and considered that the mandate of heaven could not be resisted by human beings. As the counterpart of Confucianism, Taoism had more influenced on garden design. Laotze (Laozi) advocated maintaining the ordinary course of events and thought that man should respect the law of nature. Mencius (Menzi) combined the thoughts of Confucius and Laotze on nature and considered that the law of heaven controlled the development of both human society and nature, and man should respect nature, which was created by heaven. It was because the domination of the thought of "man and nature in one" that the ancient Chinese believed planting and other elements of gardens, as parts of the second

---

[24] Dorothy Graham, *Chinese Gardens: Gardens of the Contemporary Scene: An Account of Their Design and Symbolism* (New York: Dodd, Mead and Company, Inc., 1938), p.18.

nature built by man, should maintain a state of "pure nature."

The metaphor of moral integrity and nature was popular in the Spring and Autumn period (770-481 BC). It resulted in the viewing of nature from the point of view of ethics. It also humanized nature by endowing nature with moral integrity, and led to the respect of nature. "Lofty mountains and flowing water" have been the symbol of noble and unsullied morality and Shanshui (mountains and water) have been the substitute for natural scenery in China. Thus Chinese garden design emphasized the natural state of garden elements such as plantings, mountains, water, etc., from the beginning and it should not be surprising that planting design in Chinese gardens developed in a naturalistic style.

The cosmology of the deity emerged at the end of the Chou (Zhou) Dynasty (1122–771 BC) and was popularized in the Chin (Qin) Dynasty (221–207 BC) and the Han Dynasty (202 BC–AD 220), as the result of the diversity of the schools of the thoughts in the Warring States period (403–221 BC), and also as the means of escaping from the suffering reality of the times.

The Legends of the Kunlunshan Mountain and of the Celestial Isles in the Eastern Sea are two major systems in the cosmology of deity. It was said that the Kunlunshan Mountain was connected to heaven, a supernatural being lived on its summit, and the hanging garden built by the emperor Huangdi was on its slope. Penglai, Fangzhang and Yingzhou were three mythical islands where the immortals lived and which vanished and reappeared in the mist above the Eastern Sea.[25] This legend about mythical islands might have been developed from the natural phenomenon of mirages appearing above the sea that can still been seen occasionally in the coastal areas of Northeast China today. It was the origin of the "three islands in a lake" pattern in Chinese garden design. Since Chinese gardeners strive to recreate these mythological lands that appeared in a "natural" style, it is not surprising that planting, as one of the essential garden elements, was considered as "natural" and should manifest no artificial trace.

4. Basic categories and characteristics of Chinese gardens and their planting design

Chinese gardens can be grouped into three basic categories: private gardens, imperial gardens and grand natural landscape gardens, such as temple gardens, monastery gardens and ancestral hall gardens. Private gardens are noted for their flexible layout and tranquil atmosphere, and gardeners cultivate most plants in private gardens. Imperial gardens are much larger in scale, more formal and sumptuous, and even though their design made every effort to show the imperial manner, they are still in a naturalistic style in general. Grand natural landscape gardens are celebrated for using natural scenery as background

---

[25] Zhou, *The History of Chinese Classical Gardens*, pp. 11-16.

and carefully take advantage of some man-made structures, such as temples, monasteries, ancestral halls and pavilions to add the finishing touch. These gardens are usually rustic and celebrated for the precious plants in their courtyards and some aged, rare trees around the buildings. Most of the plants in these gardens grow naturally and have been preserved by man.

In general, Chinese gardens have four major characteristics: originated from nature, but higher than nature; the combination of architectural beauty and natural beauty; the pictorial and poetic temperament and interest; the implication of artistic conception or atmosphere.[26]

5. Factors that influence the development of planting design in Chinese gardens

The major factors that influenced the development of planting and other aspects of Chinese garden design are: natural environment, economics, society, politics, philosophy and technology.

Studying the works of the ancestors and learning from nature are the two basic methods of the training of landscape painters and gardeners. Fantastic scenic mountains, grotesque aged pines, jagged rocks, galloping streams, mirror like rivers and lakes, floating clouds, emerging mist, etc., have been favorite source materials of Chinese landscape painting. Almost all the celebrated Chinese landscape painters traveled widely and tried to master the essence of nature, and Chinese painting and gardens were actually their interpretations of Chinese natural landscape. The diversity of plant materials is also one of the reasons that resulted in the diversity of planting design in different regions of China. Therefore, Chinese natural environment has a direct influence on the planting design of Chinese gardens.

Most Chinese gardens were built in the middle or the later periods of a dynasty when the economy of the whole society developed to a certain standard. Since families have been deemed highly important by Chinese societies, a majority of gardens were private gardens. Even the imperial gardens could be regarded as gardens for the imperial family. The tension of a hierarchical society, frustration in officialdom and the desire to gain satisfaction from nature instead also contributed to the building of private gardens. (One of the most famous of these gardens is the "Unsuccessful Politician's Garden" or "Humble Administrator's Garden" in Suzhou). These factors were more or less reflected in the planting design of Chinese gardens.

The development of the technology of plant cultivation also affected planting design in Chinese gardens. The influence of cosmology has been mentioned before in the section

---

[26] Zhou, *The History of Chinese Classical Gardens*, pp.20-23.

entitled "The Origin of Planting Design in Chinese Gardens."

6. Stages of development

The development of Chinese gardens and planting design can be divided into these episodes (See Appendix also): Period of formation —Han Dynasty (202 B.C.–A.D. 220) and times before; period of transition —Three Kingdoms (220–280), Southern and Northern Dynasties (386–589); period of efflorescence —Sui Dynasty (590–618) and Tang Dynasty (618–906); and period of maturity —from Song Dynasty (960—1279) to Qing Dynasty (1644–1912).

During the period of formation (before A.D. 220), the mainstream of garden development was the improvement of imperial gardens. Very few private gardens appeared and most of them followed the pattern of imperial gardens, and there was no obvious difference in design between these two categories of gardens. The functions of gardens shifted gradually from hunting, communing with the deity and practical agricultural production to the enjoyment of "natural" beauty, yet the cultivation of plants was still mainly for agricultural production instead of aesthetic appreciation. The species of plants for aesthetic appreciation were very limited, and technologies of plant cultivation were at a preliminary level.[27]

The second episode of development ranged from the Three-Kingdoms period (220–280) to the Southern and Northern Dynasties period (386–589). The focus of gardening changed from the "reproduction" of nature to the representation of nature. Some functions of gardens, such as hunting or accessing the deity gradually disappeared and aesthetic appreciation became the dominant function. The creation of artistic conceptions was in an embryonic state. Temple gardens emerged and private gardens developed rapidly. Planting in gardens also began to emphasize artistic effect.

Chinese gardens and planting design reached the period of full bloom during the Sui Dynasty (590–618) and Tang dynasty (618–906). The difference between imperial gardens and private gardens became obvious. Some literati took part in the building of gardens, and poems and paintings began to influence garden design. The technologies of plant cultivation developed to an advanced level, and people bred new plant species by means of plant introduction, plant domestication and plant grafting. They also developed the technology of transplanting flowers and trees, and began to highlight the aesthetic properties of plants. Numerous varieties and species of plants appeared, and a number of books on plant classification and plant cultivation were published.

The episode of maturity refers to the period from the Song Dynasty (960–1279) to the

---

[27] Zhou, *The History of Chinese Classical Gardens*, p.338.

Qing Dynasty (1644–1912). Garden design transformed from "depicting reality" to "depicting feeling," and imperial gardens began to take inspiration from private gardens. The technologies of plant cultivation developed further and got systematically generalized on the basis of previous periods. A variety of books on gardening were published. The exchange between Chinese gardens and Western gardens also started in the Qing Dynasty (1644–1912). But the development of theoretical explorations in gardening stagnated in the late Qing Dynasty (1644–1912), and the technologies and crafts of gardening returned to the state of pure oral instruction. Most of the existing traditional Chinese gardens were built in this episode.

The development of Chinese gardens and planting design can be understood better with these criteria: in general, the scale of gardens evolved from large to small; the garden scene developed from extensive and grand views to subtle and typical views; the creative method transformed from purely "depicting reality" to the combination of "depicting reality" and "depicting feeling," and then to the dominance of "depicting feeling." For example, in the Qin Dynasty (221–207 B.C.) and the Han Dynasty (202 B.C.–A.D. 220), the gardens were full-size reproduction of natural scenes; from the Tang Dynasty (618–906) to the Qing Dynasty (1644–1912), the miniaturized landscape prevailed; in the mid and later Qing (1644–1912), reproducing segments of real landscape, such as parts of mountains and streams, was used to inspire the imagination of the observer and to achieve the effect of "recognizing a leopard by a pattern of spots on its skin".

7. The distribution of Chinese gardens

Gardens exist extensively in China, but they concentrate in these areas (Figure 3.2): the area near Xian, the area near Luoyang, the area near Hangzhou and Suzhou, the area near Beijing and Chengde, the area near Guangzhou and the area near Guilin.

The area near Xian was the political, economic and cultural center of China in ancient times. The capitals of five dynasties, Western Zhou (1122–771 B.C.), Qin (221–207 B.C.), Han (202 B.C.–A.D. 220), Sui (590–618) and Tang Dynasties (618–906) were built in this region. It was the cradle of Chinese gardens: early Chinese gardens were born and developed here. Luoyang was another important city in the past. It has a central location and was the capital of the Eastern Han (25–220), of the Kingdom Wei (220–265) in the "Three Kingdom" period (220–280), of the Western Jin (265–317) in the Jin Dynasty (265–420), etc. Its warm climate is favorable for the growth of a variety of plants. A great number of famous gardens were built in this area in the Sui Dynasty (590–618) and the Tang Dynasty (618–906).

Hangzhou and Suzhou were hardly influenced by the civil wars in the past. The agriculture and handicraft industries were rather developed in this region. Merchants, nobles and literati preferred to live here. The natural environment in this area also enjoys exceptional advantages: fertile soil, warm climate, plenty of rainfall and a number of lakes and rivers. All these contributed to the advanced development of private gardens in this region, especially in the Ming Dynasty (1368–1644) and the Qing Dynasty (1644–1912).

In northern China, gardens mainly concentrate in Beijing and Chengde. Beijing has been the capital for six dynasties, including the Ming (1368–1644) Dynasty and the Qing Dynasty (1644–1912). A number of imperial gardens were built in Beijing even though its natural environment was not very favorable. Chengde was chosen as the site of the Summer Retreating Palace in the Qing Dynasty (1644–1912) for its excellent natural scenery. Most of the existing imperial gardens are located in this area.

In southern China, gardens concentrated in the delta area of the Pearl River near Guangzhou and the area near Guilin. Probably because Guangzhou has been a trading port since the Ming Dynasty (1368–1644), the gardens in this region received and demonstrated more foreign influence than other areas. Gardens in the areas near Guilin are basically natural scenery gardens.

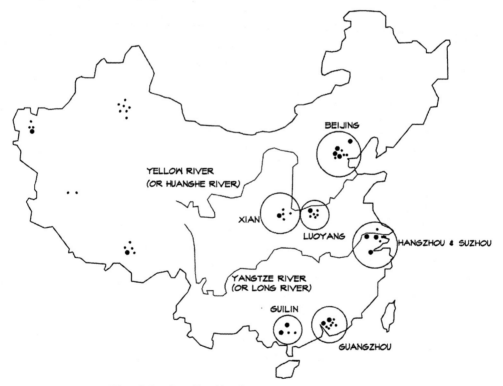

Fig. 3.2 The distribution of Chinese gardens

CHAPTER 4
COMPARING CHINESE GARDENS AND JAPANESE GARDENS AND THEIR PLANTING DESIGN

1. Historical affiliation

To some Westerners, Chinese Gardens and Japanese Gardens may seem similar. In fact, even though Japanese Gardens have developed from Chinese origins, they have adapted to Japanese climate, geography, history and culture, and evolved into a distinct style that has unique features. Japanese Gardens have been relatively well known in the West, while little is known about Chinese Gardens. This may be due to many reasons. One of the reasons may be Japan started the Meiji Reform and opened to the West as early as 1868, while China started its reform and opened to the West as late as 1979. To better understand the differences between Chinese Gardens and Japanese Gardens, we'll start with the common ground of the two.

The earliest communications between China and Japan might have been as early as the Qin Dynasty (221–207 BC). The first emperor of China, Qin Shihuang, united China again as one empire. He had done many grand scale projects: connected the defense walls of the seven warring states and turned them into the Great Wall, built the Afang Palace (one of the greatest palace; unfortunately it was burned by peasant rebels later), unified the weighing and measuring systems, unified the Chinese written language, built his own tomb structures. His tomb structures are some of the greatest underground constructions in human history. Today, only his secondary tombs have been evacuated and opened to the public; his main tomb has not been evacuated yet. The vivid life-sized sculptures of his terra cotta soldiers and horses in his secondary tombs still stun many visitors to Xian today. He also built his royal garden in the "three islands in a lake" pattern and tried to reach the mythical islands and the immortals. He enjoyed his life and ruling so much that he wanted to live forever. In order to reach the mythical islands and get elixir, the medicines that would make him live forever, he himself traveled to the coast of the East Sea of China several times. He sent out a sorcerer, Xu Fu, to search for elixir. Xu Fu knew he probably could not find elixir. So, he asked the emperor for 3000 young men and women and a lot of supplies, including plant seeds. He started the journey, and disappeared from China. Nobody knew exactly where he went eventually. Some guessed he probably went to the coast of the East Sea and the Korean Peninsula, and sailed across the ocean to Japan. Some modern scholars in both China and Japan even speculate that he indeed went to Japan and met the natives there. If more evidences discovered later confirm that this theory is true, that probably would be the first communication between the two nations.

In 552, Buddhism spread to Japan through Korea. In 607, emperor Sui Yangdi of the Sui Dynasty (590–618) was building his landscape parks near his capital city of Luoyang. This pleasure park is important to Japanese landscape development, because the Japanese ambassador's report on this park had a profound influence on Japanese landscape design and the first imperial Japanese landscape design seems to stem directly from it. The head of this Japanese embassy was Ono no Imoko sent by empress Suiko. The beauty of the royal park he saw at Luoyang astonished him. Before that, many Japanese had learned about China and the Chinese products from Korea and from Buddhist monks, but they had not actually seen China and the Chinese landscape arts. Buddhism had indeed been a powerful carrier for Chinese arts and culture to Korea and Japan. Ono no Imoko returned to China again soon after. This time, he was accompanied by a group of scholars. After his trip to China, he founded the art of flower arrangement in Japan. The placing of flowers on Buddhist altars might have inspired this. Four years after Ono no Imoko's trip to China, a Korean craftsman whose face and body were spotted with white arrived in the capital of Japan. His name was Michiko no Takumi, sometimes referred to as Shikomaro, the Ugly Artisan. Japanese thought he might have leprosy and tried to cast him on an island in the sea and left him there to die. He told them that he had landscaping skills and could be beneficial to the country. They spared his life and ordered him to build a "bridge of Wu," or a bridge in Chinese style. This order indicated there might have been some attempts to build for the empress a park in the "lake and island" pattern. Based on existing evidence, the Ugly Artisan probably built a park in the "lake and island" pattern for the empress. This became a basic pattern for the Japanese landscape parks for the next several hundred years.[28] The planting design in these landscape parks was naturalistic. Since Ono no Imoko's visits to China, there were a steady stream of Japanese students and scholars to China to learn Chinese arts and culture. They were pretty much like today's oversea students and scholars. Some of the Chinese scholars also traveled to Japan for academic exchange, or moved to Japan to escape war or persecution. They brought with them landscape paintings and skills, arts of sculpture, calligraphy and architecture.

---

[28] Kuck, Loraine E. *The World of Japanese Garden: From Chinese Origins to Modern Landscape Art.* Weatherhill, Inc., 1968. pp. 65-69.

2. Differences between Chinese gardens and Japanese gardens and their planting design

Three hundred years of the Tang Dynasty (618–906) brought profound influences on Japanese architecture and landscape arts, some of these influences are still evident today, as seen on the relatively straight rooflines and stone lanterns in the Japanese gardens. In Song Dynasty (960–1279), Chinese landscape paintings and prose reached a new height. Zen Buddhist monks brought some of these paintings to Japan. Later, the Mongol invasion made many of the fine paintings available in common Chinese market, some of these paintings reached Japan. These advanced arts of the Song Dynasty inspired the Japanese Muromachi painters. Even though Muromachi painters were developed in a different space and a different time (15th century, after the Song Dynasty's fall), they were closely related to the Song Dynasty Arts. Many of the early Muromachi painters were completely Song (Dynasty) style artists.[29]

There were two major styles of paintings in China: "Gong Bi," literally translated as "neat pen," a style emphasizes depicting the realty and every detail of an object or a scenery; "Xie Yi," literally translated as "depicting meaning and feeling," a style focuses on depicting the essence and spirit of the object or scenery and the feeling of the painter. In this style, painters sought to use the minimum numbers of lines and strokes to catch the essence of an object or scenery. Exaggerated forms and bold lines were use. Details were not as important as in the "Gong Bi" style. Many of the Song and Muromachi landscape paintings were in the "Xie Yi" style. Both traditional Chinese and Japanese landscape paintings were frequently drawn in black ink on semi-absorbent paper (Xuan Ji) or silk. The black ink could have many different shades of gray depending on the amount of the water added. Sometimes accent color like red, green, blue or yellow were added. The brush was handled in the same way as calligraphy: definite and final. It could not be erased or drawn over to cover a mistake. Japanese painters and Zen monks (many of them were talented painters also) combined landscape paintings and Zen Buddhism and created a very unique Japanese garden style: the Zen gardens. We could view them as landscape painting done with different materials: sands, rocks and plants. Loraine Kuck even named them "Painter's gardens." Zen paintings and gardens frequently had Zen symbolism: In Zen paintings, houses, villages and small human figures were frequently shown at the foot of a huge cliff, which symbolizes the ordinary world, from which the painter or Zen monk was constantly trying to lift himself; the tiny human figures showed their relative importance in the universe; a monastery was often shown in the

---

[29] Kuck, Loraine E. *The World of Japanese Garden: From Chinese Origins to Modern Landscape Art.* Weatherhill, Inc., 1968. p. 149.

background, in a somewhat higher ground; a long climbing path meandered to the peak symbolized the long and hard path to enlightenment. In Zen gardens, rocks symbolized cliffs or peaks and raked gravels symbolized valley or water. The marks on the rocks could symbolize paths to the cliffs or peaks of enlightenment for the pilgrims. The Zen paintings or gardens were not meant to be the representation of a specific scene, but an attempt to generalize the common essence and quality of all scenes observed by the painters, and a means to convey this observation and feeling to others. Only a limited number of plants were used in Zen gardens. The shrubs were trimmed into round shapes and the colors of plants were basically green. Large areas of sand were used to create dry style Zen gardens. They were acceptable and became popular in Japan. This might be because that most areas of Japan had a long rainy season and abundant water supplies, and the owner of a dry style garden knew that if he walked out of the door, he could easily find a pond, a stream or a river. The dry landscape created in Zen garden was rare and could hardly be found in natural scenes. It could be tightly controlled and requires very small and limited spaces and could be very attractive to a Japanese. On the other hand, a dry style gravel garden was probably not even considered in China, because many areas of China, especially the northern parts of the country, had a constant and real threat of drought. A dry gravel garden would probably hardly become popular in China.

After about one thousand years of evolution and maturation, Japanese gardens finally outgrew the Chinese influence in Ashikaga (1336-1572) and Tokugawa (1603-1867) periods. Because of the invasions of the Mongols and dynasty changes, Chinese changed the style of paintings and gardens and also shifted their focus and excelled in other areas of the arts: Ming Dynasty architecture, ceramics, furniture, etc. Mongols never invaded Japan. Japanese architecture continued its development from the Tang dynasty style and it did not follow the more decorative and complicated Chinese Ming dynasty style. Japanese paintings were not interrupted by the Mongols and continued their development from the Song dynasty style. Chinese gardens and Japanese gardens also developed along different directions. The differences between the two Garden styles also became more and more obvious. Since the Japanese Meiji (Ming Zhi) reform in 1868, through the hard work of many Japanese landscape designers and intense cultural exchanges with the West, Japanese landscape arts have been introduced to many parts of the world and Japanese gardens have been recognized worldwide for their simplicity, abstraction and symbolism. Although Chinese gardens and Japanese became two distinct garden styles, the communication between the two almost never stopped. For example, in late Ming dynasty (1368–1644), Ji Cheng wrote a book entitled "The Craft of Gardens (Yuan Ye)." (See annotated bibliography at the end of this book). This book generalized many of the design principles of Chinese gardens, but all copies of the books were destroyed or lost in China because of civil unrest and invasion of the Manchus. Finally, a copy of this book (printed in Chinese) was found in Japan, and all the current prints of this book in China were reprinted based on the copy found in Japan. Many design principles described in "The Craft of Gardens," like "borrowing scenery," "Heavenly Creation" and "Taking Advantage" (see detailed discussion in later portion of this book), were used in both Chinese gardens and Japanese gardens.

Along with Zen Buddhism, the appreciation of tea also spread from China to Japan. Japanese developed the tea appreciation into a tea ceremony and also created a unique Japanese style of gardens: Tea Gardens. The tea ceremony was a well-mannered ritual that is always performed indoors. The Tea Garden is the outdoor approach to the tearoom. The tea plant is *Thea sinensis*, a native of China. Tea is a drink made form its leaves that had the power to induce wakefulness. Tea was known in China since early times. In the Tang Dynasty (618–906), it was already a common drink and was imported to Japan. In the Song Dynasty (960–1279), Buddhist monks in Changan drank tea in a ceremony honoring Bodhidharma. Changan was the capital of Qin (221–207 BC) and Tang (618–906) dynasties and is now called Xian. In Japan, a Zen monk, Shuko (or Juko, 1423-1502) developed drinking tea into a ritual ceremony. This ceremony took place at the back of one of the buildings in the Silver Pavilion garden. The basic purpose of the tea ceremony was to instill the virtues of courtesy, imperturbability, purity and urbanity. The tea ceremony is one way for friends to gather. The tea ceremony itself is only an introduction; the conversation that happens after the ceremony is more important. The tea ceremony was one vehicle that saved Muromachi aesthetics. Instead of becoming monks as those in previous periods, people turned to the tea ceremony to seek peace and beauty. Rikyu's idea on simplicity made it accessible to ordinary people. The tea hut might be modeled after the Grass Cottage with thatched roof as described in the famous Chinese poet, Po Chu-I (Bai Juyi) in the Tang dynasty (618–906), whose poems were also popular and favored in Japan. The entire tea garden sought to create a rustic atmosphere and pure and plain beauty. Woodwork was not painted and the wood grain would show; the walls were mud-plastered but without the white finish; the windows were filled with bamboo lattices and oiled paper; the fences were also made from bamboo; the path that lead to the tea room was composed of natural stepping stones. The tea garden and tearoom represented an escape to the wild from the daily pressure from outside world. Such scenes seeking plain and pure beauty were once popular topics in Chinese poems and paintings. Today they can still be found in the Japanese tea garden, but rarely in any Chinese gardens. The existing Chinese gardens were mostly built in the Ming (1368–1644) and Qing (1644–1912) dynasties and were of different styles.

Sometimes the path to the teahouse is divided into inner and outer portions. The outer part represented the world outside, and the inner part represented the wild and natural world, the hiding place from the outside mundane world. The qualities sought in a tea gardens are: rustic solitude, tranquility, finish of ageing as shown in weathered stones, lichen and mosses that built up through ages.[30]

In addition to Zen gardens and Tea gardens, there are many other differences between Chinese gardens and Japanese gardens:

Both are naturalistic style gardens, yet Chinese gardens typically occupy a larger space. Japanese gardens strike to achieve maximum artistic effect in a concise space. Chinese garden design emphasizes path and movement in the gardens; garden designers seek to achieve the view changes as one moves through a garden. Path is an indispensable part of Chinese gardens. Many Japanese gardens, like the Zen gardens, emphasize the beauty of static view.

Fig. 4.1 A multi-story stone lantern in a Japanese garden

Japanese designers and craftsman have developed some very unique small items, like stone lanterns, stone basin, Buddhist sculptures, wells, stepping stones, bamboo fences, and used them extensively and repeatedly in the gardens and form some kind of "pattern" language (Fig 4.1). These small items may have originated in other countries, but Japanese designers have advanced their use to a higher level. These items are inexpensive, easy to make and transport, and they fit extremely with a small garden space and often form a very unique feature and pattern. Many of these smaller items were once favored in Chinese gardens, but were discarded later and can rarely be seen in existing Chinese gardens.[31]

In the Ming (1368–1644) and Qing (1644–1912) dynasties, Chinese garden designers shifted the direction of garden development and excelled in other areas of garden design. Most of the existing Chinese gardens were built in these two dynasties. Chinese designers improved the techniques and technology in architecture, more curved roof hips and eaves

---

[30] Kuck, Loraine E. *The World of Japanese Garden: From Chinese Origins to Modern Landscape Art.* Weatherhill, Inc., 1968. pp. 149-201.

[31] Tsu, Frances Ya-sing. *Landscape Design in Chinese Gardens.* San Francisco: McGraw-Hill Book Company, 1988. pp. 31-37.

appeared, and many different types of garden architecture, like covered walkways, pavilions, kiosks, chambers, were used extensively and integrated very well with the garden space. The relationship between inside and outside space, sequences and relationships of different garden spaces became the focus of design. Garden architecture was occupied space and had many practical functions: courtyards for children to play, pavilions and chambers for meeting friends and discussing poems and prose, etc. Garden space also adapted to different regions and climate; for example, the courtyards in Northern parts of China were designed as larger "warm courtyards" so that the sun could shine into the courtyards in the cold winter, while the courtyards in Southern parts of China were designed as smaller "cool courtyards" so that the garden walls could block the low angle summer sun and formed cool shadow areas in the courtyards. The streets (some designers call them "cool streets") in traditional residences in Southern China were also very long and narrow for the same reason. Garden architecture details also developed to an advanced level: various lattice windows, moon gates and "bottle gates" appeared. For example, there were many different kinds of lattice windows, like fan shape, square shape, etc. With so many different geometric patterns formed by lattice, they could be compiled into one big book. I also think that these geometric patterns of various lattice windows can be used in developing the parterres or Knot gardens of the formal planting design: you can get the inspiration from the geometric form and patterns and then use different materials, like hedges or colorful flowers to make them and the outcome should be good. The garden walls in Chinese gardens were often painted white and used as background to show the lines and shadows of plants in the sunlight or moonlight. Because several of the emperors of the Qing dynasty (1644–1912) had seen and liked the private gardens in their trips to Suzhou and other cities in South China, they "copied" and sometimes enlarged the same garden space or space sequences in the royal gardens, but used different colors and finish and improved them: in China, during Qing dynasty (1644–1912), the use of color in gardens and architecture had very strict control per the hierarchy of the government officials. For example, ONLY the emperor could use the orange yellow color as shown in the roof tile color of the Forbidden City. Using the wrong color could be a "crime" punishable by death.

In Japanese gardens, the garden architecture continued the development from the Chinese Tang dynasty (618–906) style. The existing Japanese garden architecture still show many features of Tang dynasty style: relatively straight hips and eaves, large overhang of the eaves, plain colors, etc. Japanese gardens also used fewer garden architecture, and many gardens, like the Zen dry style gardens, were designed to be viewed from the house, and not to be occupied or even stepped on. Chinese calligraphy is used in both Chinese gardens and Japanese gardens on the columns or walls as couplets or along the beam or lintel as a horizontal scroll to hint at the theme of the scenery, but it is used more extensively in Chinese gardens. The treatment of the ground, or the "bottom surface" of gardens are different in the two styles: In Japanese gardens, the "bottom surface" is formed by pavement, gravels, pebbles, stepping stone, grass, moss, and groundcover, the soils are rarely exposed. In Chinese gardens, the "bottom surface" is composed of pavement, grass, ground cover and swept earth. Swept earth is used mostly in North China, where the climate is dry. Pavement is made of tiles, brick or broken china pieces to form some geometric pattern or shape of flowers or animals.

Rocks are used by both styles, but the ways to choose and use rocks are different: In Japanese gardens, rocks are relatively smooth and smaller in size. They are harder, heavier and denser metamorphic granites and cherts. A few rocks can be scattered in gardens in half-buried, horizontal or vertical form, and used with sand or gravels. Rocks are used to create a sense of timelessness, so the more signs of ageing, the better. The grouping and composition of the group is very important. In Chinese gardens, rocks are usually lake rock with rough surface. They are sedimentary rocks that show signs of beaten by water over the years, to show the Taoism teaching of "softest things overcame the hardest things." They are frequently piled up as "cliff" or rock outcrops to symbolize cliffs, peaks or remote mountains, and they are often combined with plants to form a rock-plant combination as a main feature of a garden.[32]

Even though Japanese and Chinese have many common favorite plant materials and the symbolism, like lotus, cherry, peach groves, "three friends in winter" (pines, bamboo and plum), plants are handled differently in the two styles: In Japanese gardens, shrub were pruned into round shapes to show the mass and to maintain the controlled "perfect beauty." The flowers of the shrubs are less important. Plants are used for forms, mass and shades. Flowers play a relatively minor role. In Zen gardens, colors are limited to mostly green colors to create an atmosphere for mediation. Trees are often handled in naturalistic style. In Chinese gardens, both trees and shrubs are often allowed natural growth to show their lines and colors. Even though they may be trimmed or pruned, yet the intention is still to create some kind of naturalistic look. Shrubs and trees with colorful flowers, foliage and fruits are often used. Flowerbeds in irregular shape formed by rockery are often filled with colorful perennials like peonies and begonias.

Both styles pursue the antique feeling as well as grace and strange forms of plants. For examples, pines in asymmetrical spread form are often used at the edge of cliffs or the edge of water to show their graceful form. Both styles use limited plant materials, but the reasons may not be the same. The Chinese gardens use limited plant materials mostly because of plants' symbolism, while Japanese gardens use limited plant materials mainly to pursue simplicity, abstractions and plain and pure beauty. The symbolism of plants is

---

[32] Engel, David H. *Creating a Chinese Garden.* Portland, Oregon: Timber Press, 1986. pp. 19-41

not as strong as in Chinese gardens. In Chinese gardens, walls are higher and are used to block the noise from the urban neighborhood and prevent outsiders from looking in, while in Japanese gardens, walls are lower and they are used to block view lines and prevent insiders from looking out.

CHAPTER 5
COMPARING CHINESE GARDENS AND ENGLISH NATURALISTIC GARDENS AND THEIR PLANTING DESIGN

1. Historical development of English naturalistic gardens

There are three major schools within the naturalistic gardens and planting design: English naturalistic gardens or English landscape gardens, Japanese gardens and Chinese gardens and their planting design. We have compared Chinese gardens and Japanese gardens and their planting design in previous chapter; let's do a comparative study of Chinese gardens and English naturalistic gardens and their planting design in this chapter.

The early English gardens were pretty much like the rest of the Europe and Near East and were Formal Gardens. In the eighteenth century, English Landscape Movement started the English naturalistic gardens and planting design, and quickly spread throughout the Europe. There were probably several main factors that influenced the eighteenth century English Landscape Movement.

First of all, in seventeenth century, the news came through Holland that all Chinese gardens, including the emperor's gardens were done in a naturalistic manner. This news changed many European designers' ideas and aesthetic views, and brought the fundamental conceptual change that naturalistic gardens and planting design were acceptable and they could be beautiful. Because of the difficulties in communications, however, specific design information and in-depth discussions of Chinese gardens were not available. English designers turned to other sources and their own creativity for specific design information and filled in the blanks. Secondly, the writings and landscape paintings of the suburb of ancient Greece and Rome provided the specific "blue prints" for English Landscape Movements and planting design. Thirdly, the passing of the Acts of Enclosure and reclamation of wasteland, swamp and scrub made large pieces of land available for landscape development, and made it possible to exploit new landscape ideals. The Industrial Revolution was first started in England in the eighteenth century and its development was faster in England than in other countries. The Industrial Revolution brought urbanization and the concentration of population and related problems like pollution in large cities. Many people were nostalgic for previous rural lifestyles and missed rustic landscapes, the countryside and the wilderness. The landscape of the countryside and the wilderness had become something they missed and wanted. Gardens and parks created in the Landscape Movement could satisfy this need. Lastly, compared with the rest of the Europe, Near East and Middle East, England had a temperate climate and more rainfall, the efficiency provided by the formal gardens and planting design was less important. It was also easier for English landscape designers to develop the naturalistic style gardens and planting design because of this advantage.

In the seventeenth and eighteenth centuries, many Europeans were fascinated by Chinese civilization. This phenomenon was called "Chinoiserie." It referred to philosophy, arts, things and ideas in the "Chinese manner." In addition to the insatiable demand for Chinese silk, tea, and porcelain (china), and translations of Confucian and Taoist classics, many Europeans also had the desire for meandering streams and paths, elegant bridges, pagodas and pavilions. Most European information about Chinese gardens was impressionistic and secondhand at that period. European garden designers sometimes had to used Western details and techniques to fill in the blank in creating the "Chinese" style that they heard about or read about. In 1665, a Dutch mission to Beijing published a book with illustrations on Chinese gardens; this book was later translated into English. In 1685, Sir William Temple first mentioned Chinese landscape design in one of his essay, "Upon the Gardens of Epicurus." It compared the formal gardens with symmetry and ruled lines with the naturalistic Chinese gardens with irregular forms, or *Sharawadgi,* a term Temple made up and with no Chinese roots. It is believed that many prototypes as described by Temple's *Sharawadgi* came from an album brought back from China by Father Matteo Ripa. This album is still in the British Museum today. Temple wrote: "The Chinese scorn this [formal] way of planting…But their greatest reach of the imagination is employed in contriving Figures, where the Beauty shall be great and strike the Eye, but without any Order of Disposition of Parts, that shall be commonly or easily observed." The idea of breaking away from formalism was formed and the seed of the English landscape revolution was planted. Stephen Switzer was the first one to translate and apply Temple's *Sharawadgi* into practicable, naturalistic landscape design. Alexander Pope also applied the Chinese-style principles of "pleasing intricacy" and "artful wilderness" in his garden designs. In 1710, Ashley Cooper wrote in "The Moralists" that people should "no longer resist the passion for Things of a natural kind: where neither Art, nor the conceit of Caprice of Man has spoiled the genuine order…Even the rude Rocks, the Mossy Caverns, the irregular unwrought Grottos and broken Falls of Waters, with all the horrid Graves of Wilderness itself, as representing nature more, will be the more engaging, and appear with Magnificence beyond the formal Mockery of Princely Gardens." Joseph Addison supported Cooper's view and first introduced the word "landskip," a word that eventually evolved into landscape, a term that is still used in modern times.[33] Williams Chambers visited Guangzhou (Canton) when he was young. He designed a 10-story Chinese pagoda as "eye-catcher" in the garden for George III at Kew in 1757, and published a renowned book entitled "Dissertation on Oriental Gardening" in 1772. In 1782, Lord Macartney, an admirer of the English Landscape Movement, led the first official British embassy to China. He was very enthusiastic about the Chinese imperial gardens that he saw: "There is no beauty of distribution, no feature of amenity, no reach of fancy, which embellishes our pleasant ground in England that is not to be found here…"

In the late seventeenth century, many English visitors went to Italy; they learned not only the formal Italian gardens, but also the appreciation of the whole Italian landscape with its ancient Roman ruins and subtleness. Many writings on these travels occurred, including: Richard Lassels' *The Voyage of Italy*. These writings were also sources of inspiration for the English naturalistic planting design.

In early eighteenth century, the English gardens and planting design started to shift away from the formal style garden and planting design. By 1719, Alexander Pope wrote in his letter to the Princess of Wales: "In laying out a garden, the first and chief thing to be considered is the genius of the place." He also believed that "All gardening is landscape painting…" This methodology and idea was very similar to that of Chinese landscaping, except that the two garden styles were based on two different styles of paintings from two different cultures. The paintings of the Greek and Rome countryside done by Nicolas Poussin (1594-1665), Claude Lorrain (1600-1682) and Salvator Rosa (1615-1673) became the "blueprints" for the newly developed English naturalistic landscaping.

The development of English Landscape Movement could be divided into several phases:

The first phase is the Preparation Phase in the seventeenth century and the early eighteenth century as we discussed earlier. In this phase, people's ideas and aesthetic views changed and the seed of naturalistic gardens and planting design and English landscape revolution was planted.

The second phase was the Transitional Phase from 1720s to 1740s, as represented by Charles Bridgeman and William Kent, a coach painter, interior designer, architect and landscape designer. Alexander Pope heavily influenced Kent. Statues, pavilions, temples and other garden architecture were important parts of the gardens in his garden design.

---

[33] Loxton, Howard (Editor). The Garden: A Celebration. David Bateman Ltd., 1991. p.64-65.

Bridgeman and Kent mixed the elements of previously used formal gardens and those of the naturalistic gardens and opened gardens' view into the surrounding countryside. They "leaped the fence and saw all nature was a garden." As described in the essay "On Modern Gardening" by Horace Walpole, written between 1750 and 1770. Bridgeman opened up the views to the countryside through the use of *ha-ha*, a sunken, retaining wall and ditch; sometimes a metal fence was added at the bottom of the ditch (Fig. 5.1). *Ha-ha* could keep deer and domestic animals from crossing into the gardens while allowing continuous view into the countryside; it played an important role in the development of the English naturalistic park. The *Ha-ha* was introduced into England by a French gardener in the 1690s, and it was called *ah-ah* in France. The same principle is still used today in zoos to remove the visual barrier between visitors and animals. In 1731, Alexander Pope celebrated Bridgeman and summarized the new naturalistic garden design style with a poem entitle "Of Taste:"

> *To build, to plant, whatever you intend...*
> *In all, let Nature never be forgot...*
> *Consult the Genius of the Place in all;*
> *That tells the Waters or to rise, or fall...*
> *Calls in the Country, catch op'ning glades...*
> *Paints as you plant, and as you work, designs...*

The third phase was the Mature Phase from 1750s to 1780s, as represented by Lancelot "Capability" Brown and his followers. Grass, trees, sky and reflecting water were the main components of the park designed by them. For many people, these are the English style gardens / parks on their mind. Brown got the nickname for his habit of trying to analyze a site to bring out its "capabilities." He broke away from formal gardens; gardens were no longer handled in the same way as architectural elements. The landscape and planting design brought the countryside right up to the house. After Brown's death, Humphry Repton continued Brown's effort from 1788 to 1818, but reintroduced flower gardens around the house. Repton was famous for his "Red Books." He always carried his "Red Books" in which he had the "before" and "after" sketches of a site that he could show his clients.

The last phase was the Picturesque Movement from 1780s to 1820s. Leaders of this movement criticized Brown and Repton for the tameness of their designs. They sought romantic wilderness as demonstrated by asymmetry, remote mountains, rushing water and collapsed ruins. The basic features of the Picturesque Movement were roughness, sudden variation and irregularity as demonstrated in Salvator Rosa's paintings (1615-73).

Many of the existing English gardens and parks were worked on and modified by leaders of various phases at different time.

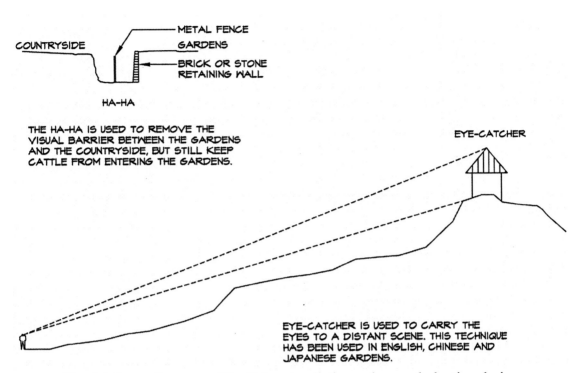

Fig. 5.1 Some features of English naturalistic gardens and planting design

The use of shrubbery became more common as the English Landscape Movement developed. The shrubs often formed serpentine borders close to a walk. The plants were arranged from low to high, with herbaceous plants and low shrubs at the front, and higher shrubs rose in gradation and the taller ornamental trees at the back. Evergreen shrubs and deciduous shrubs were either completely separated or mixed together to create contrast. The shrubs were not trimmed into hedged enclosure as in the formal gardens. Because of the temperate climate and availability of plants, English gardens sometimes tended to grow too many different species of plants. Eventually, the shrubbery planting in English naturalistic gardens developed into two basic patterns: The first pattern was the "mingled" or "common" manner. The shrubs were planted in rows and formed different tiers, with the lowest at the front and gradually rose to the tallest at the back. Sometimes perennials were placed at the front as the first tier. The second pattern was "selected" or "grouped" manner. One species was selected and planted together to form a mass and to create a powerful impact. [34]

Eighteenth century England was inundated with literature on both sides of the arguments regarding formal gardens and naturalistic gardens. Many missionaries and plant hunters to China confirmed the information that even the Chinese Emperor's royal gardens were decorated with naturalistic planting; this reinforced the case for naturalistic landscaping. The English naturalistic landscaping became very popular and eventually dominated all of Europe in the eighteenth century. Central Park in New York, designed by Calvert Vaux and Frederick Law Olmsted, was a remote descendant of this style. It was inspired by Joseph Paxton's Birkenhead Park in England, designed with Edward Kemps in 1843.

2. Comparing Chinese gardens and English naturalistic gardens and their planting design

Now that we have a basic understanding of the English naturalistic gardens and planting design, we can compare it with the Chinese naturalistic gardens and planting design so that we'll have a better understanding for both.

Both English naturalistic gardens and Chinese naturalistic gardens advocated and emphasized the use of poems, prose and paintings in garden and planting design. Alexander Pope (1688-1733) thought that garden should follow the same rules as paintings; he started to integrated poems, paintings and gardens in his own gardens and his friend's gardens; many English naturalistic gardens were inspired by the paintings of Nicolas Poussin (1594-1665), Claude Lorrain (1600-1682) and Salvator Rosa (1615-1673). This coincided with the ideas of Wang Wei (699-759), Chinese poet and garden designer of the Tang dynasty. Many Chinese gardens were also modeled after Chinese Landscape paintings, and poems and verses had been an integrated part of Chinese gardens. The methodologies in the two styles were the same to some extent, but the content and style of the paintings and poems used were different.

Both styles used "words" directly in gardens to suggest or hint the theme of a garden theme. In English gardens, sometimes, stone plaques and urn presented verses were used. In Chinese gardens, words or calligraphy were used extensively. You can find them in almost every Chinese garden. Poems, verses or prose were either hanged on garden walls, or placed at pavilion columns or as horizontal scrolls. They were not intended to describe every detail, but rather to suggest or hint the theme and to stimulate people's imagination. These words contributed greatly to the creation of artistic conception and people's

---

[34] Hobhouse, Penelope. *The Story of Gardening.* DK Publishing, 1st edition, November 1, 2002. p.32, pp.205-239.

understanding of the garden theme.

Both styles tried to recreate nature in gardens. English naturalistic gardens were a more faithful reproduction of nature; sometimes, English gardens were almost not different from the surrounding countryside. English garden designers stressed to blend the gardens and parks well with the surrounding nature. Early Chinese "lake and islands" pattern gardens were larger and were probably more faithful reproduction of nature than later Chinese gardens. Later Chinese gardens became smaller and tried to symbolize nature, and became a more condensed version of "nature." The goal was to create gardens that originated from nature, but higher than nature. Chinese garden designers were not very interested in blending the gardens with the immediate surrounding; they strived more to create the "nature" that they experienced, either through travel or observations from the landscape paintings. They wanted the gardens to suggest the scene of famous but remote mountains, and to stimulate similar feelings that they experienced when they traveled these remote mountains.

Both styles tried to create an illusion of a larger garden in a limited space, but the methods were different. English naturalistic gardens achieved this goal through revealing: removed the fence through the use of *ha-ha* (Fig. 5.1), revealed the surrounding countryside and brought them into the gardens. Garden spaces were often a series of outdoor green "rooms" enclosed by plants. Chinese gardens achieved this goal through concealing or a combination of concealing and revealing: Many of the existing Chinese gardens were urban gardens. The entire garden was typically separated from the noisy urban streets by tall garden walls. Chinese garden designers avoided exposing the entire garden at a glance. They often divided a garden into many different sizes of spaces enclosed by garden walls, garden architecture, rockery and plants. These spaces were organized and linked together by meandering paths. You would not expect what you'll discover beyond a moon gate, or after you walk to the other side of an artificial hill formed by rockery. It seems liked you were really in a very large area and you had walked through so many different spaces of various sizes, yet in fact you are still walking within a very limited garden area. Buildings were integrated into garden; Ambiguity between indoor and outdoor space was another technique to create an illusion of larger garden space. Many buildings or garden structures, like pavilions, kiosks and chambers had very open "side surfaces" and the space under the roof were "gray spaces"- spaces between indoor and outdoor. Sometimes, in a larger garden space, Chinese landscape designers would use densely planted trees and shrubs to conceal the garden walls, but leave a view line to a distant scene like a tower or a pavilion on a hill top to create an illusion that you are in a very large space enclosed by woods. Designers for both styles did understanding the principle of concealing and revealing very well. For example, Lancelot "Capability" Brown would use plants in natural form and organize them to create a unified but multidimensional scheme. He would use woodland to conceal boundaries and unsighted views and leave "gap" in planting to show good views.

Both styles use garden architecture, but in different ways. In English naturalistic gardens, statues, garden house, pavilions or classical buildings were scattered in the green landscape formed by plants, they were used to create a rustic feeling or an artistic atmosphere; buildings were primarily used for ornamental purpose, not as rest stops. Sometimes, plants became background for these buildings. In some garden areas, benches and trellis were used; Occasionally, a large lawn area enclosed by densely planted shrubs and trees would be used as open gallery to display various statues or sculptures. Thomas Whateley was probably the first Westerner to suggest the use of rock in the garden in his book "Observations on Modern Gardening" (1770). Overall, rockery was rarely used in English gardens. In Chinese gardens, a large number of pavilions, kiosks and chambers were used, and they were often grouped together and connected by covered walkways to form a series of garden spaces and a complex. Buildings had both practical functions and aesthetic values. They were inseparable parts of garden to serve the various needs of the owner, such as meeting friends, discuss poems and literature, etc. Statues or sculpture were rarely used, but rockeries were used extensively. The first use of rock was probably in Tu Yuan, the Rabbit garden, built in Western Han (202 BC–AD 9). Over time, rockery had evolved into an elaborate art in Chinese gardens. Sometimes a strange rock could be used as a specimen or an "abstract sculpture" and became the focus of a garden space. Benches were often designed as components of pavilions and chambers to create a rest stop for visitors; benches were used more frequently in spaces that had nice scenes. Some modern researchers used films and photos to study people and they discovered that people like to stay longer at places where they can sit. It seems like the designers for these classical Chinese gardens put this observation into practice long before the modern research and discovery. These classical gardens were originally designed as either the "backyard" of a rich family or a retreat of the emperor, buildings were closely integrated with garden spaces and an entire garden is designed as a livable habitat for various human needs.

Planting design in both styles were naturalistic, but they were done in different manners. Lawns were used at the courtyard of the Medieval European Gardens. English landscape designers advanced the use of lawns to a higher level. In English gardens, large areas of lawns often dominated a garden space and they became a main feature of English naturalistic garden. These large lawn areas also had many practical functions: they could be used for wedding, tea parties, etc. Trees were carefully placed to form a pleasant composition. Shrubs did not arrive until the later stage of English landscape movement. The landforms in many English gardens were very gentle slope or valleys planted with grass. Undulating naturalistic landforms were common scenes. Symbolism of plants was not very strong. In Chinese gardens, lawns were rarely used. Plants were used either against the white washed garden walls to show their lines and shadows, or placed with rockery to form a rock-plant composition, or used to enclosed garden space. Symbolism of plants was very important in the selection of plant materials. The landforms were rougher than English gardens. Rockeries were often used to form an artificial hill or cliff. Pavilions were built on top of these artificial hills. The paths to these hilltop pavilions were very rough and meandering. Both styles tried to avoid arranging plants or garden paths in a straight line or a geometric manner.

Water was handled differently in these two styles. In English gardens, streams were often dammed to form one or two large lakes. Grass, trees, garden architecture, lakes and sky formed the basic elements of an English garden. The edge of water was formed by gentle grass area, and people could walk up to the edge of the water and access it; shrubs were rarely placed at the edge of water. Floating plants or aquatic plants were rarely used on water surface. In Chinese gardens, lakes or ponds were often created by artificial means, and designers always wanted to connect a large pond or lake with narrow and serpentine streams to create contrast. The origin of water was always covered, either by plants or rockery to create an endless feeling. Lotus or other aquatic or floating plants were frequently used on water surface. Golden fishes were also placed in many Chinese gardens. Various forms of bridges were placed over the streams or ponds, and pavilions were often placed at the water edge. The edge of water is formed by covered walkway, chambers, pavilions, soil or rockery. Shrubs or climbers were often used to cover portions of the edge of the pond.

In English gardens, temple, obelisks, bridges, pagodas, grottoes and ruins were often used as "eye-catcher" to attract visitors' attention and carried their view line to a distant picturesque scene (Fig 5.1). For example, William Kent, a leader in the English Landscape Movement used an "eye-catcher" at Rousham, Oxfordshire. It is a triple arch, placed at a hilltop about one mile away. There were many similar examples in Chinese gardens, even though the term "eye-catcher" might not have been used: Chinese designers often placed a pagoda, tower, or pavilion at a distant hilltop to form an "eye-catcher." For example, at the royal Beihai Park, a White Dagoba was placed at the summit of Qiongdao, or the Jade Islet as an "eye-catcher." It was also the highest point for the city of Beijing for a long time. This scene was shown in an eighteenth century European painting of a Chinese imperial boating party. For smaller private gardens, sometimes it was hard to place an "eye-catcher" within the garden because of the garden size, then the garden designers would try to take advantage of the technique of "borrowing scenery" to use a pavilion or a pagoda on a hilltop outside of the property as "eye-catcher." Sometimes, a large tree with strange form on a distant hilltop or a tree hanging from a cliff would be use as an "eye-catcher" also.

CHAPTER 6
THE PRINCIPLES, CONCEPTS AND METHODS OF NATURALISTIC PLANTING DESIGN WITH CHINESE GARDEN AS CASE STUDIES

1. Plant materials

a. Most commonly used plants

According to the practical system of classification we have mentioned earlier in this book, the most commonly used plant materials in Chinese garden can be put in these categories:

Trees (Mass Planting): Trees handled by this planting method were usually found in imperial gardens and temple gardens. They were used to create large-scale spatial effects. Topography and landform are important factors to be considered in grouping and locating the trees (Table 6.1. All tables are placed at the end of the book as part of Appendixes. This is typical for the entire book).

Trees (Special Effects): Trees that are highly individualistic, spectacular, and characteristic and trees that are flowering or have good autumn color, fragrance, or fruit are used as specimens or sometimes as accents in mass planting (Table 6.1 and 6.2).

Shrubs (Group Planting): Acting as decoration or points of interest in the gardens. They can also create a middle layer of plantings under trees (Table 6.1 and 6.2).

Shrubs (Special Effects): Like trees of the similar qualities, shrubs that have beautiful flowers or leaf colors could create similar special effects in plantings (Table 6.1 and 6.2).

Shrubs (Barriers): Shrubs were often used in traditional Chinese gardens as barriers to create spaces that were physically divided but visually connected.

Shrubs (Edgings): The use of shrubs as edgings of ponds, footpaths, rockeries and buildings is a frequent occurrence in Chinese gardens.

Ground Cover: Plants used as groundcover under groves or shade trees must be able to grow well without full sunshine. These may include ferns, herbs and some low growing shrubs.

Vines and Climbers: They are used to cover a wall or act as foils against rocks, fences, or act as specimens in a garden scene.

Aquatic and Sub-aquatic plants: This category includes floating plants, marginal plants and plants that grow in wet conditions (Table 6.1).

Bamboo: Bamboo is an indispensable plant material in Chinese gardens. We'll discuss it in detail in Chapter Seven.

2. Cultural Influence

The raindrops of the night, which fall upon the banana leaves, are like the tears of the weeping mermaid (pearls). When the morning breeze flows through the willows, the latter bend like the slender waists of dancing girls.

Before the window one plants bamboo, and between the courtyards pear trees...

These lines are taken from *Yuan Ye (The Craft of Gardens)*, which was written by the famous garden designer, Ji Cheng, in 1631. They express the interaction between human beings and plants, winds, moonlight and other natural phenomena. These paragraphs also reflect the Chinese way of humanizing plants and viewing them as friends.

Indeed, poem, prose, paintings and other literal forms have a significant influence on traditional Chinese planting design. First of all, cultural influences on Chinese garden and planting design are manifested in the essential ideas and creative approaches. Chinese gardens and planting design, like Chinese poetry, prose and painting, emphasize the creation of artistic conception (conceptual idea, artistic atmosphere, or "Yi Jing" in Chinese). The idea is considered as the most important thing and should always go first in writing an article or building a garden. A writer or a painter or a garden designer should always have a well-thought-out plan before the actual writing, painting or garden building process. Many creative methods of gardening and planting design were borrowed directly or indirectly from poetry, prose or landscape painting.

Let's look at another example: As we have mentioned earlier, China is the country that has the richest flora in the world. Between 1899 and 1911, the famous plant hunter Ernest Wilson discovered and collected about 5,000 species, including 65,000 specimens from the wilds in China, more than 1,000 species were established in Western Cultivation.[35]

This collection has greatly enriched the plant materials for Western garden

---

[35] Keswick, *The Chinese Garden: History, Art and Architecture*, p. 176.

designers, yet Chinese garden designers seem to have been completely unaffected by the discoveries. They continued to develop only the plants that had been domesticated long time before, and continued to love the species that their ancestors had loved since the ancient times. Why? There are basically two reasons: (1) The conservatism that had impeded the development of Chinese society since fifteenth century; (2) The Chinese tradition of treating plants as symbols of ideas, emotional states, will, personality and moral qualities. The newly discovered plants lack the symbolic and historical associations and are considered less valuable and suitable for gardens.

Planting design in Chinese gardens has very strong relationships with poetry, prose and painting. In a sense, poetry and prose supplied the creative concepts and act as the source of inspiration for planting design. Landscape paintings often become the "blue prints" of planting design: the layout and design were adopted from and related to traditional landscape paintings. This amalgamation of art forms (gardening, literature and painting) is an important characteristic of Chinese gardening, especially planting design.

a. Plants and iconography

The most commonly used plants in Chinese gardens are not just objects; they are in fact a kind of "icon" with connotation and can illustrate man's feeling and aspiration, and sometimes even become the source of them. Plants are humanized to indicate a certain feeling, desire, virtue and character. They are used to create aesthetic effects and also to communicate to viewer the intention and concept of the designer.

For example, mulberries have been domesticated since ancient times, and their leaves have been used to feed the silkworm, which produces silk. Probably because "silk" and the word "missing each other" have the same pronunciation ("Si" in Chinese), and mulberries are related to silk, they are often used in poems and stories about lovers as "tree of missing each other" or "tree of love," implying the "yearning between lovers." Mulberries were mentioned in an ancient poem in *Shih Ching (Si Jing*, or *Book of Poems*, written in the Spring and Autumn period, 770–481 B.C.), in which a young girl begs her lover not to visit her at night:

> *I beg of you Chung Tzu*
> *Do not climb into our homestead.*
> *Do not break the willows we have planted...*
>
> *Do not climb over our wall,*
> *Do not break the mulberry-trees we have planted...*

Do not climb into our garden,
Do not break the hardwood we have planted...[36]

Another plant frequently mentioned in Chinese poem is willow, which has been used to make basket and ropes. Its leaves can be infused in water to make tea. The bark and leaves of some species are ingredients in preparations to relieve dysentery, bruises, goiter and rheumatic pains. Buddhists also regard the willow as a holy plant and use its twigs to purify water. Willows are normally planted near water, and water usually associated with women. The swaying willow trees also look like the waists of dancing ladies. All these made willow trees closely related to the description of the female in Chinese literature, such as: "having an eyebrow as slim and beautiful as a leaf of willow."

Spring is the season to appreciate orchids (*Cymbidium spp.*). Orchids are called "ancestor of fragrance"; their fragrance is subtle and yet pervasive, discreet yet interesting, suggesting honorable friendship and uprightness. This fragrance would spread across a room without causing special attention, yet every one would feel the loss when it disappears. Some orchids have curved and balanced leaves, which look like fine brush strokes; other orchids have sheath-like leaves, suggesting both gracefulness and strength.

Tree peony also flowers in the spring in south China, but flowers in the summer in northern part of the country. It is called the "King of Flowers," and its glorious profusion of blooms suggests nobility, wealth, rank, prosperity, honor and beautiful women. Unlike other plants, it was first introduced into the garden for pure show instead of for practical uses, even though its bark was found to have a medical function and was prescribed for blood disorders later.

The peony came into gardens relatively late and is not mentioned in *Shih Ching (Book of Poems)*, or the *Book of Rites* (written in the Spring and Autumn period, 770–481 B.C.), or the *Li Sao (Encountering Sorrow*, written in the Warring States Period, 403–221 B.C., by the famous poet Qu Yuan), and not even in the literature of the Han Dynasty (202 B.C.–A.D. 220). Its first literal record appeared in the writings of Hsieh Ling-yun (Xie Ling-yun) in the fourth century, who is called "Chinese first landscape poet" by Maggie Keswick. The peony he described seemed to be still a wild flower. The first description of the peony in garden was by Li Po (Li Bai), the famous poet of Tang Dynasty (618–906). The peony first appeared in imperial gardens, and then began to be planted near private houses, and soon became popular all across Chang–an, the capital city of the Tang

---

[36] Trans. by Arthur Waley, *Book of Songs*. (London, First Published in 1937, First Grove Press Edition, 1960), p.35. Copyright 1996 by Grove Press, Inc. Used by permission of Grove/Atlantic, Inc.

Dynasty (618–906). Between 684 and 705, the cultivation center of the peony moved to Luo Yang, where double-petal varieties and other hybrids and cultivars were developed. A Festival of Ten Thousand Flowers was declared every year in Luo Yang City, which continues to present times. Po Chi-i (Bai Ju-i), a poet in the early ninth century, described such a flower festival:

> *Cheap and dear—no uniform price*
> *The cost of the plants depends on the number of blossoms*
> *The flaming reds, a hundred on one stalk;*
> *The humble white with only five flowers...*
> *If you sprinkle water and cover the roots with mud*
> *When they are transported they will not loose their beauty.*[37]

Lotus (*Nelumbo nucifera*) is a plant that flowers in summer. It has both practical and ornamental uses, as well as symbolic meaning. Almost every educated Chinese will relate lotus to "Ai Lien (Lian) Shuo" ("On the Love for Lotus") by Chou Tun-i (Zhou Dun-i), a famous eleventh century scholar. All students in high school, even in modern China, memorize it:

Rising from filthy mud without being polluted, reposing purely above the crystal-clear water, empty inside and upright outside, its stems do not strife or offshoot. Its delicate scent spreads in the air far and wide. Resting there with its sparkling immaculateness, the lotus is to be viewed from a distance, but not to be humiliated and played with.

Thus, lotus is regarded as a symbol of purity and truth for rising spotlessly from its bed of mud.

Lotus tubers are crispy, juicy and sweet, and can be eaten raw or cooked as a syrup, soup or vegetable, or sliced and preserved and eaten as a sweet. Its seeds are also edible, and its leaves can be used to wrap things in or be cooked to make syrup or used for flavoring.

In Chinese, lotus is call "lien (lian)" or "ho (he)". "Lien" sounds similar to the word for "unite", and "ho" sounds like the word for "harmony." Therefore, the lotus has relations to both meanings and is usually considered as a symbol for friendship, happy union and peace. It was considered by Confucianists as a model for the "superior man," and was also a Taoist symbol and used as the emblem for "Ho Hsien-

---

[37] 'The Flower Market' in *Chinese Poems*. Translated by Arthur Waley, (Unwin Brothers Limited, London, 1962), p.132.

ku (He Xian-gu)," one of the eight immortals. It was made full use of by Buddhists: it stands for the soul struggling up from the material world, and its open petals formed the seat of Buddha.

Fig. 6.1 Lotus in the wind: Guangzhou Botanical Garden

Lotus can create great seasonal transformations in Chinese gardens. In spring, its leaves are small, green and floating on the top of water. When summer heat comes, these plants grow up and rise high, their leaves stretch on the curved stems and form a new, green layer above the space, swaying with winds. The fragrance of its flowers also spreads out (Fig 6.1). When raindrops fall onto the leaves of lotus, they form crystal clear water balls. If the leaves sway in breeze, these water balls roll back and forth like pears of various sizes. When a large number of Lotuses are planted in a pond, the swaying leaves and the dancing "pearls" formed by raindrops can form a spectacular scene.

Because of the aforementioned reasons, lotus has been use extensively in Chinese Gardens. For examples, it has been used in the pond in front of the Reflection Tower and pond in front of the Mountain In View Tower in the Unsuccessful Politician's Garden.

Lotus is "the flower of summer," while the chrysanthemum is "the flower of autumn." Chrysanthemums have changed radically through times since their domestication: The earliest species are yellow, but by the Tang Dynasty (618–906), white blooms and even a purple variety appeared. In the Song Dynasty (960–1279), more and more varieties were developed by crossing and grafting. In the twelfth century, monographs on chrysanthemum appeared. In the flower encyclopedia of 1708, more than 300 different chrysanthemums are mentioned. They gained lovely names that related to the forms and colors of the flowers. For instance, "Jade-saucer-gold-cup" refers to a grand white flower with a yellow center; "Heaven-full-of-star" refers to a small flowered, yellow-headed kind.

Exhibitions or shows of different kinds of chrysanthemums are often held. Even now there is an annual "Chrysanthemum Exhibition" held every autumn at the

"Memorial Park of Revolutionary Martyrs" in the City of Canton (Guangzhou). Thousands of chrysanthemums representing hundreds of species or varieties are shown in the event.

The flowers of chrysanthemums can be made into fragrant tea, or grains of medicine. The essence from these plants is said to be able to give long lives to people. Probably because chrysanthemums flower in autumn, a season when all other flowers (except plums) wither, they are related to longevity, and are called "late fragrance," "those who survive all others" and "those who defy frost." Chrysanthemums grow well in temperate or subtropical zones, and they are the symbol of autumn in both north and south China.

b. Some set compositions of plants

When severe winter comes with cold wind from the north, all other flowers wither and fall, except plum (*Prunus* spp.) Plum, bamboo and pine are called "Three Friends in winter." They symbolize the true friendship between virtuous people that revealed in hard times. The plum blooms luxuriantly in winter, even in snow, suggesting an unconquerable spirit and heralding the coming of spring. Plum can also be combined with orchids, bamboo and chrysanthemums to form another conventional composition-"Four Virtuous Gentlemen."

Some fruit trees also have symbolic meanings. Pomegranates (*Punica granatum*) have red fruits containing innumerable seeds. They became auspicious symbols of fertility, implying prosperous offspring. Peach (*Prunus persica*) is chosen as emblems of spring, love, marriage and immortality. There was a legend regarding a specimen of peach in the gardens owned by Hsi Wang Mu (Xi Wang Mu), the Taoist's Mother Goddess of the West. The fruits of this specimen were said to ripen every three thousand years and to be able to confer immortality on people who tasted them. Pears (*Pyrus* spp.) also signify longevity, but a more modest one, because pear trees was said to live up to three hundred years. Pear trees suggested good government as well, since the Duke of Shao administered justice beneath a pear tree in 1053 B.C. Finger lemon (*Citrus medica*) is called "Buddha's hand," it is another emblem of longevity. Persimmon (*Diospyros* spp.) has orange-gold, soft fruits that taste sweet when ripe, implying joy in Chinese culture. Loquat (*Eriobotrya* spp.) pronounces as "Pi Pa," which is the same as a plucked string Chinese classical music instrument with a fretted fingerboard. This musical instrument often appeared in poetry and prose, and loquat is related to it. This is probably the reason for the constant recurring of loquat in Chinese gardens, especially the gardens of the literati. Banana (*Musa* spp.) is related to an ancient story: a penniless scholar once used its wide leaves to write on for want of getting better, thus banana was considered as "the tree of self-improvement." The melancholy sound of rain dropping on its leaves was depicted over and over in music, poetry and prose. This became the inspiration of a favorite garden theme.

In the past, the use of plants was even related to the hierarchy of the society. For instance, five trees were planted in cemeteries according to the hierarchy of the owner: poplars for commoners, *Sophora japonica* for scholars, *Koelreuteria* for governors, *Thuja* for princes, and pines for the ruler. But these applications did not prevent them from being used in pleasure gardens.

Some other plants also have their own symbolic meanings. For example, Narcissus (*Narcissus taezetta* var. *orientals*) signifies "fairy girls riding the waves." Rose (*Rosa* spp.) blooms profusely and means ever blooming; camellia (*Camellia* spp.) and azalea (*Rhododendron* spp.) suggest wild atmosphere and are used to decorate rockeries (or artificial mountains) in gardens. Chinese parasol tree (*Firmiana simplex*, or *Sterculia platanifolia*) is the perch of the phoenix in Chinese legend. Its seeds are edible and are use to make moon cakes at the mid-autumn festival. It constantly appeared in Chinese landscape painting, sheltering a study hall with an aged pine. The eighteenth century poet Yuan Mei wrote about Chinese parasol tree ("Wu-tung", or "Wu-tong" in Chinese) in his verse:

> *Half bright, half dim, are the stars;*
> *Three drops, two drops, falls the rain.*
> *Now the Wu-t'ung tree knows of autumn's coming*
> *And leaf to leaf whispers the news.* [38]

The deciduous Chinese parasol tree is also preferred in small courtyards. Its crown creates a cooling sunshade in summer, and will let sunshine penetrate through its bare twigs in winter. Its shadows on the floor are reminiscent of Chinese painting. Its smooth and clean bark can stand heavy human contact. Its large leaves are easy to collect and can also be left on the ground for appreciation, as described in Yuan Mei's verse which we mentioned earlier.

Exotic plants are also used in traditional Chinese gardens. They were first brought into the gardens purely for curiosity. With the time passed, some of them gradually gained symbolic meanings and found their place in Chinese gardens.

---

[38] Trans. by Robert Kotewall and Norman L. Smith in *The Penguin Book of Chinese Verse*. (Penguin Books Inc., 375 Hudson St, New York, NY 10014), 1962. p. 68. Reproduced by permission of Penguin Books Ltd.

In the past several centuries, western culture has been introduced and absorbed and also brought some "new" symbolic meanings for plants in Chinese gardens: Rose (*Rosa* spp.) expresses love; camellia suggests beautiful women, etc.

From the above discussion, we can see that the iconography of a plant is usually generated from its graceful form and habit, the pronunciation of its name, a legend, an allusion or literary quotation or other historical associations. Plants are selected carefully and can be used as the center of interest with reference to their traditional meaning. Sometimes a plant becomes the theme of a garden scene. Garden scenes or garden architecture are often named after plants, such as: the Spring Home of Begonia, the Loquat Garden, the Magnolia Hall, the Willow-shaded Winding Path (Walking Gallery), the Pines and Breezes Pavilion, Lotus Breeze from all Sides Pavilion, Far-reaching Fragrance Hall, and Lingering and Listening Tower as well as Listening to the Rain Studio (both names came from a line of the ancient poet Li Yishang's verse: " Leave the leaves of lotus there so that the sound of rain drops pattering on them can be heard.") in the Unsuccessful Politician's Garden.

A plant without historical association or traditional symbolic meanings is just an object, even if it has graceful form and pleasing color. The iconography of plants is more important than the objects (plants) themselves. Planting is also a vital factor in the transformation of a Chinese garden:

The joy of a garden comes from the fresh and cool feeling that a creek brings in the summer, from the remote sound of a leaping fish in the evening fog, from the snow falling on tree branches in the winter, from the scent of lotus and other flowers. It also comes from the eternal transformations of time and space, from the charm of contrast - from the singing noise of a cicada that highlights the silence of a grove, from the rustling sound of breeze that intensifies the tranquility.

3. Aesthetic Considerations

a. An important aesthetic concept: "Yi Jing"

Before the discussion and analysis of the aesthetic consideration of Chinese planting design, we need to explain "Yi Jing", because it is the most important aesthetic concept in all Chinese artistic creation and appreciation, and also the most vital aesthetic concept of Chinese gardening and planting design. If one does not understand "Yi Jing", he can hardly understand Chinese gardens, and he can hardly understand Chinese planting design. The word "Yi Jing" will appear again and again in the following discussion. That's another reason that we need to explain it as clearly as possible here.

"Yi Jing" is one of those Chinese words that one can understand, but is really hard to explain, especially in a language other than Chinese. The common translation of "Yi Jing" from a Chinese-English dictionary is: "artistic conception". This is only part of the meaning, which is far from enough. Let's try to go further in the explanation here. "Yi Jing" is composed of two Chinese characters: "Yi" and "Jing", both in the fourth tone (There are four tones for each Chinese pronunciation). "Yi" means "idea, meaning, sense, significance, intention, desire, will, wish, trace, hint and suggestion, etc.", we can generalize it as subjective idea, thought and emotion; "Jing" means "realm, area, circumstance, condition, situation and boundary, etc.", we can summarize it as objective life, scenery and situation. "Yi Jing" is produced by the combination of subjective "Yi" and objective "Jing" in artistic creation. The designer smelts his idea, thought and emotion with objective life, scenery and situation, so as to stimulate a similar emotional excitement, idea, thought and associations in an observer's mind.

The concept of "Yi Jing" arose long time ago, but the theoretical explanation appeared relatively late. In Tang Dynasty (618–906), poet Wang Changlin proposed to criticized poetry by means of the theory of three "Jing"s (realms): those depicting the forms of mountains and water belong to the "Objective Jing (Realm)"; those expressing the emotion of the author with the help of the description of scenery belong to "Emotional Jing (Realm)"; those manifesting the aspiration of the author belong to "Yi Jing". In recent times, Wang Guowei has put forward two kinds of realms: "the Realm with Me (the author of the poem)" and "the Realm without Me". "The Realm with Me" means to observe objective scenery from "my (the author's)" point of view; therefore the whole scenery carries "my" emotional coloring. "The Realm without Me" means to observe "myself" from the point of view of the objective world. Thus it is hard to distinguish which part is "me", which part is the objective world. These theories are about poetry, but they are also true for Chinese gardening and planting design. The two realms mentioned by Wang Guowei and the "Emotional Realm" and "Yi Jing" defined by Wang Changlin, are all the production of objective world and subjective emotion and thought; therefore, they all belong to the "Yi Jing" referred to by the Chinese artists.

"Yi Jing" is an essential criterion for the aesthetic evaluation for Chinese planting design and other artistic creation: A good artistic production should have its "Yi Jing"; an excellent one should have a "Yi Jing" of high level. With the help of "Yi Jing", an observer in the gardens can sense not only the scenery viewed by his eyes, but also the "scenery beyond the objective scenery" coming up in his mind. He obtains not only aesthetic enjoyment through his sensory organs, but also continuously arousing feeling and thought as well as intellectual associations, or "meaning beyond the scenery."

A very unique technique use in Chinese garden and planting design is the use of antithetical couplet or poems directly in a garden scene. The couplet appear in pair and are rhyme and antithetical to each other. They are often inscribed on wood, stone or bamboo to bring out the "Yi Jing" or the theme of the scenery. At the Fragrant Snow and Azure Sky Pavilion in the Unsuccessful Politician's Garden (Fig 6.2) a pair of

Fig. 6.2 The Fragrant Snow and Azure Sky Pavilion in the Unsuccessful Politician's Garden (looking north)

antithetical couplet has been inscribed on bamboo pieces that hangs on two of the pavilion's columns and one horizontal scroll: The couplet on the right reads "The forest becomes quieter because of cicada's noise"; The couplet on the left reads "The mountain appears more serene owing to the birds' singing"; The horizontal scroll on the top reads "The Fragrant Snow and Azure Sky Pavilion". In this case, the garden is treated as a three-dimensional painting and antithetical couplet bring out the "Yi Jing" or the theme of the design. We can find two more examples in the Unsuccessful Politician's Garden:

Fig. 6.3 "Who to Sit with" Pavilion

At the Jade Spring Well, a poem of entitled "Jade Spring" written by a famous poet, Wen Zhengming, has been inscribed on the side of the well. The poem has made the well an attraction for visitors. The name of "Who To Sit With" Pavilion comes from a line of a famous ancient poem: "Who to sit with? Bright moon, clear breeze and me." The words "Who To Sit With" Pavilion has been inscribed on a horizontal scroll and hanged inside the pavilion. In both of these examples, literature has been directly transformed into garden scenes and became the themes of the design (Fig 6.3).

b. "Heavenly creation" and "taking advantage"

Fig. 6.4 Borrowing scenery and utilizing the smell of plants in the Unsuccessful Politician's Garden

Another important aesthetic principle we need to explain here is that a Chinese garden and its planting should look like heavenly creation even though they are made by human beings. A good garden designer should be ingenious at taking advantage and borrowing scenery according to the time, space and specific condition, and master the skill of choosing the suitable size and form. At the Unsuccessful Politician's Garden, plants are carefully arranged to frame the view of the Northern Temple Tower outside the garden in a great distance. This is a very successful example of borrowing scenery. In this case, the scenery borrow is the Northern Temple Tower, which is outside the property line of the Unsuccessful Politician's Garden (Fig 6.4).

c. Antiquities, strangeness and grace

Fully taking advantage of the old existing trees is one application of this principle. This is also because antiquity, strangeness and grace are considered as very important aesthetic properties of trees. Some ancient Chinese gardens have trees that are hundreds or even thousands of years old, they were not considered as obstacles for building a new garden or rebuilding an old one, but as treasures and were made full use of. Artificial mountains, rockeries, ponds and houses were designed according to the locations, sizes, forms and habits of old existing trees, all these factors were skillfully combined together in the design. Examples are the old Ginkgo tree in the middle area of the Lion Grove and the several maple trees in the middle area of the Unsuccessful Politician's Garden.

d. Design for five senses: the creation of sound effects

Chinese garden and planting design are not solely a visual art. They also involve the senses of hearing, smelling, touching, etc. Besides this, the seasonal and weather changes (spring, summer, autumn, winter, rain, snow, overcast or sunny day, etc.) can change the "Yi Jing" of the space and deeply influence the feeling of people, all these factors affect the garden indirectly with plants as their media. For example, some classical gardens in Suzhou take advantage of the sound of natural wind or rain to create ever-changing and volatile feelings of space, and have a distinctive style. In the Unsuccessful Politician's Garden, the name for the Pine and Breezes Pavilion comes from the soughing of the wind in the pines, which makes the space feel more serene and creates the wild atmosphere sought by the designer; the names for the Listening to the Rain Studio and the Lingering and Listening Tower come from the "Yi Jing" of rain drops pattering on the leaves of banana. Several banana trees were planted in the back of the Listening to the Rain Studio, they can be seen through the windows of the studio and are very impressive, especially when the spring rain comes. Similar technique is use at the Surging Wave Pavilion.

e. Taking advantage of the color and smell of plants

In addition to utilizing the sound effects created by wind or rain on antique pines and banana trees as well as lotus leaves to give different artistic feelings for people, garden designers also expressed their ideas by means of the colors or smells of plants. In gardens for literati, a place for reading books and cultivating the heart and the culture of nature, evergreen trees were used as background, and few colorful flowers were used as ornament in order to create a serene atmosphere. The white wall and gray tiles works as paper, antique trees (pines, bamboo, plum-blossom trees, orchids) and strange rocks work as pens. They work together and create a graceful garden scene, a "three dimensional Chinese landscaping painting". In the scene "Golden Lotus Reflecting Sunshine" in the Summer Retreating Mountain Villa and in the Loquat Garden in the Unsuccessful Politician's Garden, the designer also influences the feelings of people with the help of colors of plants. "Golden Lotus Reflecting Sunshine" is located at the west of Good Luck Isle; thousands of lotuses were planted there. When shined on by the sun, they look more splendorous and look as if a piece of ground covered by gold. The Loquat Garden is located at the southeast of the Unsuccessful Politician's Garden, a number of Loquat trees were planted in the garden, and the fruits have golden color. When the fruits get ripe, the golden scene dominates the whole garden; therefore, the garden is also called "Golden

Fruit Garden."

There are also numerous of examples of taking advantage of the smell of the plants. The fragrance of plants puts the body and mind at ease, makes people feel as if they were in the countryside. At the Osmanthus Fragrance-Smelling Studio in the Lingering Garden, Osmanthus trees were planted all around. In the blooming season, the fragrance of the flowers assails one's nose and creates an exquisite "Yi Jing". The Lotus pond in the middle of the Unsuccessful Politician's Garden directly faces the Far-reaching Fragrance Hall. When summer comes, the lotus bloom, and the delicate fragrance is blown into the hall by the breeze and spreads all over. The name of the hall also comes from "Far-reaching Fragrance Spreading Out." The Fragrant Snow and Azure Sky Pavilion is located at a small mound in the Unsuccessful Politician's Garden. Several tall arboreal trees and many plum blossom trees were planted around the pavilion. When severe winter comes, the snow-fighting plum trees bloom. The fragrance of the flowers combined with the auspicious snow makes the pavilion a good place to go and appreciate wintry scenery.

f. Emphasizing the beauty of lines

Plants themselves contain beautiful lines of nature: soft or hard, thick or fine, curved or straight. Chinese arts emphasize the use of lines, and Chinese planting design is not an exception of this rule: plants are judged according to the beauty of lines they contain. A number of principles regarding the use of lines in planting design were borrowed from Chinese landscape painting. For example, plum trees are chosen according to the beauty of lines formed by their branches: A plum tree is beautiful for being curved, if it is straight, it has no good appearance. It is beautiful for being crooked, if it is upright, it creates no scenery. It is beautiful for being loose [thin in density], if it is dense, it has no form.[39]

g. Light and shadow(s)

Different light can create different effects. In classical Chinese gardens, plants are used with other garden elements as well as natural light to create the contrasts of brightness and darkness, of light and shadows, etc. These contrasts combine with the closeness or openness of the space to exaggerate the environmental atmosphere. For instance, in "Crisscross Ancient Tree Branches Court" of the Lingering Garden, a very

---

[39] Baihua Zhong et al., *A General View of Chinese Garden Art* (Jianshu Province: The People's Press of Jianshu, 1987), p. 247.

old pagoda tree is located in the small courtyard. The shadows of the old pagoda tree and other plants are projected against the white wall; they form a graceful picture on the wall.

By utilizing these physical properties of plants, garden makers can create a unique "Yi Jing". Let's use bamboo as an example: If bamboo is planted properly in a garden, when the sun rises, we get cool shade; when the moon appears, we get clear shadows; when wind comes, we get fresh sound; when rain drops, we get clear and melodious rhythm; when dew congeals, we get clear light; when snow ceases, we get the fresh delight.[40] This "Yi Jing" focuses on the aesthetic perception of the "clear" and is very graceful. At the North Corridor of the Lion Grove, numerous bamboos are planted around the corridor; the corridor itself is also built of bamboo. This technique also creates a very unique "Yi Jing".

h. Transformation

Chinese garden designers fully realize that changes are eternal and constant, while the "stable" or the "static" is only temporary in nature. Therefore, they do not intend to keep the springtime profuse blooms of plants all the time. On the contrary, they utilize the properties of plants to create scenery of different seasons. Plants are used as the medium for seasonal transformation. For example, the Ge Garden in Yangzhou is famous for its artificial mountain of four seasons; the formation of the four season artificial mountain is closely related with the use of plants. At the entrance of the garden, lake rocks were placed along the road, with bamboo planted among them. Groups of evergreen Osmanthus trees are planted on the other side. The green colors of bamboo and Osmanthus symbolize the coming of the spring. On the horizontal plate of calligraphy at the gate of the garden, one can find the Chinese characters for the Ge Garden. The character of "Ge" in Chinese is "个", which is similar to the shape of three leaves of bamboo. This gives the garden a deeper symbolic meaning: In Chinese landscape painting, the way to paint the leaves of bamboo is to "write" a number of "个", the character of "Ge", grouping or overlapping. This rule is called the knack of "Ge" in Chinese landscape painting.

Having passed the spring mountain, and made a detour and crossed the Hall of Osmanthus, one can see another artificial mountain facing water. A clear stream comes out from a "valley." Leafy trees are planted on the top of the mountain. Half way up the mountain are hanging vines. Lotus flowers in the clear pond are blooming and reflecting

---

40 Zhong, *A General View of Chinese Garden Art*, p. 247.

sunshine. All these compose the "Yi Jing" of the summer mountain.

High and steep rockeries dominate the autumn mountain. The plants used here are mainly maples so as to create an autumn atmosphere.

At the winter mountain, round "snow rocks" are used, the pavement is also white stone. The scene is decorated with plum trees and heavenly bamboo so as to set off the "Yi Jing" of the winter mountain.

Garden architecture, rockeries and still water surfaces are relatively stable elements in a garden, while plants change with seasons and their ages. The seasonal changes and growth of plants create not only seasonal changes for gardens, but also differences of proportion and scale of space with time, and make the static architectural environment more variable and seasonal.

i. The way of planting: regularity and irregularity

Fig. 6.5 Bamboos are arranged naturalistically near a moon gate at the Lingering Garden

Normally, the Chinese way of planting pursues a naturalistic layout and avoids regularity. Garden designers study nature and try to reproduce or represent nature in planting design through contrast: the sparse layout of trees contrasts with the dense one, the large trees combine with the smaller ones, the tall trees mix with the short ones. They try to achieve this purpose: that even though the trees are artificially planted, yet they should look like natural vegetation. The northwest area of the Lingering Garden is one example. Similarly, several bamboos are planted near a moon gate at the Lingering Garden; they are so naturalistically arranged and appear to grow naturally there (Fig 6.5).

Under special situations, in order to be in harmony with the environment, trees can be planted in a uniform and neat geometric form, like the pine trees at the front yard of the Avoid Complacency Hall in the Summer Retreating Mountain Villa.

According to different sites and environments, trees can be planted in these ways in Chinese gardens: Single Planting, Group Planting, Mass Planting, Strip Planting and Artificial Forest.

j. Single planting

Single Planting can be used for these purposes: (1) To act as the focus of a garden scene; (2) To set off garden architecture; (3) To decorate garden space; (4) To create shade; (5) To be used at transitional spots, such as: the end of a bridge, the beginning of a garden path, the turning point of the edge of a pond, to act as either a foil or a focus of garden scene. If a single tree is located in a relatively large and open space, and the designer wants to exhibit the overall beauty of the whole tree, a suitable viewing distance should be considered. The ideal viewing distance is four times to ten times the height of the tree.[41]

Single planting can fully express the color, smell or form of a tree. It is also applied in small spaces for close appreciation and to act as the theme of a courtyard. The single tree should take a corner location and avoid the central position. Its height and density should fit the size of the courtyard. For example, at the Net Master's Garden, a single tree is planted at the corner of the courtyard behind the Cold Spring Pavilion. Several lake rocks scatter around the tree and form a scene for the garden (Fig 6.6). A single pine tree is planted at the corner of another courtyard at the Net Master's Garden utilizing the same technique. At the Crisscrossing Ancient Tree Branches Court of the Lingering Garden, the courtyard is extremely small and in an "L" shape. In the southeast corner of the courtyard, there is an old pagoda tree. Its branches are dry, but still antique and strong. It is the theme of the courtyard, the name "the Crisscrossing Ancient Tree Branches Court" came from it. The Ancient Pagoda Tree Court at the Pleasure Boat Studio in Beihai Park is a

Fig. 6.6 A single tree is planted at the corner of the courtyard behind the Cold Spring Pavilion at the Net Master's Garden

[41] Youxiang Sun, *Garden Art and Garden Design,* (Beijing: Department of City Landscaping. Beijing Forestry University, 1986), p. 107.

similar case. As its name suggest, the theme of the court is an ancient pagoda tree, which is planted in the southwest corner of the court. It has no luxuriant foliage, but has antique and strong branches. The Court of the Stone Forest in the Lingering Garden is extremely small and irregular. Oleander and Big Leaf Hydrangea are planted there, but the domain of the space is a white bark pine in the southwest corner of the courtyard, which is tall and big, forceful and straight, leafy and verdant. It provides shade for the courtyard and also decorates the space. At the Spring Home of Begonia in the Unsuccessful Politician's Garden, begonia and bamboo are planted, and the begonias are the major objects for appreciation. A tall and big elm tree is also planted in the southeast corner of the yard as an embellishment. Garden designers sometimes take advantages of the crooked branches and luxuriant and well-spaced leaves of a tree, and plant it on a cliff or artificial mountain so as to set off the dangerous and precipitous cliff (Fig 6.7). Single planting can also be

Fig. 6.7 The Crape Myrtle on the artificial cliff of the Grace- Surrounding Mountain Villa

used on the edge of a pond to create lively reflection on the water surface. It can be used for vines as well (Fig 6.8). Sometimes a single tree is also used as a decoration near a grove or artificial forest, acts as a transitional element or is used to break the monotony of a single species of the grove and enrich the content for appreciation (Fig 6.9).

What single planting expresses is the beauty of an individual tree, while what group planting, mass planting, strip planting and artificial forest express is the overall beauty of the entirety of trees. A single tree often occupies a prominent location in composition; therefore, it should have outstanding individual beauty.

Gong Xian, a painter in the Ming Dynasty, said: A tree standing alone should have a spreading canopy and most of its branches should grow downward and its form must be unique.[43] A single pine should be strange, while pines in a group should not have too much difference.[44] As Gong Xian indicated, in the composition of a painting, a single tree should have an outstanding form. A tree with a spreading crown is relatively suitable to be used as a single tree. This is also true in selecting the species and form of a tree for single planting in gardening. A single tree in a garden should have a prominent and strange form and figure, while trees in a grove can have normal or simple form and figure. A tree without a

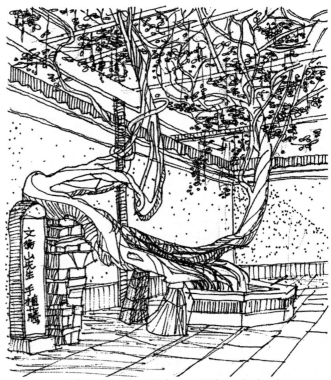

Fig. 6.8 The Chinese Wisteria in the Unsuccessful Politician's Garden[42]

spreading crown may not be suitable to be used for single planting. The most important factors in the aesthetic consideration of a single tree are its figure, posture and form. A tree with one or more of the following properties is considered suitable for single planting: (1) A tree with particularly big bodily form. Some trees, such as *Ficus macrocarpa, Cinnamomum camphora, Platanus acerifolia* and *Quercus dentata*, etc., have a widely spreading crown and a big trunk. They can appear grand and vigorous. (2) A tree with an outline that is rich in changes, with a graceful and beautiful form and posture, with pleasing lines in branches. Examples are: *Acer palmatum, Betula japonica, Sabina chinensis, Pinus tabulaefoimis*, etc. (3) A tree with luxuriant blossoms and gorgeous colors, such as: *Delonix regia, Cossampinus malabarica, Magnolia denudata,*

---

[42] It is also translated as The Humble Administrator's Garden.

[43] Xian Gong et al., *The Theory of (Chinese) Landscape Painting*, (Taibei, Taiwan: Art book Publishing Company, 1975), p.205.

[44] Gong, *The Theory of (Chinese) Landscape Painting*, p.219.

Prunus persica variegata, Prunus mume variegata. (4) A tree with strong smell or rich fruits or autumn leaves, like *Osmanthus fragrans, Malus pumila, Liquidambar formosana, Sapium sebiferum, Ginkgo biloba, Acer truncatum, etc.*

Fig. 6.9 The magnolia tree in the north area of the Lingering Garden

A tree used as single planting for shade probably should have spreading crown and grow fast. A tree in cylindrical or circular cone shape, or a tree with loose form may not be suitable for single planting to create shade. A single tree should not be put in the geometric center of a garden, but at the natural center of gravity instead, so as to respond to and balance other garden elements. It can be planted on the edge of a river, a lake, a pond, etc. and utilize the water as its background so that people can see far and appreciate distant scenery from under its shade. It can also be planted on a highland or artificial mountain so as to enrich the outline of a garden.

Locality is an important factor to be considered in single planting. If we do not use local or native species, we may not be able to obtain the tremendous and spreading crown of a tree required for single planting. For instance, *Populus alba* can achieve tremendous and spreading crown in the northeast area of China, but its crown is no longer tremendous if it is planted in Beijing, and it will even become a shrub if it is planted in the eastern area of China. *Platanus acerifolia* grows extremely big and has a crown that can spread about 90 feet in the eastern area in China, but it will become a small arboreal tree if it is planted in Beijing, and it even becomes a shrub because of the cold climate if it is planted in Shenyang area.

A single planted tree does not exist lonely in the garden composition, but integrates with surrounding scenery in the garden composition. It can be a foil or focus for the surrounding scenery; it can also be a transitional form for dense forest, group planting or bush.

A single tree is an exposed plant; therefore trees requiring high humidity or warm microclimate are not suitable to be used for single planting. For example, *Larix* spp. and *Pinus koraicnsis* are shade plant and require high air moisture. If they are chosen for single planting, they cannot grow well and cannot even survive. These kinds of trees need to grow in a forest environment with relatively high humidity and certain shade.

When we lay out the single planting for a garden, we should first take advantage of the existing old tree on the site. If the site has a big tree that is hundreds of years old, we should make the composition of the garden integrate with this favorable natural condition, and use the existing old tree for the single planting in the garden. This is the best way of "taking advantage of the site" and can save us a lot of time to achieve the expected artistic effect. If there is no old tree to utilize, we can save a middle age tree (10-20 years old) and use it as the single tree of the scene. It will still help us to achieve the expected effect faster than a newly planted tree. If there is no tree to utilize on the site, as a last resort, we can transplant a big tree to the site. If transplanting is not possible because of the economic situation, we can design two kinds of single planting schemes: short term single planting and long term single planting: use trees which grow fast for short term single planting, such as: *Albizzia falcata* and *Albizzia procera*; For long term single planting, we can plant 3-5 trees in a group at the beginning, and handle them as shrubs or small arboreal trees in group planting. With the time passes, we can save one in the group that grows well and use it as a single tree, and move the other trees out of the site.

k. Group planting

Group planting normally is composed of two to nine or ten trees, and if shrubs are included, the total number of plants can reach fifteen or so. On one hand, plants in group planting are a unified entity. A designer should consider the beauty of the entirety. On the other hand, a designer should also express the individual beauty of each plant in the unitary composition. Group planting is different from mass planting: First of all, group planting is composed of fewer plants than mass planting. Secondly, in the design of mass planting, the overall beauty of the mass is the major factor in consideration; a designer does not have to express the beauty of each individual plant. In group planting, the beauty of both the individual plant and the whole group need to be expressed. Thus, the plants used for group planting should have some special characteristic of form, or color, or smell or flowers, etc.

Group planting has two basic functions: (1) To set off garden architecture; (2) To decorate garden space. In the first case, the garden architecture is the domain or the center. Plants should be planted around it, and they should be at different distances from the architecture. The layout of plants should maintain balance, but rigid symmetry should be avoided. For example, the Fragrance Snow and Azure Sky Pavilion in the Unsuccessful Politician's Garden, there are several tall arboreal trees surrounding the pavilion, some of them are far from the pavilion; some of them are very close to it. They are not in a symmetrical layout, but their size, distance and location are carefully considered and they maintain an asymmetrical balance. At the Surging-Wave Pavilion in Suzhou, there are six major arboreal trees around the pavilion, and the trees maintain an asymmetric balance.

The Embroidery Pavilion in the Unsuccessful Politician's Garden is located on an artificial hill, the five arboreal trees around it are arranged in such a way: the smaller ones are planted farther away from the pavilion, and the bigger ones are planted closer to it, so as to maintain an asymmetric balance. If you draw a line to connect any two plants, the intersection for these lines is the location of the pavilion. This is also roughly the gravity center of the composition.

If group planting is used to decorate a garden space, the trees can be the focus of a garden scene. In group planting, a designer can apply trees of the same species, or trees of different species according to different situations. If the purpose of group planting is to provide shade, then tall arboreal trees with spreading crown are suitable plants, and preferably they should be of the same species. If the plants in group planting are used for appreciation, they can be arboreal trees and shrubs in combination. They can be planted on top of a mountain, or on a piece of flat land. They can also be combined with rockeries and perennial plants to form a plant community, or the rock-plant combination in Chinese gardens. Now we'll discuss following kinds of group planting: two-tree combination, three-tree combination, four-tree combination, five-tree combination and the combination of six trees or more.

l. Two-Tree Combination:

The two-tree combination should obey the principles of the unity of opposites: the two trees should be harmony with each other, but they should also contrast with each other.

Planting two trees with too great a difference will fail. For example, if an arboreal tree and a shrub, or a weeping willow and a cypress are planted together, the aesthetic effect will not be good, because the two trees are completely different. Therefore, we must first ensure the two trees are in harmony with each other, and then consider the contrast between them. If two trees of the same species are planted together, it is easy to get harmony, but if they have very similar size and form, the effect can be very stiff. Thus, two trees of the same species should have some difference in posture, form or size so that their combination can be lively. Gong Xian, a painter in the Ming Dynasty, wrote some very incisive comments on the situation: When two trees are grouped together, if one tree has exposed roots, the other should have concealed roots. If one tree is planted at a higher ground, the other should be planted at a relatively lower ground. If one tree has relatively straight trunk, the other should have relatively twisted trunk. If one tree has upward branches, the other should have downward branches. If one tree has a "flat" canopy, the other should have a "sharp" canopy. In a two-tree combination, their branches should have some contrast. Their canopies should "face" outwards and yet they should have some connection through their branches.[45] The same principles are also true for multi-tree combination.

These instructions are on drawing trees in Chinese landscape painting, but they have had a very strong influence on Chinese traditional gardening and planting design. The ideal distance between two trees in a group should be close to the radius of the canopy of either of the trees, so that they can form an entity. Under special situations, the distance between the two trees can be larger. For instance, there are two arboreal trees in the court of the Magnolia Hall in the Unsuccessful Politician's Garden, one big and one small, the bigger one is *Magnolia denudata,* which is the major object for appreciation in the court, the smaller one is *Osmanthus fragrans,* which acts as a foil. The distance between the two trees is larger than the radius of the crown of the smaller tree, but they can still form an entity because they are located in the same small court enclosed by high walls. Therefore, they can still be considered as two trees in a group, instead of two trees in single planting. From this example, we can also observe that if two trees are planted together in a courtyard, they should be of different sizes, and they should each take a corner location, and their layout should not be symmetric. The courtyard of the Five Pine Gardens in the Lion Grove is another example.

m. Three-Tree Combination:

If three trees are of the same species, or of two different species but with similar outlook, their combination can be harmonious. The two different species should both be evergreen, or both deciduous, or both arboreal trees, or both shrubs. The three trees in a group should not be of three different species, unless the different species have a very similar appearance.

Gong Xian wrote in his article on painting three trees in a group: In a three-tree combination, one tree can be a "host," while the other two can be "guests." There should be contrast between the host tree and the guest trees. If "host" has twisted trunk grow downwards, the two "guests" should have relatively straight trunk and grow upwards, vice versa. If the "host" has exposed roots, the two "guests" should have concealed roots, vice

---

[45] Gong, *The Theory of (Chinese) Landscape Painting,* p. 205. p. 216.

versa. The two "guests" should have similar branches when the "host" should have different branches. The "host" should have lower roots and closer to the viewer. The two "guests" should be placed closer to each other while the "host" should be placed farther from them. All three trees should not be placed too far apart to avoid the ruthless feeling.[46]

When three trees are planted in a group, they should have contrast and difference in their size, posture and form. The following situations should be avoided:

Three trees are placed along a straight line, three trees form an equilateral triangle, and three trees are of the same species and have very similar size, posture and form. The big one forms a subgroup, and the medium and the small one form the other subgroup; The two subgroups have almost the same "weight", and form a rigid balance; Three trees are of two different species; the big one and the small one are of the same species and form one subgroup, the medium one is of the other species and forms the other subgroup. The two subgroups are composed of trees of different species and size, and have almost no similarities; Three trees are of two different species, the small one and the medium one are of the same species and form a subgroup, the third one is of different species and forms the other subgroup. The two subgroups form a rigid balance and are isolated from each other.

Here are some ways to form a entity in contrast for three tree combination: Three trees are of the same species, the big one and the small one form a subgroup, the medium is a little farther from them and forms the other subgroup. The three trees are not planted along a straight line, and their locations form a scalene triangle. The two subgroups are composed of trees of the same species and have similarities beside their differences (Fig 6.10). Three trees are of two different species (e.g. two *Osmanthus* and one *Lagerstroemia indica*); the first subgroup is composed of the big one (*Osmanthus fragrans*) and the small one (*Lagerstroemia indica*). The other subgroup is formed by the other *Osmanthus fragrans*. Both subgroups have *Osmanthus fragrans*, but the second subgroup has no *Lagerstroemia*. Thus, the two subgroups have both similarities and differences, and form an entity in contrast.

HOST (MEDIUM SIZE)

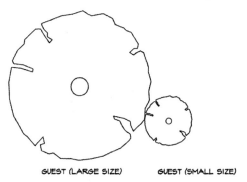

GUEST (LARGE SIZE)   GUEST (SMALL SIZE)

Fig. 6.10 Three-tree combination

[46] Gong, *The Theory of (Chinese) Landscape Painting,* pp. 205—206. p. 216.

n. Four-Tree Combination:

Four trees in a group should be of only one or two species, they should not be of more than two species, unless the different species have very similar outlook. If the four trees are of the same species, they should have some differences in form, posture, size, height and distance between each other.

Following are some situations that should be avoided in the four trees combination: The four trees should not form a square, a straight line, or an equilateral triangle. The four trees should not be divided into two subgroups as the following: one is composed of three small trees and the other is composed of one big tree, or one composed of three big trees and the other is composed of one small tree. They also should not be divided into two subgroups of two. If they are of the same species, the four trees should not have too similar sizes and posture. If the four trees are of two different species, we should not equally divide them and have two trees for each species. We also should not put three trees of the same species in one subgroup and the fourth tree in the other subgroup, because such two subgroups are tended to be isolated from each other. The fourth tree of the other species should not incline to one side in the layout; it should not be the biggest one or the smallest one either.

We recommended some layouts for four-tree combination: the four trees can be divided into two subgroups, one is composed of three trees, and the other is composed of one tree. The biggest tree should be in the three-tree subgroup, and there should be also some contrast within the subgroup. The one-tree subgroup should be composed

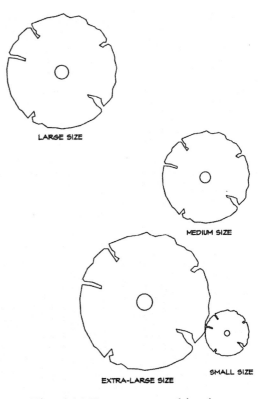

Fig. 6.11 Four-tree combination

of the second biggest or the third biggest tree (Fig 6.11). The layout of the four trees can be a scalene triangle or a quadrilateral with different sides and angles. These are two basic layouts for four-tree combination. The contour of the planting spot can also be different.

o. Five-Tree Combination:

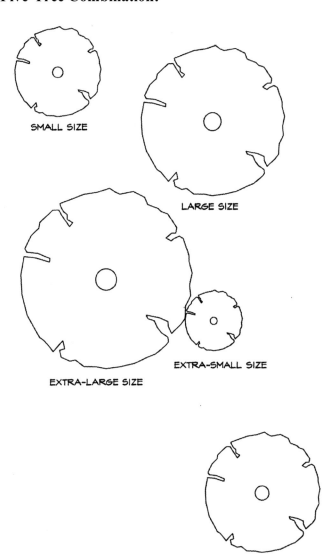

SMALL SIZE

LARGE SIZE

EXTRA-SMALL SIZE

EXTRA-LARGE SIZE

MEDIUM SIZE

Fig. 6.12 Five-tree combination

The five trees in a group can be all of the same species, or be all arboreal trees, or be all shrubs, or be all evergreen trees, or be all deciduous trees. Under this kind of situation, the form, posture, size and distance between each tree should be different. The ideal way is to divide the five trees into two subgroups, one consisting of three trees, and the other consisting of two trees. The three-tree subgroup can take advantage of the principles for three-tree combination, and the-two tree subgroup can utilize the principles for two-tree combination. The two subgroups should each form a moving tendency, and their moving tendencies should be balanced and respond to each other (Fig 6.12).

The five trees can also be divided into such two subgroups: one consists of four trees and the other consists of one tree. The single tree should not be the biggest one or the smallest one. The two subgroups should not be too far away from each other, and their moving tendency should be related.

The basic plans for the layout of five-tree combination are: a scalene triangle, or a quadrilateral, or a pentagon with different sides.

The following situations should be avoided in five tree combination: If the five trees are of two different species, they should not be divided into one subgroup consisting of one species and the other subgroup consisting of the other species, because two such subgroups are difficult to get harmony and balance and can be isolated from each other.

p. The Combination of Six or More Trees:

The more trees are there in a group, the more complicated their combination will be. But we can break the group into subgroups and utilize the principles for combinations of fewer trees. Single planting is a basic type; two-tree combination is the other basic type. A three-tree group can be viewed as the combination of a two-tree subgroup and a one-tree subgroup. A four-tree group can be regarded as the combination of a three subgroup and a one-tree subgroup. A five-tree group can be considered as the combination of a four-tree subgroup and a one-tree subgroup, or the combination of a three-tree subgroup and a two- tree subgroup. If we get familiar with the combination of five or less trees, then we should have no problem in the combination of six or more trees. It was written in the *Jiezhi Yuan's Guide for Painting:* If we get familiar with the combination of five or less trees, then we can handle the combination of numerous trees on the analogy of the principles. The secret of success is contained in them (the principles for the combination of five or less trees).[47]

In fact, the most important principle of group planting is to pursue contrast and difference within the entity, to pursue harmony when the contrast is too strong, and to pursue contrast when there are too many similarities. Therefore, we cannot use too many species for a combination of few trees. When the number of the trees increases, the number of species can be slowly increased.

A six-tree group can be divided into a two-tree subgroup and a four-tree subgroup. The four-tree subgroup can be divided again into a three tree "mini" group and a one tree "mini" group.

If the six-tree group contains both arboreal trees and shrubs, it can be divided into two subgroups of three trees.

A seven-tree group can be divided into a subgroup of five trees and a subgroup of two trees, or a subgroup of four trees and a subgroup of three trees. The number of species used should not exceed three.

An eight-tree group can be divided into a subgroup of five trees and a subgroup of three trees, or a subgroup of two trees and a subgroup of six trees. The number of species used should not exceed four.

---

[47] Sun, *Garden Art and Garden Design,* p.126.

A nine-tree group can be divided into a subgroup of three trees and a subgroup of six trees, or a subgroup of five trees and a subgroup of four trees, or a subgroup of two trees and a sub group of seven trees. The number of species used should not exceed four.

For a group composed of less than fifteen trees, the species used should not exceed five, unless the appearance of the different species is very similar.

Above are some principles for group planting. They are important, but they should not be taken as rigid dogma. These principles should be used flexibly and factors such as the site condition and the space available for planting should also be considered in actual planting design.

One species can dominate a garden space in group planting. Different species can also be applied if we want to get different scenes in different seasons, or the contrast in colors, form, and postures, etc., but all these different species should be able to obtain harmony with each other and form an entity in contrast.

Fig. 6.13 A rock-plant composition: Cloud-Crown Peak in the Lingering Garden

In traditional Chinese landscape painting and gardening as well as planting design, trees, shrubs, perennials or annuals and rockeries are often combined together to form a rock-plant composition (Fig 6.13). This composition is usually rather complicated and can create a lively and naturalistic scene of plants, which is actually a plant community and can be very beneficial to the growth of plants. Preferably, this kind of rock-plant community should take a relatively high location for the convenience of drainage. It will also make the rock-plant combination outstanding in the composition. The rock-plant combination can also take advantage of the white walls of the garden as background and form a "picture" with a certain theme, or "Yi Jing". Moon gates and circular openings and lattice windows are often used as the "frame" of the "picture". The rock-plant combination is often used at the corner of a courtyard to create artistic interest, or the changing point of a walking gallery, or the corner of garden architecture to soften the transition between architecture and garden space.

q. Mass planting

Mass planting usually consists of more than twenty trees, and what it expressed is the overall beauty of the entirety. Mass planting can be divided into "pure mass planting" which consists of one species of trees, and "mixed mass planting", which consists of different species of trees. "Mixed mass planting" can be composed of five layers: arboreal layer, sub-arboreal layer, big shrub layer, small shrub layer, and perennial ground cover. The habits, colors, smells of plants and the overall outline of the mass should be considered in mass planting. Here is one example of mass planting in the Yangtzi River basin area (Fig 6.14 and 6.15): The first layer is *Acer palmatum*, whose leaves turn red in spring and autumn. The second layer is *Osmanthus fragrans* var. *aurantiaca*, which flowers in late September and has strong fragrance. The third and the fourth layers are *Jasminum*

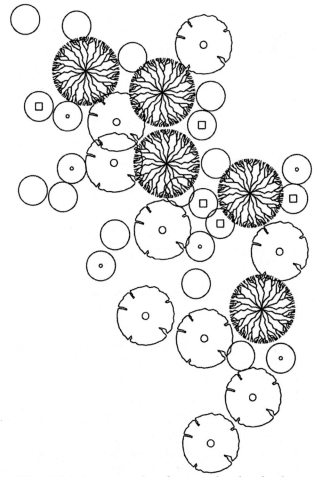

Fig. 6.14 An example of mass planting in the Yangtze River basin area

odoratissimun, which is an evergreen shrub and creates fragrance, *Gardenia jasminoides grandiflora*, which is evergreen shrub and flowers in late June and create strong fragrance, and *Juniperus chinensis*. The ground cover is composed of *Hermerocallis flava*, which flowers in June, *Hosta plantaginea* var. *plena*, which likes shade and flowers in September, *Beletla striata*, which likes shade and flowers from May to June, and *Lycoris radiata*, which flowers from September to October. These plants in mass planting bloom in different seasons and create an effect of seasonal changes.

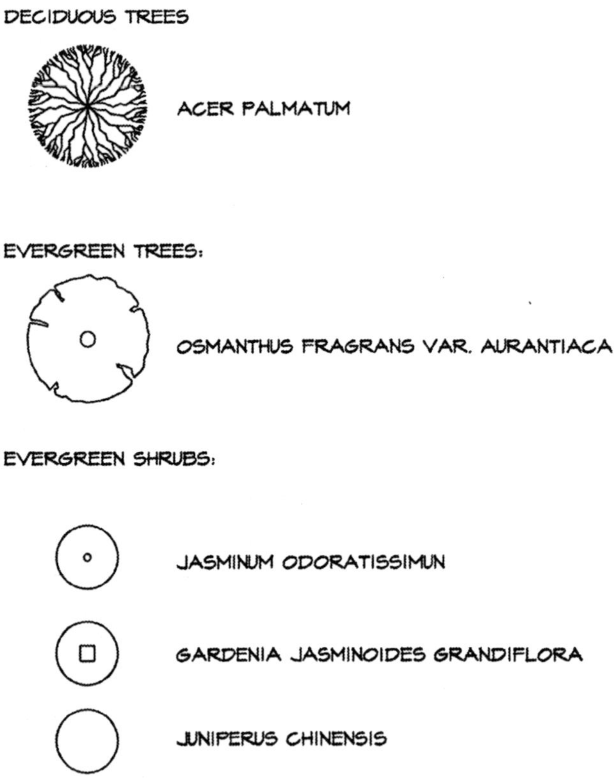

DECIDUOUS TREES

ACER PALMATUM

EVERGREEN TREES:

OSMANTHUS FRAGRANS VAR. AURANTIACA

EVERGREEN SHRUBS:

JASMINUM ODORATISSIMUN

GARDENIA JASMINOIDES GRANDIFLORA

JUNIPERUS CHINENSIS

Fig. 6.15 Legend for Fig 6.14

If we use small trees of different species for mass planting, we would get an unstable mass planting, because the growing speeds of different species may be different.

r. Strip planting

Strip planting is mass planting in strip shape. It can be used to separate different areas within a park, or used to separate a park from an urban area, or planted along rivers or roads to provide shade. We need to pay attention to the overall outline and the distance when we use strip planting.

s. Plants and mountains

The selection and layout of plants should be harmony with the size and form of the mountain. If there is more soil than rock in an artificial mountain in a traditional Chinese garden, the mountain will be mostly covered by relatively tall deciduous trees and relatively short evergreen trees. The trees as well as shrubs and perennials form the main body of planting. They cover the soil and rock and sometimes the edge of a pond. The whole mountain will look luxuriant and wild if it is viewed from a distance. In the mountain, the sunshine is partly blocked by the leaves and interweaving branches of the trees. The mountain in the middle area of the Unsuccessful Politician's Garden is one example. Normally there are three layers of plants for a mountain: trees, shrubs and groundcover, but sometimes the shrub layer or the groundcover layer can be omitted. The two layer plantings can interlock with the three layer plantings and make a composition with variety. Relatively more species of plants will be involved in this kind of planting, and the number of deciduous trees will usually exceed that of evergreen trees. Normally gardeners will let plants grow freely in this situation so as to create a wild atmosphere. If there are more rocks than earth in an artificial mountain, fewer trees, shrubs and groundcover will be used so as to display the forms of the rocks. The plants will also be planted sparsely. Examples can be found in the Pleasure Garden, the Lion Grove, the Lingering Garden and the Grace Surrounding Mountain Villa. The combination of deciduous trees and evergreen trees will have more freedom and will not stick to one pattern. For instance, in the Pleasure Garden and the Lion Grove, evergreen trees are planted on the main elevation of the mountain, while deciduous trees are planted at the back of it to act as foils. On the contrary, in the Lingering Garden, deciduous trees are planted on the main elevation of the mountain while evergreen trees are planted on the back of it. When they are planted on a cliff, no matter whether there is water under the cliff or not, the trees should have crooked branches so as to set off the cliff. In fact, in order to obtain more sunshine, the branches of the trees will normally grow and spread outwards. If they are properly pruned, they will naturally inclined outwards from the cliff and form a graceful posture.

t. Plants and garden architecture

Plants near garden architecture can not only provide shade, fragrance and act as objects for appreciation, but also enrich the composition of the elevation of the garden architecture (Fig 6.16 and 6.17). Plants around garden architecture should have unique colors, or smell, or form. We should not use too many plants around garden

Fig. 6.16 The front yard of the Five Peak Immortal Hall in the Lingering Garden

architecture, and should keep a certain distance between big trees and garden architecture so as not to influence the appearance of the architecture and the use of natural light for its rooms.

Fig. 6.17 The Mountain in View Tower in the
Surging-Wave Pavilion

If garden architecture faces water, shrubs should not be planted around its side facing water so that people can appreciate the scene of the water easily. Few plants should be planted along the side facing water so as not to block the view. Tall arboreal trees can be planted on the side of the architecture to provide shade and act as foils.

Trees or some other plants should always accompany a pavilion in a garden so that it will not stand alone, no matter whether it is located on a mountain or along the edge of water. There are basically two ways to layout plants and a pavilion:

Fig. 6.18 The Listening to Rain Pavilion in the
Unsuccessful Politician's Garden

(a) Build a pavilion in a grove, like the Pavilion for Free Whistling in the Lingering Garden, the Orange Pavilion and Far Away Looking Pavilion in the Unsuccessful Politician's Garden.

(b) Plant few tall arboreal trees around the pavilion, decorated with some short plants, like the Green Ripple Pavilion. The Embroidery Pavilion and the Listening to Rain Pavilion (Fig 6.18) in the Unsuccessful Politician's Garden, the Slender Bamboo Pavilion (Fig 6.19) and the Flying Waterfall Pavilion in the Lion Grove.

The plants in front of windows for viewing the scenery should have luxuriant but well-spaced branches and leaves. Outside the windows for adopting natural light in the backyard or courtyard of a house, bamboo or some other evergreen plants should be planted so as to cover the enclosing wall and give people a fresh feeling. An opening in a wall or a lattice window on the wall of a walking gallery or a hall of flower studio is used to connect the inside room and the outside area and enlarge the

Fig. 6.19 The Slender Bamboo Pavilion in the Lion Grove

space, and make it convenient to appreciate scenery (Fig 6.20). Therefore, the plants outside the opening or lattice window should have few branches and a graceful form, such as banana or bamboo with thin foliage so as to only partly cover the opening or lattice window and create a partly hidden and partly visible scenery and poetic

atmosphere, or "Yi Jing." One example is located at the Net Master's Garden, several bamboos are planted loosely outside the lattice window, and the garden scene outside the window is partly hidden and partly visible. The couplet to the right of the window reads: "Bird resting on the jade (referring to the green bamboo) and the spring cloud appears to be warm." The couplet to the left of the window reads: "The eave protect the banana trees while the night rain

Fig. 6.20 Lattice windows are used to connect the inside and the outside: a scene in the Unsuccessful Politician's Garden

feels to be cool." The lattice window, the combination of the bamboos and the couplet forms a very special poetic atmosphere, or "Yi Jing."

u. Plants and water

Fig. 6.21 Use plants with weeping or drooping forms to cover the bank of the pond and create a lower layer of planting

Plants floating on the water, plants growing out of water and plants growing on the edge of water can enrich the composition of the water surface. On the edge of a pond, tall deciduous trees are usually used as a mainstay, decorated with some relatively short plants and a few evergreen trees. The branches of the deciduous trees often incline outwards and form a graceful posture. If the bank of the pond is relatively high, gardeners usually use plants with weeping or drooping forms to cover it and create a lower layer of planting (Fig 6.21). Plants between a pond and a garden path should be placed sparsely. It is common to plant several arboreal trees and few short plants so as to enrich the scenery along the edge of the pond and not to block the view.

The reflection in a pond can form a graceful "picture", no matter whether it is in hot summer or in chilly winter, in a morning with mist or in an evening with the moon, or on a day with a breeze. Therefore, few or no aquatic plants should be used in water under a garden bridge, or near a pavilion facing water. If they are used, their growth should be controlled so as not to damage the reflection in the water. Plants like the water lily that has small leaves and will not grow too high above the water can be used for small pond. Algae are seldom used, except for feeding and otherwise providing an environment for fish.

Plants or rockeries are often used to cover the origin of water to create an endless feeling. For example, the water areas in the Unsuccessful Politician Garden include both large areas of water and narrow streams to create contrast. The origins of streams are often covered with rockeries.

v. Flower beds and potted landscapes (bonsai)

Flowerbeds are widely used in traditional Chinese gardens. They can often be seen in front of a studio or behind a house, beside a walking gallery or near a garden path. No matter whether they are composed of lake rock or yellow stone, they take naturalistic form. Only very few flower beds are built with bricks and stones to form a regular shape. A naturalistic flowerbed will take irregular forms and compositions in both plan and elevation. It will form a "natural" picture together with the plants and rockeries.

Potted landscapes are also common objects for appreciation in tradition Chinese gardens. They have great flexibility and can be used both indoors and outdoors.

The characteristic of potted landscapes is that it can mimic the actual mountain, water or antique trees in a much smaller scale and represent them inside a little pot, and form a three dimensional "landscape painting" which is alive. Potted landscapes in different sizes are often placed on a platform in front of a studio in traditional gardens.

4. Functional aspects

As we have partly mentioned before, functional aspects are also considered in Chinese planting design in addition to cultural influences and aesthetic considerations.

a. Food and plants

Even though it is not the most important factor considered, a number of plants are used as food in traditional Chinese gardens. Examples are the Loquat (*Eriobotrya japonica*), Lotus (*Nulumbium speciosum*), Chrysanthemum (*Chrysanthemum* spp.), Pomegranates (*Punica granatum*), Pears (*Pyrus* spp.), Persimmon (*Persimmon* spp.) and Banana (*Musa* spp.), etc.

b. Transitional functions

Plants can be applied as transitional objects between buildings, between architecture and garden space, between water and land, etc.

c. Providing shade

As in other gardens of the world, plants are also utilized to provide shade in Chinese gardens.

d. Enriching the change of spatial layers and deepening the depth of the field in gardens

As in other gardens, plants can enrich the change of spatial layers and deepen the depth of field in Chinese gardens. The luxuriant but well-spaced branches and leaves of plants can form a "net" or "gray space." If the distance between a viewer and the scenery remains the same, we add this layer or "net" between the viewer and the scenery; the depth of the field will feel deeper, even though the actual distance is still the same. Besides this, if we look at scenery through a luxuriant but well-spaced "net" of branches and leaves, the scenery will become partly hidden and partly visible. It can also obtain different level of implicit sense because of the density change of the "net." In the middle area of the Unsuccessful Politician's Garden, if a viewer looks at the Fragrant Island (a boat-like house) from the Willow-shade Winding Path (a walking gallery), the branches of the trees become the close scenery, the crooked bridge forms the middle scenery, and the Fragrant Island is the third layer or the farthest scenery. In the Net Master's Garden, if a visitor looks at the pavilion and the walking gallery in the opposite bank through the luxuriant but well-spaced branches, they will become more implicit and far-reaching. Similar technique is used in the Lingering Garden.

e. Defining space

As in other gardens, if the "net" formed by the trunk, branches and leaves of plants becomes dense to a certain extent, it can transform into a kind of "interface," or "boundary" or "side surface." This "interface" can define space. Even though it is not as clear, concrete and dense as the interface formed by architecture and garden walls, yet it has its own characteristic. If we consider the barrier provided by architecture and garden walls as dense, then the barrier formed by the combination of these two kinds of barriers must be partly enclosed and partly penetrated. For example, the space in the middle area of the Lingering Garden is defined by the combination of these two kinds of interfaces. The interfaces can be divided into East Interface, South Interface, West Interface, and North Interface, according to their locations. The East Interface and South Interface are mostly formed by architecture, and plants only work as decorations. The West Interface and the North Interface are formed mostly by trees. The West Interface is relatively dense, and the North Interface is relatively thin. Thus, the middle area of the Lingering garden becomes a garden space that is partially enclosed and partially penetrated.

In some circumstances, luxuriant trees can even play a major role in defining space. For instance, when buildings are too sparse to form an interface effectively, the densely planted trees can compensate for the shortage of architecture and play a major role in defining space. The middle area of the Unsuccessful Politician's Garden is one of these cases. Even though there are several garden buildings there, they look sparse and cannot define the space effectively because they are too far away from each other. Therefore, the garden designers had to take advantage of the luxuriant trees to compensate the shortage of architecture, and let plants play a major role in defining space.

When architecture, mountains or rockeries surrounding a garden area are not high enough to create a feeling of strong space, trees with luxuriant branches and leaves can also be utilized to compensate the shortage. Under this kind of situation, we can densely plant arboreal trees and try to form a high, relatively thin interface above the lower, relatively dense interface formed by architecture, artificial mountains and rockeries so as to reinforce the feeling of space. At the Garden of Harmonious Interest in the Summer Palace, even though the interfaces composed of buildings and walking gallery surrounding the lake form an enclosed "ring," yet the feeling of space is not strong enough because the lake is very large and the architecture is rather low. Fortunately, arboreal trees reaching to the skies are planted in the area outside the "ring" and they form a relatively thin interface above the interface formed by architecture, and reinforce the feeling of space. The space at the northern area of the House Between Boats in the North Sea Park (the Beihai Park) are formed by interfaces composed of artificial hills and rockeries. The heights of the hills are limited and the terrain slopes gently. It is a problem that the feeling of space is not strong enough. Trees with luxuriant leaves and branches planted on the slope compensate this shortcoming. The trees form a special "interface" and play an extremely important role in reinforcing the feeling of space.

f. Exaggerating the difference in contour

A number of traditional private gardens are built in urban areas, where the land is usually flat. In order to create contrast, lakes are often dug out on the site, and the excavated soil is used to build artificial hills. In order to exaggerate the difference in contour between the hills and the lake as well as other areas in the garden, tall arboreal trees are often planted on the higher part of the artificial hills.

g. Other practical functions

Plants can also be utilized to make tools, works of art, or used in construction in Chinese gardens. A good example is bamboo.

5. Ecological Factors

a. Natural order and "heavenly creation"

The idea of "man and nature in one" is actually the dominant philosophy for garden building in ancient China. Natural order or law was highly respected, and reproducing or representing nature, the "Heavenly Creation," has been the goal of garden design. Traditional Chinese gardeners did not have the science and technology that we have today, and they did not look at "ecology" at a global scale as we do today. What they counted on were long-term observations, experience and philosophy accumulated through generations of experimentation and practice by trial and error. These experiences and philosophy are still valuable and can be utilized today.

b. Plant selections and ecology

Plant materials used in Chinese gardens have been strictly selected. Most of the plants used are native or naturalized species adaptable to regional climates. This is stressed in order to minimize maintenance work. Exotic plants are cautiously used, and artificial microclimates are sometimes created to provide them with favorable conditions. For example, the whitewashed wall is often used as wind shelter for banana, which was once an exotic plant.

As in other kinds of gardens, topography, orientation, water supply, soil moisture, soil type, prevailing winds, temperature, the habit and natural setting and ultimate size of plants, as well as the relationships between plants also determine the choice of plants in Chinese gardens. At the corner of a building or a courtyard, shade-tolerating Camellia (*Camellia* spp.), Nadina (*Nadina* spp.), Chinese little boxwood (*Buxus* spp.), Osmanthus (*Osmanthus* spp.), Chinese Holly (*Ilex* spp.) and Glossy Privet (*Ligustrum lucidum*) are often planted. On hilly areas, the drought-tolerating Pine (*Pinus* spp.), Elm (*Ulmus* spp.), Cypress (*Cupressus* spp.), Chinese Jujube (*Ziziphus jujuba*) and Yucca (*Yucca* spp.) are usually found. Near watercourses or ponds, the plants that prefer moist soil, like Willow (*Salix babylonica*), Terocarya (*Terocarya stenoptera*), and Pomegranate (*Punica granatum*) are planted to embellish the water scene.

c. Micro "Ecosystem"

"The forest becomes more quiet because of the voice of the cicadas, the mountains become more serene because of the singing of the birds." Fish, birds, insects and plants are all considered as organic components for Chinese gardens. The singing of birds and the voice of the insects can create a feeling of serenity, instead of dead silence for a garden.

The traditional Chinese garden can be viewed as a balanced micro "ecosystem." Its components are the result of generations of experimentation and selection by trial and error. The hills, water, plants, fish, fowl and architecture form a cycle of resources that operates in a compatible way. The fish feed on aquatic plants, and limit their growth. The waterfowls feed on the fish; they also fertilize the plants. The architecture acts as a windshield and sun shelter. An established Chinese garden can maintain a delicate, self-sustaining natural balance and become a miniature of nature.

d. Plants and maintenance

Trimming and root pruning are sometimes used, but in a way completely different from that of Western gardens. Plants are not trimmed into geometric forms, but in the way of their natural growth as observed by the garden makers. The models for trimming are usually trees of grotesque and usually balanced form that have experienced the hardship of a severe natural environment. Plants are also given time to grow to manifest their natural beauty. This unique way of taking advantage of the natural growth of plants greatly reduces maintenance work.

CHAPTER 7
THE CONCLUSION REGARDING NATURALISTIC PLANTING DESIGN WITH CHINESE GARDENS AS CASE STUDIES

After discussing the naturalistic planting design through the case studies of natural, historical and cultural context, as well as the principles and methods of traditional Chinese planting design, we'll evaluate the observations we have made, clarify the underlying theory behind the principles, rules and patterns, make some judgments on the cohesive theoretical frame works explaining the observations and give some suggestions on the future development of planting design.

1. Two major principles underlying the development of Chinese planting design

The development and creative principles and methods can be better understood with these two major principles: the idea of "Man and Nature in One" and the dominant influence of literature and painting.

a. The idea of "man and nature in one"

The idea of "man and nature in one" is the most fundamental thought that expresses the quintessential nature of Chinese planting design. It originated mainly from Taoism, and was implemented by Confucianism and Metaphysics as well as other philosophical schools.

Man is different from nature, but both man and nature are the components of a bigger "whole," the universe. The idea of "man and nature in one" contains three layers of meanings. First, since man is the product of heaven and earth, or the universe, man should obey the universal laws of the world. Furthermore, the general laws of nature are related to the supreme principles of human ethics. The ideal of life is the harmony between man and nature. Man should maintain an intimate and harmonious relation with nature. On the one hand, man needs to adjust nature and make it accord with the wish of human beings, on the other hand, man should respect nature, protect nature and its balance.[48] Moreover, the idea was also demonstrated in humanizing nature by endowing nature with human integrity and viewing nature as human beings. For examples, "lofty mountains and flowing water" are considered as the symbol of noble and unsullied morality; plum, bamboo and pine work as "three friends in winter"; plum, orchids, bamboo and chrysanthemums form "four virtuous gentlemen," etc.; This becomes an anthropomorphic view.

Not all the combinations of man and nature can create an aesthetic "Yi Jing" (artistic conception) in gardens. The combination must achieve the requirements of "one," which means an integrated and harmonious entirety.

The idea of "man and nature in one" experienced a radical advancement in the episode of transition in Chinese planting design (220-589), especially during the Jin Dynasty (265-420) and Southern and Northern Dynasties (386-589). The philosophy of upholding nature greatly influenced the prevailing customs of the society and the ideal of life for the literati and officialdom. The beauty of the ideal personality has been considered as transcending worldly views and casting off outside trammels and complying with nature. The elite viewed nature in a completely new way, and pursued the philosophy of life from natural scenery, and utilized the dialectical philosophy of opposing each other and yet also complementing each other of Taoism to recognize gardening. They consciously pursued the harmony between "Yin" (the void or the shady or the female essence) and "Yang" (the solid or the bright or the male essence) and the unity of opposites in planting design, and combined plants, mountains, water, and garden architecture into an organic "whole." The philosophy of "Man and Nature in One" had a more profound influence in planting design and other gardening activities.[49]

As we have mentioned before, the idea of "man and nature in one," the philosophy of the metaphor of nature and moral integrity and the cosmology of deity determined that Chinese planting design developed towards a naturalistic orientation from its very beginning. The philosophy of "man and nature in one" ran through and dominated the complete historical development process of Chinese planting design, and has become the kernel of the aesthetics and philosophy of Chinese gardening. With this major underlying philosophy, we can better understand the principles and methods of traditional Chinese planting design that we have discussed before: Plants are used as icons and symbolized ideas, emotional states, will, personality and moral qualities, and they are also viewed as human beings; Planting and other garden elements should "look as if they were created by heaven (nature), even they are actually built by man"; Planting design should take

---

[48] Zhou, *The History of Chinese Classical Gardens*, pp. 336-337.
[49] Zhou, *The History of Chinese Classical Gardens*, pp. 336-337.

advantage of existing old trees or other favorable natural conditions; Plants are used as media for seasonal or spatial transformation; Painters and gardeners utilize the principles of the unity of the opposite to create the rules for planting so as to produce irregular and naturalistic vegetation; Dense planting is used to cover the soil and create a wild atmosphere in mountains with more soil than rocks, while thin planting is applied to show the "natural" beauty of rockeries in mountains with more rocks than earth. All these are the specific applications of the philosophy of "Man and Nature in One" in Chinese planting design.

Chinese gardens are both viewed gardens and occupied gardens. Architectural beauty is usually combined with natural beauty. Buildings and plants, mountains as well as water, often form an organic "whole." Their harmonious and mutually beneficial aspects are emphasized, and their opposite and mutually exclusive aspects are restricted. Buildings are often parts of a garden, parts of the "Man and Nature in One." The interior architectural space and exterior garden space are also often connected to each other through windows, doors or moon gates and form an organic "whole." Garden designers pursue the highly harmonious "Yi Jing" (artistic realm) between artificial and "natural" elements, a realm of "man and nature in one." The intimate and harmonious relations between garden architecture and plants, mountains as well as water, the "natural" elements and the symbol of natural scenery, also reflect people's desire to transcend common customs and cast off outside fetters to access nature.

b. The dominant influence of literature and painting

The Chinese traditional way of thinking emphasizes synthesis and comprehension through analogy and inference. Different disciplines of arts can overstep the boundaries between them and penetrate into each other, and mix together. The relation between Chinese planting design and literature and painting is one of the examples.

Literature and painting have a dominant influence on Chinese planting design. The creation of landscape painting and literature is a process "from nature to culture," while the Chinese planting design is a reversed process: "from culture to nature" with the help of landscape poetry, prose and painting.

Chinese landscape painting, poetry and prose emphasize the depiction of spirit with form and the depiction of sentiments. Painters or literati usually travel extensively to study and comprehend the volatile natural scenery. The scenery they express in their works is not only the individual natural scenery, but also their subjective interpretation and summarized scenery. They present not only the scenery they see and feel, but also their imagination based on the reality. For example, plants in Chinese landscape painting should not only manifest their natural beauty in posture and lines and reflect the laws of their natural growth, but also a "Yi Jing" (artistic conception). A mountain in painting should be summarized and extracted to display the laws of formation of nature. This is a process "from nature to culture."

Chinese planting design can be viewed as the reproduction or representation of the summarized and extracted natural scenery of landscape painting and literature in a three-dimensional space, a process "from culture to nature."

The dominant influence of painting and literature on Chinese planting design are mainly manifested in these aspects: the emphasis of the well-thought-out plan and layout before the actual creative process, the pursuit of "Yi Jing" (artistic conception), and the reproduction of the "Yi Jing" of painting and literature in planting design by means of distinct images; The use of the name for a scenery, the horizontal inscribed board and the couplet written on scrolls and hung on the pillars of a hall to directly bring out the theme of the scenery; The reference to creative concepts, principles and methods of landscape painting and literature; The anthropomorphosis of plants by endowing them with moral integrity and symbolic meanings and viewing them as human beings; The emphasis on implicit beauty, and the use of the "net" formed by plants to create implicit beauty for a garden scene; The idea that stated meanings are only meant to suggest implied meanings and evoked meaning, which are far more important than stated meanings; The pursuit of pictorial and poetic temperament and interest and "the scenery beyond the scenery"; The communication between the designer and the observers that transcends the barriers of time and space with the help of "Yi Jing" (artistic conception); The emphasis on the aesthetic properties of the antiquity, strangeness and grace of plants; The development of planting design from "depicting reality" to the combination of "depicting reality" and "depicting feeling," and then to the dominance of "depicting feeling." All these are the results of the dominant influence of literature and painting.

c. The use of bamboo in Chinese planting design embodies both the idea of "man and nature in one" and the dominant influence of literature and painting

Bamboo is divided into internodes by nodes, and it is hollow inside and straight outside and grows upright. It has special properties, elegant forms, multiple uses, and abilities to grow in severe conditions; thus, bamboo is esteemed and considered as the representative of the noble virtues such as being upright and humble, and yielding but never breaking. The pronunciation of "node" of bamboo is the same as that of "integrity" in Chinese. This also brings out the symbolic meaning of "moral integrity," of "showing noble integrity in strong wind (severe conditions)." Bamboo is both a member of "three friends in winter" and a member of "four virtuous gentlemen." Therefore, it displays one important aspect of the philosophy of "Man and Nature in One"— the anthropomorphism of plants and viewing them as human being.

Because of all the factors mentioned above, bamboo is a favorite subject and is depicted over and over in Chinese painting, poetry and prose. It was very popular in the circle of literati; For example, Su Shi (Su Dongpo), a famous writer and poet in the Song Dynasty (A.D. 960–1279), once said: "I can live without meat as my food, but can not live for even one day without bamboo near my house." The use and vogue of bamboo in Chinese gardens are a result of the promotion of the literati and painters, and the principles of laying out, planting and maintaining bamboo are also borrowed from bamboo painting; Thus, bamboo also manifests the dominant influence of literature and painting on Chinese planting design.

The idea of "man and nature in one" and the dominant influence of literature and painting converge together and are both demonstrated through the use of bamboo in Chinese planting design.

2. Judgments and Suggestions

a. Forms vs. ideas, principles and methods

In the past years, there are a few Chinese gardens that were copied and reproduced in western countries: all the materials were shipped from China and then installed on the site. The cost to reproduce such a "Chinese" garden is usually millions of dollars.

It is necessary to restore some precious and famous traditional Chinese gardens in China, and it may be necessary to "ship," copy or reproduce a limited number of "Chinese" gardens in western countries. The techniques of copying and restoring can be used under special circumstances, but it is neither possible nor necessary for us to use these techniques in common landscape practice. In a sense, when a "Chinese" garden is shipped to a western country, it is not a Chinese garden anymore, even if it is similar in form, because it is out of its original context and transgresses the philosophy of "man and nature in one" and the basic principle of "taking advantage." For example, the Astor Court at the Metropolitan Museum of Art in New York was a "copy" of a small courtyard within the Net Master's Garden in the City of Suzhou. All the garden architecture, rockeries and plants were reproduced according to the prototype. Because the cold climate of New York is completely different from the humid and warm climate of Suzhou, the courtyard was moved indoors and covered with skylights. The Astor Court is not a Chinese garden anymore, even though its physical form is very similar to the original courtyard: the original courtyard is a part of an organic "whole." It is closely related with the other parts of the complex formed by gardens and architecture, even the whole city of Suzhou. It fits with the environment, climate and culture of Suzhou and embodies the pursuit of "man and nature in one"; While the Astor Court is isolated from its surrounding environment and even the whole New York City. It does not fit with the environment and climate, and needs to be put in a "greenhouse" and be protected by modern technologies. It demonstrates another idea: "man vs. nature." The site is different from the original, thus, a marvelous view formed by borrowing the scenery of the middle area of the Net Master's garden is not splendid any more; The soils and water in New York are also different from those in Suzhou, thus, the plants will grow differently: a tree may become a shrub in the Astor Court, the size, smell and taste of the fruits and flowers of plants may also change. There is a banana tree in the Astor Court, but it is not used properly: it was planted in a "greenhouse," no rain drops can fall on its leaves. It can never produce the "Yi Jing" of raindrops pattering on banana leaves and cannot stimulate related literary reference. In fact, the most critical difference between the Astor Court and the prototype is in Culture: the original courtyard is the product of its culture and society. Its garden elements have not only graceful forms, but also symbolic meanings related to the culture. They can not only create physical enjoyment, but also stimulate feelings, thought and intellectual associations, or "meaning beyond the scenery." The Astor Court is not related to its local culture, and cannot create the intended "meaning beyond the scenery."

If a celebrated Chinese gardener designs a garden in New York, he will not copy a garden from China. He will use the ideas, principles and methods of Chinese gardening to design a garden according to the site conditions and the local culture. The forms of the garden may not be completely similar to those of a garden in China, but the garden will express the spirit and essence of Chinese gardens.

Similarity in spirit is far more important than similarity in forms. Mastering and applying the ideas, principles and creative methods are much more significant than copying a garden.

b. The possibilities of applying the principles and methods of traditional Chinese planting design in modern naturalistic planting design

The profession of landscape architecture has begun to prosper in modern China. Most of the planting design is not done by professional painters and literati anymore, but by architects or landscape architects instead; However, the creative method "from culture to nature" by referring to literature and painting is still valuable today and can be used in modern naturalistic planting design. We can bring a deeper meaning and create a unique "Yi Jing" (artistic conception), and produce not only physical enjoyment but also intellectual association and spiritual pleasure in planting design. The symbolism of plants is still prospering in modern China and the written culture is still strong enough to allow the literary reference to be made. It is also possible to transplant this creative approach to the Western world: the symbolism may vary with different cultural context, but it will still bring both physical enjoyment and intellectual associations and spiritual pleasure for garden lovers, visitors and observers.

The creative method "from culture to nature" requires that the designers have accomplishments in literature and painting.

As we have mentioned before, China is a country that owns the richest plant materials in the world, but the palette of plant materials used in Chinese gardens is very limited. Why? There are basically two reasons: (1) Plants in Chinese gardens are treated as symbols of ideas, emotional states, will, personality and moral qualities. Plants from the wild lack symbolic and historical associations and are considered less valuable and suitable for gardens; (2) Plants are not written words; they indirectly express their symbolic meanings through images, colors and smells. In order to retain the symbolic meanings, the palette of plants has to be limited, and the same plants have to be used repeatedly to some extent. If the palette is increased, the strength of the symbolism of each plant will probably diminish. If the species used in gardens are not controlled, the symbolic meaning of plants will gradually disappear; therefore, we should maintain a relatively stable palette of plant materials for planting design to keep the symbolic meanings.

The anthropomorphism of plants and nature should be encouraged and elaborated, since it will bring out the symbolic meanings and result in the respect of plants and nature. The pursuit of antiquity, strangeness and grace of plants and the emphasis on transformation are still significant today. The rules for single planting, group planting, mass planting and strip planting should be passed on, but we should apply them according to site conditions and should not take them as rigid dogma. The creation of sound effects, the emphasis of the beauty of lines, taking advantage of the color and smell of plants and the use of light and shadow are still important techniques today. Plants in a garden can still be used to produce food, to provide shade, to enrich the changes of spatial layers and deepen the depth of the field for a garden scene, to define space, to form a micro "ecosystem," and to work as transitional elements in gardens. Bamboos remain a required part in Chinese gardens, and can also be used in Western landscaping.

The pursuit of "Yi Jing" and the principles of "heavenly creation" and "taking advantage" are not only significant to contemporary Chinese planting, but also valuable to other schools of planting design in the world.

ANNOTATED BIBLIOGRAPHY

1. Planting Design

Austin, Richard L., Robert P. Ealy. *Elements of Planting Design*. John Wiley and Sons. 2001. Covers the ecology and process of planting design, with some technical information and graphic.

Carpenter, Philip L., et al. *Plants in the Landscape.* New York: W. H. Freeman and Company, 1990. A collection of papers on plants and planting design. Refers to almost every aspect of planting design. A list of plants from eastern Asia.

Clouston, Brian, ed. *Landscape Design with Plants.* Boca Raton, Florida: CRC Press, Inc., 1990. A collective book on planting design for different purposes, regions and situations. Each section written by a different author. Very comprehensive.

Grant, John A. and Carol L. *Garden Design Illustrated.* Seattle: University of Washington Press, 1954. Includes discussions on draft (naturalistic planting), on plant materials, curves and contours, garden colors, and a specific example and some supplementary examples.

Hackett, Brian. *Planting Design.* New York: McGraw-Hill Book Company, 1979. A comprehensive book on Western planting design. Includes history of planting design, natural plant relationships, appearance and uses of plants, planting design and ecology, planting design and habitat, design methods and planting design for different purposes.

Robinson, Florence Bell. *Planting Design.* Illinois: The Garrard Press, 1940. A classic on Western planting design. Includes: design factors, such as color theory, the use of colors, texture, the attributes of mass, ecological factors, local factors and individual factors as well as applications.

Sun, Youxiang. *Garden Art and Garden Design.* Beijing: Department of City Landscaping. Beijing Forestry University, 1986. A handy book for students of Forestry. Some patterns of natural planting of trees (In Chinese).

Walker, Theodore D. *Planting Design.* Arizona: PDA Publishers Corporation, 1985. A very practical book on Western planting design. Some design principles and functional uses of plants. The process of planting design. Preparing planting plans and specifications. Wonderful illustrations. Some working drawings and details of planting design.

2. Plant Materials and Plant Identification

Anderson, A. W. *How We Got Our Flowers.* New York: Dover, 1966. Stories about plant hunters in the Far East. With a section on the Chrysanthemum from China.

Brickell, Christopher (Editor-in-Chief) and The American Horticultural Society. *Encyclopedia of Garden Plants.* New York: Macmillan Publishing Company. 1989. A illustrated guide to over 8,000 trees, shrubs, vines, flowers, foliage and water plants, and cacti and succulents, with over 4,000 full color photographs. Include symbols for cultivation and hardiness, size and shape, preference of sun or shade, moisture level, and PH requirements for each plant. An excellent book for plan identification.

Chandler, Philip. *Reference Lists of Ornamental Plants for Southern California Gardens.* Southern California Horticultural Society. A comprehensive ornamental plant list for Southern California by "the dean of Southern California gardening."

Cox, E. H. M. *Plant Hunting in China.* London: Oldbourne, 1945. Interesting stories of the well-known plant hunters of Britain, Europe and America.

Farrington, Edward I. *Ernest H. Wilson, Plant Hunter.* Boston: Stratford, 1931. Fascinating stories of "Chinese" Wilson, who introduced hundreds of plants from China, Japan, etc.

Lancaster, Roy. *What Plants Where.* Dorling Kindersley Limited, London, 1995. A very good book for plant identification, includes one close-up color photo for each plant. Use very simple symbols to describe light level, hardiness, acidity, average spread and height.

Loewer, Peter (Author and Copyright Holder). *Tough Plants for Tough Places.* Rodale Press, 1992. Discuss climate, soils, watering and plant care, and 25 garden design case studies. Many line drawings of specific plants.

Pei, Sheng-ji. *Botanical Gardens in China.* Hawaii: Harold L. Lyon Arboretum, University of Hawaii, 1984. A three-page-long section on the history of Chinese plants.

Philips, Roger and Martyn Rix. *The Botanical Garden, Volume II, Perennials and Annuals.* Firefly Books Ltd., 2002. A very good book for plant identification regarding perennials and annuals, with color close-up photos for each plant discussed.

Siren, Osvald. *China and the Gardens of Europe of the Eighteenth Century.* New York: Ronald Press, 1950. Some data on Chinese native flowers.

Stiff, Ruth L.A. *Flowers from the Royal Gardens of Kew.* University Press of New England, 1988. A collection of color drawings for some decorative plants.

South China Plant Research Institute of Chinese Science Institute, ed. *Records of Plants in Guangzhou.* Beijing: Science Press, 1956. An inclusive records of plants in Guangzhou, contains illustrations of the forms of plants.

Stuart, David and James Sutherland (Author and Copyright Holder). *Plants from the Past: Old Flowers for New Gardens.* Viking Penguin Inc., 1987. Includes historical reference for some plants, a few good knot gardens, labyrinth gardens, and parterre.

Sunset Books and Sunset Magazine, *Sunset Western Garden Book*, Fifth Edition. Fourth Printing, March 1990. Lane Publishing Co. A very comprehensive encyclopedia of plants in western United States, with color photos and figures.

Wilson, E. H.. *A Naturalist in Western China.* Volume I and II. London: Cadogan Books, 1986. The original works of Wilson. Extensive descriptions of the Chinese natural environment.

Wright, Michael. *The Complete Handbook of Garden Plants.* The Rainbird Publishing Group Limited. 1984. Includes over 900 species and varieties of garden plants, more than 2500 full-color illustrations. Discusses climate and hardiness map, pest and disease, trees, shrubs, perennial climbers, borders and bedding perennials, bulbs, corms, tubers, rock plants, annuals and biennials, water plants. An excellent tool for plant identification.

Ying, Shao-shun. *Colored Illustration of Herbaceous Plants of Taiwan, Volume One.* Taiwan: Yin, Shao-shun, 1980. Color photos and the names of herbaceous plants in English and in Chinese. An index in English and an index in Chinese.

3. Design and General Landscaping

Boisset, Caroline. *Vertical Gardening.* Mitchell Beasley Publishers, 1988. Climbing plants, hanging plants, trellises, wall planting, terraces, window boxes with color pictures and brief description.

Ching, Frank D.K. and Ching Francis D. *Architecture: Form, Space, and Order.* John Wiley and Sons, 2nd edition, February 1996. Wonderful illustrations of form, space, organization, circulations and design principles.

Colby, Deirdre. *City Gardening: Planting, Maintaining, and Designing the Urban Garden.* Michael Friedman Publishing Group, Inc. Climate and hardiness zones, soils, codes, budgeting, planting procedure and maintenance, design, formal and informal styles and finishing touches, etc.

Cox, Jeff. *Landscape with Nature: Using Nature's Designs to Plan your Yard.* Rodale Press, Emmaus, Pennsylvania. Includes discussion on learning from nature, creating a natural garden, elements of the natural gardens, with some good sketches and color photos.

Engel, David H. *Japanese Gardens for Today.* Tokyo and Rutland, Vermont: Charles E. Tuttle Company, 1959. A book on how to make a Japanese garden in the West for today.

Hobhouse, Penelope. *Color in Garden.* Little Brown and Company, 1985. Discussed the nature of color and various colors and related plants, with many color photos.

Hobhouse, Penelope and Elvin McDonald (Editor). *Gardens of the World: The Arts and Practice of Gardening.* 1991. A collections of articles on rose and rose gardens, formal gardens, tulips and the spring bulb, Japanese gardens, flower gardens, tropical gardens, country gardens and public gardens with color photos and drawings.

Hobhouse, Penelope. *Penelope Hobhouse's Garden Designs.* Henry Holt and Company, Inc. May 1997. Includes color photos, drawings and discussion on 23 gardens designed by Penelope Hobhouse and her partners.

Hobhouse, Penelope. *The Story of Gardening.* DK Publishing, 1st edition, November 1, 2002. Discusses gardens in different cultures and periods, with beautiful color photos and reproductions of garden painting and a section on plants on the move.

Jellicoe, Geoffrey and Susan. *The Landscape of Man: Shaping the Environment from Prehistory to Present Day.* London: Thames and Hudson Ltd., 1975. An excellent book for students in Landscape Architecture, with sections on Landscape and Architecture in different cultures. Many valuables photos.

Kuck, Loraine E. *The World of Japanese Garden: From Chinese Origins to Modern Landscape Art.* Weatherhill, Inc., 1968. Very detailed discussions of the history of Japanese gardens and the Chinese origins; includes a very interesting section that discusses and compare the origins of two major landscape systems in the world and case studies of famous Japanese gardens.

Loxton, Howard (Editor). *The Garden: A Celebration.* David Bateman Ltd., 1991. A good section on the history of gardens in various regions with color photos of famous gardens, and sections on plants of the garden, botanical garden, garden design, famous gardens worldwide and garden practice. A very good reference book.

Morris, A.E.J. *History of Urban Form: Before the Industrial Revolutions.* England: Longman Scientific and Technical, Longman Group UK Limited, 1979. Reprinted 1990. A good reference book for Architecture, Landscape Architecture and Urban and Regional Planning and Design, with many line drawings and photos.

Murphy, Wendy B and the Editors of Time-Life Books. *Japanese Gardens.* Time-Life Books, Inc., 1979. Pretty pictures of Japanese Gardens with picture essay about history, types and design techniques of Japanese gardens; includes an encyclopedia of Japanese plants with color pictures of plants.

Reid, Grant W. *From Concept to Form: In Landscape Design.* John Wiley and Sons. May 20, 1993. Discussed general philosophical concepts, specific functional concepts of landscape design, various geometric forms, naturalistic forms, principles and case studies.

Sawano, Takashi. *Creating Your Own Japanese Garden*. Japan Pubns, December 1, 1999. An interesting book that discusses the history, development and different styles of Japanese gardens, also includes practical guide on how to create a Japanese garden in a Western country.

Tankard, Judith B. *The Gardens of Ellen Biddle Shipman: A History of Woman in Landscape Architecture*. Sagapress. September 1996. Include many projects Ellen Shipman did, many good examples in both formal and naturalistic planting design. Good examples of the arrangement of focus and detail along a path, regarding perennial beds.

4. Chinese Gardens

Chen, Lifang. Yu, Sianlin. *The Garden Art of China*. Portland, Oregon: Timber Press, 1986. A brief history of Chinese gardening and some design principles, with a sixteen page long section on design principles for planting trees and flowers. A list of Chinese plants for different purposes and seasons.

Engel, David H. *Creating a Chinese Garden*. Portland, Oregon: Timber Press, 1986. Some design principles and an extensive list of plants by botanical names, common names and Pinyin.

Graham, Dorothy. *Chinese Gardens: Gardens of the Contemporary Scene: An Account of Their Design and Symbolism*. New York: Dodd, Mead and Company, Inc., 1938. A chronological description of Chinese gardens.

He, Zhengqian, et al. *Die Gärten Chinas*. Köln: Eugen Diederichs Verlag GmbH and Co. KG, 1983. A lot of wonderful drawings in black and white and an excellent color picture of classical Chinese gardens. Some plans and sections of Suzhou gardens (In German).

Hu, Yunhua, et al. *Penjing: The Chinese Art of Miniature Gardens*. Beaverton, Oregon: Timber Press, 1982. A description of Chinese Penjing (Bonsai) making, with a list of species used in China for Penjing.

Ji, Cheng. *The Craft of Gardens. (Yuan Ye)*. New Haven and London: Yale University Press, 1988. A translation of "the bible of Chinese gardening", Yuan Ye.

Essential Principles of Chinese garden design, but no special section on planting design. Forward by Maggie Keswick.

Keswick, Maggie. *The Chinese Garden: History, Art and Architecture.* New York: Rizzoli International Publications, Inc., 1978. A brief history of Chinese gardens. With a nineteen page long section on flowers, trees and herbs. Contributions and conclusion by Charles Jencks.

Liu, Tung-Tseng, et al. *Classical Gardens in Soochow (Suzhou).* Beijing: China Building Industry Press. 1978. Some design principles of Chinese Gardens and detailed examples. Plans, sections and black and white pictures of Soochow (Suzhou) Gardens (In Chinese).

McFadden, Dorothy Loa. *Oriental Gardens in America: A Visitor's Guide.* 1976. A description of the oriental influence on gardens and the oriental gardens in America, with sections on early plant hunters and gardens of old China and an annotated bibliography.

Morris, Edwin T. *The Gardens of China: History, Art and Meanings.* New York: Charles Scribner's Sons, 1983. A description related to poets, painters and scholars, with a sixteen page long section "On The Garden Plants: What They Were And What They Meant;" and a section entitled, "Is The Chinese Gardens For Us?"

Muck, Alfreda, and Wen, Fong. *A Chinese Garden Court: The Astor Court at The Metropolitan Museum of Art.* New York: Metropolitan Museum of Art, 1980. A brochure introducing the Astor Court—a replication of the Garden of the Master of the Fishing Nets (Wangshi Yuan) in Suzhou. With a seven-page-long section on rocks and plantings.

Norer, Gunther. *Der Chinesische Gärten.* Wien: Ariadne Verlag, 1975. A lot of elegant pictures in black and white. (In German).

Peng, Yigang. *The Analysis of Chinese Classical Gardens.* Beijing: Chinese Architectural Industry Press, 1988. An analysis of Chinese classical gardens by means of modern theories. A number of figures and analytical drawings (In Chinese).

Qian, Yun, et al. *Classical Chinese Gardens.* Hong Kong: Joint Publishing Company. Beijing: Chinese Building Industry Press, 1982. A brief description of Chinese gardening history. With many splendid color pictures of imperial gardens, private gardens (in Beijing, Suzhou and Guangdong) and natural scenic parks and temple gardens. Very comprehensive.

Ting, Bao-lian, et al. *Suzhou Gardens.* Hong Kong: Tai Dao Publishing Ltd, 1987. A brief description of each famous garden in Suzhou. A lot of marvelous color photos (In Chinese, English and Japanese).

Tsu, Frances Ya-sing. *Landscape Design in Chinese Gardens.* San Francisco: McGraw-Hill Book Company, 1988. A general view of Chinese gardening principles. Comparison of Chinese gardens and European gardens, as well as Chinese gardens and Japanese gardens. With plans of famous gardens, a chronological table of Chinese dynasties and names of Chinese Gardens in English and in Chinese.

Tung, Chuin (Tong, Jun). "Chinese Gardens: Especially in KiangSu (Jiang Su) and CheKiang (Zhe Jiang)."*T'ien Hsia [Tian Xia] Monthly.* Vol. III. No. 3. October 1936. One of the early works on Chinese gardens. Some extreme opinions of the author.

Yan, Hongxun. *The Classical Gardens of China: History and Design Techniques.* New York: Van Nostrand Reinhold Company Inc. 1982. A brief history and some design principles of Chinese gardens. With a section about Da Guan Yuan.

Zhong, Baihua, et al. *A General View of Chinese Garden Art.* Jianshu Province: The People's Press of Jianshu, 1987. A collection of articles on Chinese gardens. With an article entitled, "The Artistic Appreciation of Plants in Suzhou Classical Gardens." (In Chinese).

Zhou, Weichuan. *The History of Chinese Classical Gardens.* Beijing: Qing Hua University Press, 1990. The first complete and comprehensive book on the history of Chinese gardens, with summaries for each chapter and a bibliography of ancient Chinese literature related to Chinese gardens (In Chinese).

5. Others

De Blij, Harm J. *Man Shaping the Earth: A Topical Geography.* Santa Barbara, California: Hamilton Publishing Company, 1974. An outstanding book for students in Geography, Geology and Landscape Architecture. Contains ten topics: landscapes, climates, population, culture, regions, politics, farming, manufacturing, cities and oceans. Some information about China.

Domrös, Manfred and Peng, Gongbing. *The Climate of China.* New York: Spring-Verlag, 1988. Includes detailed information on climate in China.

Feng, Huazhan and Qi, Zhirong, ed. *Feng Zikai's Comments' on Arts.* Shanghai: Fudan University Press, 1985. A collection of articles on arts by the famous Chinese artist, Mr. Feng Zikai. Includes some articles on the origin of arts, Chinese paintings and western paintings (In Chinese).

Feng, Zikai. *Painting and Literature.* HongKong: Far East Book Publishing Company, 1934. A collection of Mr. Feng Zikai's articles on literature and paintings (In Chinese).

Gao, Zhennong. *The Buddhism of China.* Shanghai: The Press of Social and Scientific Institute in Shanghai, 1986. An inclusive book on Buddhism of China. Contains: the origin of Buddhism, the introduction of Buddhism into China and the relationships between Chinese Buddhism and Buddhism in other countries (In Chinese).

Gong Xian, et al. *The Theory of (Chinese) Landscape Painting.* Taibei, Taiwan: Art Book Publishing Company, 1975. A remarkable collection of articles on tradition Chinese landscape painting by authors of different historical periods (dynasties).

Hsieh, Chiao-min (Xie, Jiaomin). *Atlas of China.* San Francisco: McGraw-Hill Book Company, 1973. A splendid book containing landform and vegetation maps of China.

Jing Jia, Tang, ed. *Chinese Painting.* Tokyo: Bien Li Tang, Ju Shi Hui She, 1986. Many excellent traditional Chinese landscape paintings. (In Japanese that is readable for Chinese to some extent).

Li, Zehou. *The Path of Beauty: A Study of Chinese Aesthetics.* Beijing: Morning Glory Publishers, 1988. A comprehensive, chronological book about traditional Chinese aesthetics, with a section on the landscape paintings of the Song Dynasty and the Yuan Dynasty. Several excellent traditional Chinese landscape paintings are reproduced.

Radice, Betty (Translator). *The Letters of the Younger Pliny.* Penguin Books., 1969. A collection of the letters of the Younger Pliny, divided into ten sections (ten "book"). Covers many aspect of the life in ancient Rome, including some discussions of garden and planting design.

Wang, Zhenhua. "The Meaning and Image of Hua Xia [an ancient name of China]— The Specific Techniques and Connotation of Chinese Architecture." *New Exposition and Argument of Chinese Culture: Art Section.* Taibei: Lianjin Publishing Company, 1981.

Includes a section about the natural, economic, social, political, and ideological factors that influenced the development of Chinese architecture.

Ye, Duzheng et al., ed. *The Climate of China and Global Climate.* New York: Springer–Verlag, 1987. The proceedings of the Beijing International Symposium on Climate. Includes climate history in the past 2000 years and beyond, land surface processes related to climate variation, etc.

APPENDIXES

APPENDIX 1
TABLE FOR SYMBOLISM OF SOME PLANTS IN CHINESE GARDENS

Botanical Name	Common Name	Symbolism
Bambusa spp.	Bamboo	1) "Three Friends in winter," they symbolize the true friendship between virtuous people that revealed in hard times 2) "Four Virtuous Gentlemen" 3) The pronunciation of "node" of bamboo is the same as that of "integrity" in Chinese: Representative of integrity and the noble virtues such as being upright and humble, and yielding but never breaking.
Camellia spp.	Camellia	1) Suggest wild atmosphere and are used to decorate rockeries (or false mountains) in gardens 2) Suggest beautiful women
Chrysanthemum spp.	Chrysanthemum	1) Related to longevity, and are called "late fragrance," "those who survive all others" and "those who defy frost" 2) "The flower of autumn" 3) "Four Virtuous Gentlemen"

Citrus medica	Finger lemon	"Buddha's hand," it is another emblem of longevity
Cymbidium spp.	Orchid	1) "Ancestor of fragrance", suggesting honorable friendship and uprightness 2) "The flower of spring" 3) "Four Virtuous Gentlemen"
Diospyros spp.	Persimmon	Implying joy in Chinese culture
Eriobotrya japonica	Loquat	1) Pronounces as "Pi Pa," which is the same as a plucked string Chinese classical music instrument with a fretted fingerboard, often appeared in poetry and prose 2) "The Golden Fruit"
Firmiana simplex, or Sterculia platanifolia	Chinese Parasol Tree	The perch of the phoenix in Chinese legend
Koelreuteria bipinnata	Chinese Flame Tree	Used to relate to the hierarchy of the society: planted in cemeteries for governors
Magnolia denudata	Yulan Magnolia	Purity
Morus alba	Silkworm Mulberry	"Tree of missing each other" or "tree of love"
Musa spp.	Banana	1) "The tree of self-improvement" 2) The melancholy sound of rain dropping on its leaves is inspiration of a favorite garden theme
Narcissus taezetta var. orientals	Narcissus	Signifies "fairy girls riding the waves"
Nelumbo nucifera	Lotus	1) A symbol of purity and truth for rising spotlessly from its bed of mud 2) A symbol for friendship, happy union and peace 3) Special meanings for

		Confucianists, Taoist and Buddhists 4) "The flower of summer" 5) The sound of rain drops pattering on their leaves is a garden theme
Paeonia suffruticosa	Tree Peony	"King of Flowers," and its glorious profusion of blooms suggests nobility, wealth, rank, prosperity, honor and beautiful women
Populus spp.	Poplar	Used to relate to the hierarchy of the society: planted in cemeteries for commoners
Pinus spp.	Pine	1) "Three Friends in winter" 2) Used to relate to the hierarchy of the society: planted in cemeteries for the ruler
Prunus spp.	Plum	1) "Three Friends in winter" 2) "Four Virtuous Gentlemen" 3) Suggesting an unconquerable spirit and heralding the coming of spring
Prunus persica	Pears	Emblems of spring, love, marriage and immortality
Punica granatum	Pomegranates	Auspicious symbols of fertility, implying prosperous offspring
Pyrus spp	Pears	1) Signify longevity, but a more modest one 2) Signify good government
Rhododendron spp.	Azalea	Suggest wild atmosphere and are use to decorate rockeries (or artificial mountains) in gardens
Rosa spp.	Rose	1) Ever blooming 2) Express love
Salix babylonica	Weeping Willow	1) A holy plant for Buddhists 2) Used to describe female in Chinese literature: "having an

		eyebrow as slim and beautiful as a leaf of willow"
Sophora japonica	Chinese Scholar Tree	Used to relate to the hierarchy of the society: planted in cemeteries for scholars
Thuja orientalis	Oriental Arborvitae	Used to relate to the hierarchy of the society: planted in cemeteries for princes

APPENDIX 2
PLANT LISTS

Table 6.1: A List of the Most Commonly Used Plants in Chinese Gardens[50]

a. Grove and Shade Trees

EVERGREEN CONIFEROUS TREES
Abies firma	Moma Fir
Abies koreana	Korean Fir
Cedrus brevifolia	Cyprian Cedar
Cedrus deodara	Deodar Ceda
Chamaecyparis obtuse	Hinoki False Cypress
Cryptomeria japonica	Cryptomeria
Pinus aspera	Brocaded Pine
Pinus brutia	Calabrian Pine
Pinus bungeana	Lacebark Pine
Pinus densiflora	Japanese Red Pine
Pinus parviflora	Japanese White Pine
Pinus pinaster	Cluster Pine
Pinus taiwanensis	Formosa Pine
Pine thunbergii	Japanese Black Pine
Platycladus orientalis	Oriental Arborvitae
Podocarpus macrophyllus	Yew Pine

DECIDUOUS CONIFEROUS TREES
Metasequoia glyptostroboides	Dawn Redwood
Pseudolarix kaempferi	Golden Larch

---

[50] List compiled by the author of this book through personal research. Nomenclature regularized to follow Hortus III.

Taxodium distichum var. *nutans*	Pond Cypress
Taxodium distichum	Bald Cypress

EVERGREEN BROAD-LEAVED TREES

Cinnamomum camphora	Camphor Tree
Ficus microcarpa nitida	Chinese Banya

DECIDUOUS BROAD-LEAVED TREES

Aesculus chinensis	Chinese Horse Chestnut
Castanea mollissima	Chinese Chestnut
Catalpa ovata	Chinese Catalpa
Celtis sinensis	Chinese Hackeberry
Fraxinus chinensis	Chinese Ash
Firmiana simplex	Chinese Parasol
Gleditsia sinensis	Chinese Honey Locust
Koelreuteria bipinnata	Chinese Flame Tree
Liquidambar formosana	Chinese Sweet Gum
Liquidambar orientalis	Oriental Sweet Gum
Nyssa sinensis	Chinese Tupelo
Phellodendron amurense	Smooth Chinese Cork Tree
Populus lasiocarpa	Chinese Poplar
Pterocarya stenoptera	Chinese Wingnut Tree
Quercus acutissima	Sawtooth Elm
Salix babylonica	Weeping Willow
Sapium sebiferum	Chinese Tallow Tree
Sophora japonica	Chinese Scholar tree
Tilia japonica	Japanese Linden
Ulmus parvifolia	Chinese Elm

b. Fruit Trees

EVERGREEN

Cherry Rosaceae	Sweet Cherries
Citrus	Lemons
Citrus medica	Citron
Citrus sinensis	Sweet Orange
Ensete ventricosum	Abyssinia Banana
Eriobotrya japonica	Loquat

Fortunella margarita	Kumquat
Ilex cornuta	Chinese Holly
Morus alba	Silkworm Mulberry
Musa acuminate	Banana
Musa paradisiacal	Banana
Myrica rubra	Red Bayberry
Prunus campanulata	Taiwan Flowering Cherry
Prunus salicina	Japanese Autumn Rosa
Prunus tomentosa	Nanking Cherry

DECIDUOUS

Apple Rosaceae	
Apricot Rosaceae	
Chaenomeles spp. (species)	Chinese flowering Crabapple
Diospyros kaki	Persimmon
Prunus salicina	Japanese Plum
Prunus persica	Peach
Prunus persica nucipersica	
Punica granatum	Pomegranite
Pyrus pyrifolia	Chinese Pear
Pyrus communis	'Yali' Asian Pear
Zizyphus jujube	Jujube

c. Leafy Trees

EVERGREENS

Aucuba japonica	Japanese Aucuba
Buxus sempervirens	English Boxwood
Fatsia japonica	Japanese Aralia
Ilex cornuta	Chinese Holly
Ligustrum lucidum	Glossy Privet
Rhapis excelsa	Lady Plam
Strelitzia nicolai	Giant Bird of Paradise

DECIDUOUS

Acer truncatum ssp. (=subspecies)	Painted Maple
Ginkgo biloba	Ginkgo

Liquidambar formosana	Chinese Sweet Gum
Sapium sebiferum	Chinese Tallow Tree
Populus tomentosa	Chinese White Poplar
Prunus mume	Japanese Flowering Cherry
Salix babylonica	Weeping Willow

d. Shrubs

EVERGREEN SHRUBS

Aspidistra elatior	Cast Iron Plant
Aucuba japonica	Japanese Aucuba
Buxus sempervirens	English Boxwood
Elaeagnus pungens	Silverberry
Fatsia japonica	Japanese Aralia
Hibisicus rosa-sinensis	Chinese Hibiscus
Ilex glabra	Winterberry
Ilex vomitoria nana	Dwarf Yaupon
Ilex yunnanensis	Yunnan Holly
Ixora chinensis	Chinese Ixora
Jasminum mesnyi	Primrose Jasmine
Jasminum odoratissimun	Sweet Jasmine
Jasminum officinale	Common White Jasmine
Juniperus chinensis	Juniper
Juniperus chinensis sargentii	Sargent's Juniper
Michelia alba	White Michelia
Nandina domestica	Heavenly Bamboo
Osmanthus serrulatus	Sweet Osmanthus
Osmanthus heterophyllus	Holly-leaf Osmanthus
Photinia serrulata	Chinese Photinia
Pinus mugo var. *mugo*	Mugo Pine
Rhododendron molle	Chinese Azalea
Taxus chinensis	Chinese Yew
Viburnum odoratissimum	Sweet Viburnum

DECIDUOUS SHRUBS

Abelia chinensis	Chinese Abelia
Berberis thunbergii	Japanese Barberry
Chimonanthus praecox	Wintersweet

Clethra alnifolia	Summersweet
Corylopsis sinensis	Chinese Corylopsis
Deutzia scabra	Rough Deutzia
Elaeagnus umbellate	Autumn Elaegnus
Forsythia viridissima	Chinese Yellow-bell
Hamamelis mollis	Chinese Witch Hazel
Hibiscus syriacus	Rose of Sharon
Ilex verticillata	Winterberry
Potentilla chinensis	Chinese Cinquefoil
Rhododendron arborescens	Sweet Azalea
Rhododendron calendulaceum	Flame Azalea
Rosa chinensis	Chinese Rose
Rosa odorata	Tea Rose
Syringa chinensis	Chinese Lilac
Viburnum setigerum	Tea Viburnum

e. Herbaceous Flowering or Aquatic Plants

Aconitum fischeri	Monkshood
Aster tataricus	Tartarian Aster
Callistephus chinensis	China Aster
Camellia japonica	Common Camellia
Chimonanthus praecox	Wintersweet
Chrysathemum spp.	
Chrysanthemum compositae	Chrysanthemum
Cymbidium ensifolium	Orchid
Cymbidium kanran	Winter Cymbidium
Cymbidium sinensis	Dark-purple Cymbidium
Dahlia pinnata	Common Dahlia
Dendranthema morifolium	Chinese Chrysanthemum
Dianthus caryophllus	Carnation
Equisetum hiemale	Rat-tail
Fomes japonicus	Fungose Plant
Fuchsia albo-coccinea	White Fuchsia
Fuchsia hybrida	Hybrid Fuahsia
Gardenia jasminoides	Cape Jasmine
Gladiolus gandavensis	Gladiolus
Hemerocallis fulva	Day-lily

Iris spp.	Iris
Liriope spicata	Dwarf Lilyturf
Narcissus tazetta var. *orientalis*	Polyanthus narcissus
Nelumbo nucifera	Lotus
Nymphaea alba	Water Lily
Orchophragmus spp.	
Paeonia spp.	Peony
Phragmites spp.	Marsh Reed
Polygonum orientale	Princess Feather
Prunus mume	Japanese Plum
Rhododendron pulchrum	Loverly Rhododendron
Rosa chinensis	China Rose
Thea sinensis	Tea
Trapa bicornis	Water Chestnut

f. Bamboos

Arundinaria amabilis	Tonkin Cane
Arundinaria disticha	Dwarf Fernleaf Bamboo
Arundinaria pseudo-amabilis	
Bambusa multiplex	
Bambusa multiplex 'Golden Goddes'	Golden Goddess Bamboo
Bambusa multiplex riviereorum	Chinese Goddess Bamboo
Bambusa oldhamii	Oldham Bamboo
Bambusa textilis	Punting Pole Bamboo
Bambusa ventricosa	Buddha's Belly Bamboo
Chimonobambusa quadrangularis	Square Bamboo
Indocalamus latiflorus	Latiflorus
Indocalamus nanunicus	
Lingnania chungii	
Nipponocalamus fortunei	
Phyllostachys aurea	Golden Bamboo
Phyllostachys nigra	Black Bamboo
Phyllostachys pubescens	Moso Bamboo
Phylostachys bambusoides	Giant Running Timber Bamboo
Pseudosasa japonica	Arrow Bamboo
Sasa palmate	Palmate Bamboo
Shibataea chinensis	

Sinarundinaria nitida	Fountain Bamboo
Sinobambusa intermedia	

g. Vines

Akebia quinata	Five-leaf Akebia
Bignonia grandiflora	Chinese Trumpet Creeper
Bougainvillea glabra spectabilis	Bougainvillea
Clematis chinensis	Chinese Clematis
Ficus pumila	Climping Fig
Hedera helix	English Ivy
Lonicera japonica chinensis	Purple Chinese Honeysuckle
Trachelospermum jasminoides	Chinese Star Jasmine
Vitis vinifera	European Grape
Wisteria sinensis	Chinese Wisteria

Table 6.2:Some Key Ornamentals Used for Four Seasons in Many Chinese Gardens

SPRING
Cymbidium orchidacae	Orchid
Magnolia	Yulan Magnolia
Narcissus tazetta orientalis	Polyanthus Narcissus
Paeonia suffruticosa	Tree Peony
Pyrus kawakamii	Evergreen Pear
Semperflorens begonias	Bedding Begonias

SUMMER
Dianthus chinensis	Chinese Pink
Gladiolus gardavensis	Gladiolus
Jasminum officinale	Poet's Jasmine
Nelumbo nucifera	Lotus
Rhodondendron japonicum	Japanese Azalea
Rosa chinensis	China Rose

AUTUMN
Chrysanthemum compositae	Chrysanthemum
Hibiscus rosa-sinensis	Chinese Hibiscus
Osmanthus fragrans	Sweet Olive

WINTER
Camellia reticulate	Net-veined Camellia
Chimonanthus praecox	Wintersweet
Dendranthema morifolium	Chinese Chrysanthemum
*Prunus mume*Japanese	Flowing Plum
Rhododendron mucronatum	Snow Azalea

APPENDIX 3
PINYIN ALPHABET, WITH EQUIVALENT LETTERS IN THE WADE–GILES SYSTEM AND SIMILAR ENGLISH PRONUNCIATION

Pinyin	Wade–Giles	English
	a	"a" in "farm'
b	p	"b" in "box"
c	ts	"ts" in "hits"
d	t	"d" in "door"
e	e	"e" in "term" with "r" silent
f	f	"f" in "fog"
g	k	"g" in "get"
h	h	"h" in "hot"
i	i	"ea" in "easy"; or "ir" in "bird" when following "c, ch, r, s, sh, z and zh" in a syllable
ie	ie	"ye" in "yes"
j	ch	"J" in "Jack"
k	k	"k" in "key"
l	l	"l" in "law"
m	m	"m" in "moon"
n	n	"n" in "nice"
o	o	"aw" in "law; or as "oo" in "look" when followed by "ng"
p	p	"p" in "part"
q	ch	"ch" in "cheese"
r	j	"r" in "rose" but not rolled
s	s,ss,sz	"s" in "star"
sh	sh	"sh" in "shoe"

t	t	"t" in "turn"
u	u	"oo" in "zoo"
v	v	used to produce dialect words or foreign ethnic minority
w	w	"w" in "wet"
x	hs	"sh" in "shore"
y	y	"y" in "yes"
z	ts,tz	"z" in "zebra"
zh	ch	"j" in "jeep"

APPENDIX 4
CHRONOLOGY OF CHINESE DYNASTIES

Xia Dynasty (2205–1766 BC)

Shang Dynasty (1766–1122 BC)

Zhou Dynasty (1122–249 BC)
    Western Zhou (1122–771 BC)
    Eastern Zhou (770–249 BC)
    Spring and Autumn period (770–481 BC)
    Warring States period (403–221 BC)

Qin Dynasty (221–207 BC)

Han Dynasty (202 BC–AD 220)
    Former (Western) Han (202 BC–AD 9)
    Xin Dynasty (AD 9–23)
    Later (Eastern) Han (AD 25–220)

Three Kingdoms
    Wei (220-265)
    Shu (221–265)
    Wu (222–280)

Jin Dynasty (265–420)
    Western Jin (265–317)
    Eastern Jin (317–420)

Southern and Northern Dynasties (Period of Disunity)
    South: Liu Sung (420–479)

Qi (479–502)
Liang (502–557)
Zhen (557–589)
North: Later (Northern) Wei (386–535)
Eastern Wei (534–550)
Western Wei (535–556)
Northern Qi (550–577)
Northern Zhou (557–581)

Sui Dynasty (590–618)

Tang Dynasty (618–906)

Five Dynasty (907–960)
Later Liang (907–923)
Later Tang (923–936)
Later Jin (936–947)
Later Han (947–950)
Later Zhou (951–960)

Song Dynasty (960–1279)
Northern Song (960–1126)
Southern Song (1127–1279)
Liao (907–1125)
Western Xia (990–1227)
Zin (1115–1234)

Yuan Dynasty (Mongols) (1260–1368)

Ming Dynasty (1368–1644)
Qing Dynasty (Manchus) (1644–1912)

Republic of China (1912–1949)
Nationalist Party (Guomingdang) in Taiwan (1945–2000)
Democracy and Progress Party in Taiwan (2000-)

People's Republic of China (1949–)

APPENDIX 5
SOME GARDENS/ATTRACTIONS DISCUSSED IN THIS BOOK

a. In the United States:

1) **Central Park**
Contact: The Central Park Conservancy
14 East 60th Street
New York, NY 10022
Tel: 212-310-6600
contact@centralparknyc.org
Web site: http://www.centralparknyc.org/

2) **The Mall, Washington DC**
Directions: The National Mall is located between Constitution and Independence Avenues. Address: Washington DC
Tel: 202 485-9880
Web site: http://xroads.virginia.edu/~CAP/MALL/home1.html

3) **The Grand Canyon**
Contact: Grand Canyon National Park
P. O. Box 129
Grand Canyon, AZ 86023
Tel: 928-638-7888
deanna_prather@nps.gov
Web site: http://www.nps.gov/grca/

4) **The J. Paul Getty Museum (The "New" Getty Center)**
1200 Getty Center Dr.
Los Angeles, CA 90049

Tel: 310-440-7300
Web site: http://www.getty.edu/

5) **The Getty Villa (The "Old" Getty Museum)**
17985 Pacific Coast Highway
Malibu, CA 90265
Tel: (310) 458-2003
Web site: http://www.getty.edu/museum/villa.html

b. In France:

1) **Versaille:** Some miles south-west of Paris
Contact: mcassandro@chateauversailles.fr
Web Site: http://www.chateauversailles.fr/en/
(Inscribed as World Cultural Heritage by World Heritage Committee of United Nations Educational, Scientific and Cultural Organization, see link: **http://whc.unesco.org/sites/83.htm)**

c. In China:

1) **Royal Gardens**
Summer Palace
15 km from Beijing City (The Capital of China), China (Inscribed as World Cultural Heritage by World Heritage Committee of United Nations Educational, Scientific and Cultural Organization, see link: **http://whc.unesco.org/sites/880.htm)**

Summer–Retreating Mountain Villa, Chende City
175 km from Beijing. Tour Buses leave from Beijing Daily.
(Inscribed as World Cultural Heritage by World Heritage Committee of United Nations Educational, Scientific and Cultural Organization, see link: **http://whc.unesco.org/sites/703.htm)**

2) **Suzhou Classical Gardens:**
(Inscribed as World Cultural Heritage by World Heritage Committee of United Nations Educational, Scientific and Cultural Organization, see link: **http://whc.unesco.org/sites/813bis.htm)**

Unsuccessful Politician's Garden (Humble Administrator's Garden):
178 Northeast St., Suzhou City 215001, JiangSu Province, China.
Tel: 0512-67539869

Lingering Garden:
79 Lingering Garden Road, Suzhou City 215008, JiangSu Province, China
Tel: 0512-65337903

Net Master's Garden
11 KuoJiaTou Xiang (Lane), Suzhou City 215006, JiangSu Province, China
Tel: 0512-65203514

Surging Wave Pavilion
3 Surging Wave Pavilion Street, Suzhou City 215007, JiangSu Province, China
Tel: 0512-651943754

Lion Grove
23 Garden Road, Suzhou City 215001, JiangSu Province, China
Tel: 0512-67278316

Pleasure Garden
343 People Road, Suzhou City 215005, JiangSu Province, China
Tel: 0512-65249317

Tianpingshan Mountain
Tianpingshan Mountain, Mudu, Wu County, JiangSu Province, China
Tel: 0512-66261382

Chinese Style Gardens in North America:

1) **Portland Classical Chinese Garden-**
   Garden of Awakening Orchids (Lan Su Yuan)
   N.W. 3rd and Everett
   Portland, OR 97208
   Tel: 502-228-8183
   Web Site: http://www.portlandchinesegarden.org/home

2)   **The Seattle Chinese Garden: Western Flower Garden (Xi Hua Yuan)**
South Seattle Community College
6000 16th Avenue SW (north entrance)
Seattle, Oregon
Tel: 206-282-8040 ext 100
Web Site: http://www.seattle-chinese-garden.org/frameset.htm

3)   **The Chinese Garden in the Huntington**
A New Chinese Garden will be created in the Huntington
Opening date is 2007.
1151 Oxford Road
San Marino, CA 91108
Tel: 626-405-2100
Web Site: http://www.huntington.org/ChineseGarden.html

4)   **Overfelt Chinese Cultural Garden**
2145 McKee Road, at Educational Park Drive
San Jose, CA
Tel: 408-251-3323
Web Site: http://www.scu.edu/SCU/Programs/Diversity/overft.html

5)   **The Chinese Scholar's Garden at Staten Botanical Garden, New York**
1000 Richmond Terrace
Staten Island, NY 10301
Tel: 718-273-8200
Web Site: http://www.chinesegardennyc.com/Homeimage.htm

6)   **Dr. Sun Yat-Sen Garden, Vancouver, Canada**
578 Carrall St.
Chinatown
Vancouver, British Columbia V6B 5K2
Canada
Tel: 604-662-3207
Fax: 604-682-4008
Web Site: http://www.discovervancouver.com/sun/
E-Mail: sunyatsen@bc.sympatico.ca

7) **Dream Lake Garden:**
Chinese Garden of the Montréal Botanical Garden
4101, Sherbrooke Street East
Montréal, Québec
Canada, H1X 2B2
Phone: (514) 872-9677
Fax: (514) 872-3765
Web Site: http://www2.ville.montreal.qc.ca/jardin/en/chine/chine.htm
Email: jardin_botanique@ville.montreal.qc.ca

Other Chinese or Chinese Style gardens in North America can be found at
the Classical Chinese Garden Society's Web Site:
http://www.chinesegarden.org/links.htm

APPENDIX 6
LIST OF FIGURES

Fig. 1.1 The trees in the Mall, Washington DC can be symmetrical and huge to match overall city design concept

Fig. 1.2 The overall planting design of Central Park, New York was set to be naturalistic at the city scale

Fig. 1.3 Trees at plaza scale can match the design concept of the plaza

Fig. 1.4 Plant one tree in front of each home to form a very unique tree-lined street

Fig. 1.5 Plants and view lines from a building

Fig. 1.6 Following existing shape- planting trees along the bank of a creek

Fig. 1.7 Following existing shape-palm trees along a road

Fig. 1.8 Habit of plants

Fig. 1.9 Form of plants

Fig. 1.10 Light and color

Fig. 1.11 Color wheel

Fig. 1.12 Lawn, low-rise decorative plants, shrubs and several pine trees soften the view of an iron fence

Fig. 1.13 Texture analysis in planting design-a texture analysis of Fig. 1.12

APPENDIX 7
ACKNOWLEDGEMENTS

First of all, I'd like to acknowledge Professor Achva Benzinberg Stein, FASLA, Director for Landscape Architecture Graduate Program at School of Architecture, Urban Design, and Landscape Architecture at City College of New York (CCNY) for her enthusiasm on the subject, her continuous encouragement and patient instructions. I'd also like to thank Mr. Robert S. Harris, FAIA, ACSA Distinguished Professor and Professor Emeritus and Interim Director for Landscape Architecture Studies of School of Architecture at the University of Southern California (USC) for his encouragement. I am also deeply indebted to Professor Marc Schiler from the School of Architecture at USC and Mr. Michael O'Brien, ASLA, senior planner at the city of Los Angeles and instructor in the Landscape Architecture Program at USC and Professor Dominic Cheung from the Department of East Asian Languages and Cultures at USC for their interest and precious time spent, their omnipresent help and valuable suggestions during the writing of my manuscripts. I am grateful to Mr. Donald B for his "discovery" of my original manuscript and his encouragement, and Mr. Al Amador, a former co-worker for keeping my original manuscript for over 10 years and make Donald's "discovery" possible. I'd also like to thank Ruth Wallach at the Architecture and Fine Arts Library at the University of Southern California and other librarians for their help in searching for many hard to find reference books.

An exploration related to a complex, historical subject cannot avoid drawing from the works of experts in the field. This research is no exception: Liu Tung–Tseng's (Liu Dun–zhen's) *Classical Gardens in Soochow (Suzhou)*, 1978, Peng Yigang's *The Analysis of Chinese Classical Gardens*, 1988, and Sun Youxiang's *Garden Art and Garden Design*, 1986, as well as Zhou Weichuan's *The History of Chinese Classical Gardens*, 1990, provided important raw materials and historical data. Hsieh Chiao–min's (Xie Jiao–min's) *Atlas of China*, 1973, and Maggie Keswick's *The Chinese Gardens: History, Art and Architecture, 1978,* are the major sources for valuable data in the section entitled "Natural Landscape" and the section entitled "Plants and Iconography." Tsu Frances Yasing's (Zhu Yaxing's) *Landscape Design in Chinese Gardens*, 1988, and *Records of the Plants in Guangzhou*, which was compiled by South China Plant Research Institute of Chinese Science Institute in 1956, Penelope Hobhouse's *The Story of Gardening,* Howard Loxton's (Editor) *The Garden: A Celebration,* Loraine E Kuck's *The World of Japanese Garden: From Chinese Origins to Modern Landscape Art,* David H. Engel's *Japanese Gardens for Today,* Frank D.K. Ching and Francis D Ching's *Architecture: Form, Space, and Order,* Florence Bell Robinson's *Planting Design* as well as Brian Hackett's *Planting Design,* have also been referred to. Even though I have been trying to be as complete as possible, it is virtually impossible to list all the books and materials that I have referred to. I want to give my heartfelt acknowledgment to all the books, materials used and their authors, no matter whether their names are mentioned or not.

Much gratitude goes to my family members in China for assisting me to obtain the latest books and magazines on Chinese gardens. I'd like to thank my father, Zhuixian Chen, mother, Yugen and my nephew, Jiancheng Chen as well as other family members for their assistance in taking some of the photos of the planting design in Chinese gardens.

The photographs, sketch and drawings not otherwise credited are the work of the author.

Last but not least, I want to acknowledge my wife, Xiaojie, for her tremendous assistance in every aspect of my research, and my daughters, Alice, Amy and Angela Chen for their understanding of my effort.

Printed in the United States
87093LV00004B/85-86/A